SOAS LIBRARY
WITHDRAWN

D0321780

STUDIES IN SOCIOLOGY AND SOCIAL ANTHROPOLOGY

2

Studies in Sociology and Social Anthropology

1. Biplab Dasgupta (Ed.). **Village Studies in the Third World**
2. A. L. Epstein (Ed.). **The Craft of Social Anthropology**
3. P. S. Majumdar. **Rural Poor in an Urban Setting: A Case Study in Capital City of India**
4. Miriam Sharma. **The Politics of Inequality: Competition and Control in an Indian Village**

The Craft of Social Anthropology

EDITED BY A. L. EPSTEIN

Introduction by Max Gluckman

Hindustan Publishing Corpn. (I),
Delhi - 110007

Transaction Books
New Brunswick, N.J.

Originally published by Tavistock Publications Ltd.,
II New Fetter Lane, London E. C. 4, United Kingdom

Republished in 1978 by Hindustan Publishing Corporation (India),
6 U. B., Jawahar Nagar, Delhi-110007, India

Distributed in United States of America by Transaction Inc.,
New Brunswick, New Jersey 08903, USA

ISBN 0-87855-280-4

PRINTED IN INDIA BY MOHAN MAKHIJANI AT REKHA PRINTERS PRIVATE LIMITED
A-102/1 OKHLA INDUSTRIAL ESTATE, PHASE II, NEW DELHI-110020

Contents

Contents

PART THREE

Preface to the Indian Edition

Intensive fieldwork is so integral a part of the discipline of social anthropology that it is surprising that books on the methods and techniques employed in them are few in number. In contrast, there is no lack of books on "methods of social research" which confine themselves to describing statistical methods, techniques of survey research including questionnaires of various kinds, coding and tabulation, scaling, etc. Manuals dealing with research techniques are certainly necessary as long as fieldwork has an important place in social science research but there is something unsatisfactory and artificial about dealing with techniques divorced from problems let alone from the main theoretical developments in the social sciences. The books rarely convey the intense excitement of fieldwork, nor the need for on-the-spot improvisation of techniques to cope with any difficult or unexpected situations that may arise. Perhaps this is because most manuals or textbooks have in mind survey research which usually only involve young investigators while the senior social scientist directing the study sits in the relative comfort of his office. This is particularly true of the way in which social science research is organized in our country.

Yet another drawback to the books on research methods in the social sciences is that they stem out of experience of fieldwork situations in the West which are not comparable with situations obtaining in developing countries. In this respect as in several others, *The Craft of Social Anthropology* is unusual: the field-situations it has grown out of are in tribal Africa, and tribal and rural India.

The book is divided into two parts, the first, entitled "Orientations and Techniques", while the second is concerned with "Selected Problems: Data and Methods". Each Part comprises four essays and each one of them is written by a well-known specialist. The book also carries an introduction by the late Professor Max Gluckman who influenced most of the contributors to this volume first as Director of the Rhodes-Livingstone Institute, Lusaka, and then Professor of Social Anthropology at Manchester.

The essays included in the volume deal with such basic concerns of fieldworkers as the quantification of data and the use of statistical methods in primitive and peasant societies (Colson, Mitchell, Barnes), genealogies (Barnes), and the extended-case method and situational analysis (Van Velsen). In the Second Part of the book are covered economic analysis (T. S. Epstein), law (A. L. Epstein), ritual (Turner) and witchcraft (Marwick). Indian readers might find Scarlett Epstein's and Victor Turner's contributions particularly useful as they deal with Indian situations.

The discovery of what is called the "method of participant observation" by Malinowski in the second decade of this century marks a watershed in the development of modern social anthropology, giving rise, as it did, to new and exciting developments in theory. The successors of Malinowski also felt the need to quantify data wherever possible in order to be more precise in their statements, and to enable hypotheses to be tested cross-culturally. The extended-case method and situational analysis is, however, a contribution of a different nature to the methods of the social anthropologist. According to Gluckman the use of this method would "bring to the monographic analysis some of the penetration which Freud brought to the study of human personality and some of the depth that many find in the novel but not in scientific analysis" (Introduction, p. xvi).

Emphasis on the importance of the method of participant observation, and of the extended-case method and situational analysis is particularly necessary in India where most of the research that is carried out in the social sciences—for a poor country, India spends a considerable amount of money on research—is of the survey type using low-level investigators for collecting data to be analysed by highly competent economists and statisticians using computers. Apart from the fact that the data collected are not very reliable, they are also severed from their cultural and social contexts. To expect sound planning on the basis of such data is unrealistic. The only corrective to this is carrying out selected community and case studies using the method of participant observation. The need for this is all the greater now as the emphasis in our development has shifted from merely achieving economic growth to tempering growth with justice i.e., paying special attention to the needs of the "weaker sections", especially in the rural areas, and to the reduction of inequalities between different sections of the population.

One of the good things that has happened in the social sciences in this country is the blurring of the distinction between social anthropology and sociology. This is as it should be for Indian society includes millions of very poor people and backward groups living in villages and in the forests as also sophisticated groups inhabiting the towns and cities. India is a multi-religious country, and the hold of tradition and history is still visible in the lives of vast numbers of her population. Under the circumstances, it does not make sense to draw a line between the study of tribes and of the other elements of the population. Social anthropology and sociology should coalesce in India, and both should work with the other social sciences including history.

To return to *The Craft of Social Anthropology*: It will prove to be essential reading for social scientists who intend proceeding to fieldwork. I warmly welcome the Indian edition.

Institute for Social and Economic Change
Bangalore 560040

M. N. SRINIVAS

Editor's Preface

THE tradition of conducting fieldwork, usually in more or less isolated and 'exotic' communities, and the theoretical perspectives that stem from it, would probably count for many people as one of the major contributions of social anthropology to social science. Against this tradition, it is not surprising that preparation for fieldwork has come to be seen as an essential part of the training of students in the subject, and fieldwork itself as a unique and necessary experience, amounting to a kind of *rite de passage* by which the novice is transformed into the rounded anthropologist and initiated into the ranks of the profession. What is all the more striking, therefore, is the curious dearth of publications devoted specifically to the problems of fieldwork.

The need here is not simply for a manual (or manuals) of field techniques as such. Techniques after all are only meaningful in relation to problems, and in inviting my colleagues to participate in this volume this was a point I asked them to bear continuously in mind in the preparation of their essays. This, of course, raises a number of difficulties right at the outset. In the first place, since the ethnographer is always likely to encounter fresh problems in the field or to develop new lines of theoretical interest, it is clear that the procedures the anthropological fieldworker should follow in his 'laboratory' can never be prescribed in absolute terms nor become wholly standardized. On the other hand, as anthropological analysis becomes more refined, it becomes increasingly important that students in the field should at least be aware of the need to collect certain basic kinds of data, and know how to set about this. These provide the themes of the essays in the first part of the volume. The second difficulty is that, given the wide range of interests of modern social anthropology, the array of techniques which different fieldworkers will want to bring to bear may vary considerably depending on their major theoretical orientations. In a volume of this kind some degree of selection is inevitable. The topics discussed in the second part constitute a number of important 'problem areas' that much of contemporary anthropology is concerned to explore. But my editorial choice has also been largely guided by the hope that the contributors, all of whom have worked together in close co-operation at varying times and places, would be able to discuss their different fields within a common frame of reference.

With these aims in mind, Elizabeth Colson's article, with its discussion of sampling and census-taking in small tribal communities, originally published in Robert F. Spencer (ed.), *Method and Perspective in Anthropology* (1954), seemed to me to provide an obvious lead into the discussion, and we are grateful to her and to the University of Minnesota Press for permission to reprint her essay here. Some of the points made in Mitchell's essay were also touched on earlier in his paper 'Quantitative Methods and Statistical Reasoning in Social Anthropology', published in *Sudan Society* in 1963. We are grateful to the Editor for allowing us to incorporate parts of it here. Our thanks are also due to the Council of the Royal Anthropological Institute for permitting us to make use of the article on 'Measures of Divorce Frequency in Simple Societies' which Barnes first published in its *Journal* for 1949, and which he kindly undertook to revise and completely re-write for this volume. I should also like to record here that Turner's essay was actually written some years ago for delivery to a departmental seminar. He has in the meantime carried his inquiries into ritual a good deal further, and has indeed published a number of important papers in this field, particularly on the theme of ritual symbolism. However, at the time I was planning the volume it occurred to me that his re-analysis of the Saora data fitted in very well with the scope and aims of our symposium, and I am very grateful to him for succumbing to my blandishments and agreeing to its inclusion here.

Ideally, of course, I should have liked to be able to gather all the contributors together so that their papers and the symposium as a whole could be discussed in a series of seminars, but, scattered as they were around the four quarters of the globe, this was quite out of the question. This fact also increased the difficulties in getting the manuscript together, but I hope that the corporate character of the book has not been altogether lost. At all events I should like to thank all my colleagues for their enthusiastic co-operation throughout and, above all, for the unusual degree of editorial licence they have allowed me.

Although we did not have the opportunity of discussing our early drafts with each other, a number of us did receive helpful comments, suggestions, and stimulation from a variety of persons, and we would like to make our due acknowledgments here as follows: J. A. Barnes to P. A. P. Moran, L. H. Day, G. Winefield, and S. E. Baume for help with the revision of his paper on divorce frequency; and to Paula Brown, J. D. Freeman, W. N. Gunson, M. A. Jaspan, Ling Wang, D. J. Mulvaney, Marie Reay, and W. E. H. Stanner for information and comment on his paper on genealogies; T. S. Epstein to Dr Margaret MacArthur for bibliographical references; A. L. Epstein to B. Sansom; and M. G. Marwick to Professor Monica Wilson, Dr Jit Singh Uberoi, and Dr Paula Brown. Marwick also wishes to express his thanks to the Colonial Office Social Science Research Council, which supported his fieldwork among the Ceŵa.

We should also like to take this opportunity of expressing our gratitude to the Trustees of the Rhodes–Livingstone Institute, Lusaka (now the Institute for Social Research, University of Zambia), under whose sponsorship most of us carried out the main body of our own field research. In the preparations for that research, in the seminars that punctuated our trips to the field, and in the arduous and sometimes protracted task of writing up, we were taught, guided, criticized, and stimulated by Max Gluckman, first as Director of the Institute and later as head of the Department of Social Anthropology and Sociology in the University of Manchester. In the circumstances, it is only fitting that he should have contributed our Introduction. We are happy to acknowledge here the great debt, personal as well as intellectual, that we all owe to him.

Introduction

THE essays in this book have arisen specifically out of a need that had become apparent for a series of texts that could be used in teaching methods of anthropological research, and that research workers could also use as a guide when they were actually in the field. The contributors are anthropologists who have had the opportunity of working closely together for many years either as officers of the Rhodes–Livingstone Institute, or in the Department of Social Anthropology at Manchester University, or both. They are thus able to discuss within a common framework modern fieldwork methods not simply as a set of techniques *per se*, but rather as tools for examining a number of problems that have come to interest them. But we would like to stress at the outset that we see our own work as firmly set in the whole development of social anthropology. Moreover, as the subject has developed and analysis has become more sophisticated, the standards by which data have to be collected constantly rise, and the problems at which these data have to be aimed become more complex and varied. We realize full well, therefore, that the themes dealt with here, in nine essays, are only a few of many that merit attention. We did in fact ask a number of other anthropologists to contribute to the volume, but unhappily, pressed by other commitments, they were unable to meet our dateline. If there are, then, the obvious and inevitable gaps, we hope at least that others will be stimulated to follow our example until every fieldworker can, in the limited compass of a few volumes, take with him adequate guides to most of the problems he is likely to encounter. As I have said, we have tried in these essays to set techniques in the framework of theoretical problems, so that those who use the book may remind themselves of what they are aiming at when they collect their material. The book should be useful not only to students in training but also to laymen who are frequently puzzled as to what anthropologists 'do' and how they actually set about their task.

My colleagues, who have developed research techniques far beyond those I myself employed when I was last in the field, have asked me to put their discussions into historical perspective as I see this.

Two main strands run through the essays presented here, representing two distinct, and seemingly strikingly different, types of technique. The one, which is stressed in the papers by Colson, Mitchell, Barnes, Scarlett

Epstein, and Marwick, is the consistent attempt to quantify variables as far as possible, and then to apply statistical calculations to these quantities. The second, which is the focus of interest of the essays by van Velsen and A. L. Epstein, is the concentration on detailed analysis of social situations and extended cases. The papers on quantitative techniques speak for themselves. In this Introduction, therefore, I concentrate on the exciting possibilities opened up by the study of extended cases, and for the benefit of students I spell out its origins. But I stress, as would all the contributors to this book, that the two modes of analysis must be used together.

Clearly, if new ranges of data are suddenly made available to a subject, its whole theory and perspective are bound to undergo a radical change. A new technique of observation may virtually create a new discipline, as Leeuwenhoek's improvements of the microscope, and later the creation of radio-telescopes, did. I consider that Malinowski's field researches had this effect on anthropology, partly because of his long residence in the Trobriand Islands, partly because he worked through the Trobriand language, and partly because his temperament led him to a deep involvement with the people he was studying. This combination led him to collect a quality and quantity of data quite different in kind from those of other scholars who had already begun to do long-term studies of specific tribal peoples. The data were above all different from those on which earlier anthropological theoreticians had relied; observations made by the casual travellers who had passed through colonial countries, or even those made by missionaries and administrators working for protracted periods in particular areas. The change in the nature of his data had a profound effect on his own thinking, and hence on the subject. Earlier, and even many later, descriptions of the individual's life concentrated on the rites of the life-cycle and rules of marriage etc., much in the way that Elwin does, as criticized in Turner's essay in this volume. But Malinowski's two books *Sex and Repression in Savage Society* (1927) and *The Sexual Life of Savages* (1929) are full of detailed information of how boys and girls grow up, their relations with their kin, the relations between spouses, etc.; and, unlike his predecessors, Malinowski did not write descriptions at the level of culture, custom, ritual, and belief. He dealt instead with how people grew up in a society of a particular culture, and how they used and rebelled against that culture.

Malinowski's data were thus akin to the raw material of the novelist, the playwright, the biographer and autobiographer, all drawing directly on social life, rather than to the kind of facts which the theoretical anthropologists of the nineteenth and early twentieth century had available to them. For those facts on which Durkheim, Tylor, or earlier Maine and Morgan, had worked, were the superficial observations collected, often through interpreters, of people making unco-ordinated observations on tribal life. Even the records made by the Haddon Expedition in 1898, and later by Rivers among the Todas, the Seligmans among the Veddas, and finally Radcliffe-Brown among the Andamanese and Australians, lacked the depth, complexity, and comprehensiveness of Malinowski's descriptions.

Malinowski explicitly discussed the difference between his data and those used by his predecessors. Indeed, in some respects much of his work has to be seen as an intellectual battle waged against his predecessors and many of his contemporaries, the successful outcome of which was to raise ethnographic fieldwork itself to a professional art. This battle was to establish that primitive life and primitive institutions were more complex, far more complex, than earlier theorists had thought. And it was in order to document this complexity that, already in the introduction to his first major book on the Trobriands, *Argonauts of the Western Pacific* (1922), Malinowski called for three types of evidence: the delineation of the organization of the tribe and the anatomy of its culture through concrete statistical documentation; the description of the imponderabilia of actual life; and the collection of documents of native mentality. He summed up a lot of these facts as 'cases', which must be continually cited to validate all general statements. In this Introduction, I discuss a change in the use of 'cases'. Of course, in the actual books written by Malinowski and his successors, the methods are not as simple as my statements of them; nevertheless, these methods exhibit a general similarity, which I have called (1961a) the 'method of apt illustration'.

Malinowski and the next 'generation' of anthropologists, in which I include myself, used so-called 'cases' in two ways. We made a large number of observations on how our subjects actually behaved, we collected genealogies and censuses, made diagrams of villages and gardens, listened to disputes and quarrels, obtained commentaries on all these incidents, collected texts from informants about customs and rituals, and discovered their answers to 'cases stated'. Out of this mass of data we analysed a general outline of the culture, or the social system, according to our main theoretical bent. We then used the apt and appropriate case to illustrate specific customs, principles of organization, social relationships, etc. Each case was selected for its appropriateness at a particular point in the argument; and cases coming quite close in the argument might be derived from the actions or words of quite different groups or individuals. There was no regularly established connection between the series of incidents in cases cited at different points in the analysis, though when incidents affecting the same persons at different points were used, careful anthropologists made cross-references. I cite an example where this was not done from Barton's *The Kalingas* (1949). Early in this book we are told that under hunting laws a pig belongs to the village whose dogs started the pig. This is illustrated with a case in which while hunters of Village A were pursuing a pig, dogs and hunters from Village B killed it. When Village A claimed the pig, Village B asserted that their dogs had started the pig, a fight ensued, and several men were killed. Many pages later, in an illustration of land tenure law, we learn that these two villages were at feud over a piece of land. It thus appears as if Village B's failure to comply with the hunting law was part of the total process of relations between the villages; and the case cited under hunting law falls into quite different perspective. In this example, the method of apt illustration may be adequate if we are interested in outlining the customs of the Kalinga, even the social morphology of Kalinga society: clearly, it is inadequate if we are trying to analyse the total process of Kalinga social life.

Anthropologists of my generation also used 'cases' in a slightly different way. They sometimes described a case first, and then extracted the general rule of custom or social relationship from it. Clearly, the more complex the case, the more could be extracted from it, as in Fortes's analysis of a collective fishing ceremony (1937) and of the great harvest festivals of the Tallensi (1936). I myself (1940) used a complex series of events, principally the ceremonial opening of a newly built bridge, to illustrate the extent to which Zulu and Whites were involved in a single social system and to demolish Malinowski's attack on Fortes and Schapera for adopting this viewpoint. We called these complex events 'social situations', and we used the actions of individuals and groups within these situations to exhibit the nature of the social structure. But it was still the social morphology that we were aiming to present.

As anthropologists began to collect this richer and more varied kind of material, they found that the data were susceptible of analysis in different types of scientific framework. For the same events are susceptible to various modes of examination: it is the types of relations between events that are sought, and not the events studied themselves, that distinguish one science from another. In the United States far more than in Europe and the British Commonwealth, anthropology diverged into differentiated disciplines, some concerned with the comparative study of social relations, some with the comparative study of culture, and some with the comparative study of personality. In the comparative study of personality there were biographical studies of particular individuals, for instance Aberle's *Psycho-social Analysis of a Hopi Life-History* (1951) and Steed's 'Personality Formation in a Hindu Village in Gujerat' (1955), and it is these that are in many ways closer to the new type of investigation of social relations that has developed among some younger social anthropologists. I emphasize here *some* younger social anthropologists; for among others there is a tendency to reduce the amount of data deployed in analysis in order to produce what are believed to be necessary and sufficient variables to construct a model explaining some particular social pattern.

Those who still wanted detailed case material (as insisted on by Malinowski in *Argonauts*), began to demand a different kind of data. The demand is marked, for example, in Freedman's penetrating analysis (1958) from published sources, including the books of Western-trained Chinese anthropologists, of the lineage in South-Eastern China. It occurs in M. G. Smith's critical survey (1956) of the analyses of lineage systems which made such advances from the time when Evans-Pritchard, Firth, and Fortes first established our knowledge of these. Clearly, one good case can illuminate the working of a social system in a way that a series of morphological statements cannot achieve. Evans-Pritchard was unfortunately unable to give in detail a single case of the waging or settlement of a feud among the Nuer; Colson's analysis (1953) of such a case among the Tonga of Zambia (Northern Rhodesia) throws considerable light on the Nuer social system.

But even Colson's analysis here of the settlement of a single case of homicide in a society that practised vengeance does not provide the kind of analysis that exhibits the fullest use of the case method. This new kind of analysis treats each case as a stage in an on-going process of social relations between specific persons and groups in a social system and culture. The refusal of one Kalinga village to recognize hunting law is related to a continuing state of feud with another village, possibly arising out of a dispute over land, possibly itself involved in a systematic state of feud. Colson, it is true, was concerned within the limits of an article to show the kinds of mechanism, inherent in Tonga culture, which tended to effect a settlement after a homicide, and I am unfairly using her here to illustrate the methodological point – that a full analysis would continue to trace the relations within the specific groups involved back in time, and then forward if possible. This is one of the main arguments van Velsen seeks to develop in his essay here; the approach he calls for requires taking a series of specific incidents affecting the same persons or groups, through a period of time, and showing how these incidents, these 'cases', are related to the development and changes of social relations among these persons and groups, acting within the framework of their social system and culture. My own view is that this kind of approach will greatly alter our view of the working of some institutions, and deepen our understanding of the significance of all custom. It will enable the subject of social anthropology to cope with what Malinowski dismissed as accidental quarrels and individual differences of temperament; it will bring to the monographic analysis some of the penetration which Freud brought to the study of human personality, and some of the depth that many find in the novel but not in scientific analysis. The test of this method lies in its application to work already done, and the published studies by younger anthropologists referred to in van Velsen's essay make it clear that the method survives this test. In our own Department, we have applied the method to a whole series of works by senior anthropologists, and always found that we came out with more understanding, and above all with more problems demanding further data from the field and further analysis. It is a measure of the skill of these senior anthropologists that they provide the data allowing this re-analysis of their work. Since I am of their 'generation', it is only proper that I should illustrate the general point here with a critique of my own book *The Judicial Process among the Barotse of Northern Rhodesia* (1955). I set out there to analyse the modes of thought of Barotse judges in deciding cases, and to relate those modes of thought to the economic and general social backgrounds of Barotse life. When I had finished the book, I felt that I had made an important contribution to the problems I had tackled, but I remained dissatisfied as a sociologist. I sensed that I was on the verge of important sociological discoveries, but was not making them. It is now clear to me that though I had woven my analysis out of many cases heard in court, some quoted at great length, I had in fact used each case as an isolated incident coming before a court. Yet each case was obviously but an incident in a long process of social relations, with its roots deep in the past; and often the protagonists in the case would be living together again, and their interaction would be affected by the court's decision. I had not studied that process of social life; and in my opinion here lies the next step in deepening our understanding of law and morality – the intensive study of the processes of social control in a limited area of social life viewed over a period of time.

I have been sketching in the background to what appears to me to be an important change in the use of ethnographic data in social-anthropological analysis. Many difficult problems inevitably arise from this use of the extended-case method, and some of these are discussed in van Velsen's essay. Some reviewers of van Velsen's own recent study of the Lakeside Tonga of Malawi (1964), which probably carries the method the furthest have found the details of the book burdensome. Heavy demands are indeed made on the reader by this kind of analysis, and I would merely comment that there is no reason why science should be easy reading. I confess however, that I do not yet see clear-cut answers to other problems such a the reliability of data on the past collected from interested parties, data that will have to be used since the anthropologist's period in the field is limited in time. I can only say on this point that I believe that ordinary historical caution can be applied; and since the method is clearly fruitful, these problems must be faced and overcome, and not cited to obstruct its development. For I believe that the mode of presenting ethnographic material through the combination of quantitative statements and extended cases is important not only in terms of fieldwork technique, but also because it will enable us to cope better with certain developments on the theoretical side of the science. To take one point: the view of a kind of consistent system that was the framework of analysis of Radcliffe-Brown has steadily ceased to be held by his successors. The works of Evans-Pritchard and Fortes markedly stressed the existence of cleavage, fission, conflict, etc., as inherent in social systems: Leach (1954), indeed, has argued that they did not go far enough. Nowadays, then, the anthropologist accepts 'conflict' as an integral part of even stable social systems. I outlined some of these ideas in *Custom and Conflict in Africa* (1955a), and developed them further in *Politics, Law and Ritual in Tribal Society* (1965). I therefore state baldly that many of the problems that are emerging, and that involve the basic problems of the endurance, stability, and different types of change in a social system existing in space-time, can only be tackled through the use of the extended-case method. Simmel's treatment of conflict, with the use of the method of apt illustration, despite its insights and high values, has basic weaknesses that emphasize my whole argument.

Just as there has been a change in the kinds of data that the anthropologist has sought to collect in the field and in the uses to which he has put these data in analysis and exposition, so has there been a change in the position of the field anthropologist himself, calling for a critical reassessment of his role as an observer. The typical anthropologist of the earlier generation came to know his informants well and in the field situation he may well have dealt with them and with his temporary neighbours as equals. But once he left the field, his informants became, as it were, merely the data recorded in his notebooks. His professional writings were aimed at his colleagues and not the people described in them, who in any case usually could not read. Furthermore, the anthropologist perceived his position in the field as being qualitatively distinct from that of the people he was studying, so that for most purposes he could assume that his presence did not affect the behaviour going on around him which he tried to record. Essentially the same customs and the same quarrels would have been followed out had he not been there to see them.

Barnes has brought out clearly in a recent discussion of the position of the modern fieldworker (1963) that these assumptions and attitudes no longer hold. The tribal peoples who have provided anthropologists with so much of their data are now often able and eager to read what is being said about themselves. They are likely to protest if they think that they are being misrepresented and their lives may be affected by the publication of facts that hitherto have been known only to a privileged few, or that everyone whispered about or knew half-consciously but no one admitted openly. A social institution in decline may even take on a new lease of life because of the inquiries made about it by an anthropologist, and an institution that relies for its success on flexibility and vagueness may be ruined if its position at some arbitrary moment of time is described in print as if it were fixed and permanent. Those anthropologists who have worked among literate peoples have often found that their informants are only too well aware of the hazards of publication.

The anthropologist is perhaps not very likely, by his mere presence, to alter or upset a well-established mode of customary behaviour. Yet his arrival has sometimes been the precipitating cause for a radical change, like the abandonment of a religious cult or the adoption of a new belief, a change that may have been latent for many years before he appeared. He then has the difficult task of analysing his own part in the social changes going on around him. Even when social conditions are stable, as he seeks more detailed data about specific events involving particular persons, so inevitably he finds himself drawn into a network of alliance and intrigue. Just as he tries to use his informants as sources of information, so they try to use him as a source of power, wealth, and occasionally knowledge. He has continually to clarify his own role in the society he is studying so that he is neither left completely in ignorance on the outside nor completely captured at the centre, where he knows so much that he can publish nothing. Anthropologists of an earlier day were often singularly reticent about the way in which they conducted their inquiries in the field. Though this often detracts from the value of their work, and in particular sometimes makes re-analysis of their data from a fresh point of view difficult, it does not make their work useless, for the facts they postulate are usually of a public and general kind whose observation and record do not depend on any particular mode of inquiry. Nowadays it becomes essential to know a great deal more about the way in which the field anthropologist has gone about his task: how well he knew the local language; whether he lived among the people as a prince or a beggar or like an 'ordinary' person; who were his friends and who told him what and when and why, and what, if anything, he did about the things he was told. In brief, the anthropologist has to take the processes of feedback into account both in the field and when he comes to publish. The field situation has really become a true social field, and the anthropologist has had to learn how to observe and to be at least a reluctant actor at the same time. Malinowski saw the essence of fieldwork in what he called 'participant observation'. But such participation implies involvement in the social life of the people, with all its conflicts and divisions. Clearly, Malinowski himself was deeply involved in the life of the Trobrianders, or at least certain sections among them, but we find in his writings little awareness of how that involvement might have shaped his analysis, for example, of Trobriand chieftainship.

I began this survey of the changing character of fieldwork and fieldwork methods with Malinowski, and it is perhaps fitting at this point that we should find that the wheel has turned full circle and we are back again with Malinowski in the Trobriands. For it seems to me that in other respects many of the developments I have touched on are already foreshadowed in his *Crime and Custom in Savage Society* (1926) which, with all its jurisprudential weaknesses, remains in my view the most striking of his books. I have often criticized Malinowski for his theoretical weaknesses: so I feel it just that I should end this *Introduction* by paying tribute to his great contribution to our methods of getting facts, and thus changing the nature of our facts. He made theoretical contributions besides this; but, by developing our methods, he made our new science, and he still points the way to both ethnographic and theoretical advances. It may be that in following up his call for 'documentation', through the use of the extended-case method, we are going into a much less tidy era of research and analysis, as the fuller implications of the method begin to be worked out. Moreover, as we appreciate more fully that customs and values are to some extent independent of one another, discrepant, conflicting, contradictory, we shall have to evolve concepts to deal with social life which are less rigid and which can cope with lack of interdependence as well as the existence of interdependence, with the haphazard as well as the systematic. As we stand now on the brink of this advance, I feel it is important that we continue to develop the monographic analysis as still an important part of our science. Continual comparative check will remain essential, but with the change in monographic analysis itself there will have to be a change in the manner of comparisons. I plead also that anthropologists will again have to accustom themselves to welcoming great ethnographic detail, including description and analysis of extended cases, as in the twenties and thirties we welcomed the rich detail of Malinowski's books.

Let me finish on a personal note. As I look back I see considerable advances in our subject; and this delights me indeed. But I feel also a measure of deep regret. My younger colleagues tell me that they see in my *Analysis of a Social Situation in Modern Zululand* (1940) the beginnings of some of the developments I have been outlining. I showed there how individuals in certain key positions could create and exploit social situations in terms of their power and their culture, and yet how certain other processes, arising from the larger society, led to standardized but unplanned relationships and associations. One of them has told me that I was there on the way to making the kind of analysis of how the many different components in a social system operate with varying weight in different types of situation. He asked why I had not followed up this line of analysis and said it would be interesting for students if I recorded the reason. Perhaps this was because it was ahead of its time, and I belonged after all to my own generation. In my own autobiographical recollection, I know that I went to study modern Zululand after working for years in the library on their indigenous culture. Bored with this, I plunged with zest into an investigation of their modern life. Had I returned to Zululand, I almost certainly would have gone farther in that direction. Instead, the chances of life took me to Barotseland, where I became fascinated by their complex, and not properly recorded, traditional political system; and then in the problems of their judicial process and jurisprudential ideas – all legitimate fields of study. But I can salute here the advances the new generation is making, and feel pleased that I may have helped them on their way. This Introduction may serve at least to map the path we all have trod.

MAX GLUCKMAN

University of Manchester
November, 1965

PART ONE

Orientations and Techniques

ELIZABETH COLSON

The Intensive Study of Small Sample Communities

THE last few years have seen a resurgence of interest in the comparative method among social anthropologists both in Europe and America. Perhaps the greatest recent contribution to comparative research has been that of Murdock (1949), who used information drawn from 250 societies to test the degree to which various social factors were correlated with kinship terminologies. The recent interest in the comparative method undoubtedly reflects the fact that anthropology has reached a new stage in its struggle to become a 'science'. With the use of the comparative method comes the application of statistical techniques, although much of the information that is available at the present time was not collected with this end in view.

The new techniques of analysis, as well as the new problems with which anthropologists are engaged, have already affected the fieldwork which is being done. Fieldworkers are producing more and more meticulous descriptions with a good deal of quantitative material to back up generalized statements, and at the same time they are narrowing their areas of investigation. This, I think, reflects a general and important trend in anthropology and in the social sciences in general.

It is towards a consideration of these new demands upon the fieldworker that this paper is directed. Kluckhohn (1939) some years ago pointed out: 'If we are to deal with any problem (such as that of the acquisition of culture by individuals) in a way which is reducible to actual human behaviors, generalizations must be given a quantitative basis' (p. 6). More recently Driver (1953) pressed this point home when he wrote, 'If we are going to use more mathematics, we must organize fieldwork with that in mind. We must obtain more quantification of every kind wherever it is possible to do so. . . . If one of the goals of ethnology is to arrive at patterns, configurations, or structures of cultures, these must be determined inductively from adequate numbers of actual facts if they are to satisfy the standards of science' (p. 53).

The worker in the comparative field is hampered very badly because he does not have 'adequate numbers of actual facts' upon which to base comparisons. Instead he must rely upon generalized statements about social institutions and compare these on an all-or-none basis, though the generalized descriptions may be incomparable in actual fact. Thus, in her article on the Arapesh which appears in *Cooperation and Competition among Primitive Peoples* (1937), Margaret Mead follows the description of the formal organization of Arapesh society with the comment that the actual functioning of the society is 'of a very different order than that implied in their structural arrangements' (p. 27). She further says that the formal structure is not observed in practice, unlike 'many primitive societies, notably Dobu' (p. 27). If we had the same type of material for other small-scale societies that Mead has for the Arapesh, it might well turn out that the formal structural arrangement of the society offers only a very general guide to behaviour which does not jibe with practice to any exact degree, and that those societies where formal structure and actual practice largely coincide are the exceptions. At present we simply do not know, and the type of comparative work which Murdock and others have attempted to do becomes questionable when viewed against this background. Murdock uses the Arapesh as one of his sample societies. Presumably he works with the formal structure of Arapesh society as he does with the formal structure of the other societies in his sample. As things stand, we do not know whether or not he is comparing comparable phenomena. It is certainly not suggested here that Murdock is unaware of this problem, witness his discussion of the criteria to be used in classifying a given society as polygamous or monogamous (1949, pp. 24–28). But much of the information available to him is inadequate for the purpose to which it is put.

I suspect, therefore, that the comparative method will contribute little further to our understanding of social organization and the field of cultural phenomena in general until we shift from the all-or-none classifications so largely used at present to a method based on the comparison of rates constructed from quantitative information collected in a systematic fashion. For this we need new standards of fieldwork. Counting noses is a tedious and uninspiring job, but perhaps the new depths of insight into human organization to which it should lead will at least partially compensate even the fieldworker for the loss of some of his old freedom.

We want, then, quantitative material to back up qualitative statements: an analysis of actual residence to accompany descriptive statements about whether residence is virilocal, uxorilocal, avunculocal, neolocal, or what have you; of actual inheritance and successions to back up stated rules of inheritance; of the number of cross-cousin marriages expressed as a proportion of total marriages; and so on through the whole gamut of social facts used to characterize a society and thus to contrast it with others.

This development should enable us to test a large number of hypotheses which have been put forward over the years about the nature of social interaction. Monica Wilson (1951) has some extremely suggestive things to say about the importance of residence patterns in determining the nature and direction of witchcraft accusations. To test her hypothesis, we need some cross-cultural information, showing the actual composition of residence units and the number, type, and direction of witchcraft accusations made by members of these units. Does cross-cousin marriage resolve some of the stresses that occur in a matrilineal society, as suggested by Malinowski? Some quantitative data on divorce frequencies for cross-cousin marriages as against non-cross-cousin marriages, as well as some better information on the incidence of quarrels between those united by a cross-cousin marriage tie, might help us to check this hypothesis. Does the joking relationship serve as a safety valve for people who are in some way in an ambivalent position with respect to each other? Radcliffe-Brown has made this suggestion, but nobody to my knowledge has actually tested it in a systematic fashion.

Nadel (1947), on the basis of his work among the various Nuba groups of the Sudan, has suggested that an intrinsic and logical correlation exists between social rigidity or inclusiveness and the incidence of suicide (p. 480). In this, of course, he is following in the footsteps of Durkheim. He points out that his information on the incidence of suicide for the different Nuba groups is inadequate. He usually cites the number of cases which his informants listed for him, or remarks that it was unknown or denied by informants of some particular group. This is enough, perhaps, to point the problem. But since he does not give the size of the population or the time period to which the information applies, it is impossible to construct a suicide rate for comparisons with other societies. I suspect on the basis of my own fieldwork among the Plateau Tonga of Northern Rhodesia (Zambia) that their suicide rate is high, and I think that the frequency may be related to the diffuse nature of the social network in which the Tonga finds himself, where he lacks the security that a more rigid formulation of rights and obligations might provide. On the basis of my material, I may be able to work out a very crude rate, with number of suicides, size of population, and period of time taken into account. But until other anthropologists produce the same sort of material for the peoples with whom they are working, I am in no position to be sure whether the Tonga takes their lives with any greater or lesser frequency than the majority of other pre-literate peoples. The Nuba material as it stands is suggestive, but useless for comparative purposes. What is needed is material of a type that allows of a direct comparison of rates. This, of course, will give the information for only one of the factors involved in Nadel's hypothesis. To test the hypothesis itself, we shall also need some means of stating objectively the degree of diffuseness or rigidity of social relationships, and to state this in such a way that it will be possible again to collect the information that will allow of the construction of rates for cross-cultural comparisons.

Gluckman (1950) has suggested that frequency of divorce is correlated with social structures of a particular type, but with the crude information at his disposal he is able to do little more than state the problem. To test his hypothesis we need divorce rates, worked out in a comparable fashion, for a series of societies with different forms of social structure. Barnes (1949; and see below, pp. 61–64) has attempted to develop a method of computing a divorce rate for non-literate societies where no records are kept of either marriages or divorces, and he has combed the literature for quantitative information in divorce. Other anthropologists working with various societies in Central Africa, under the auspices of the Rhodes–Livingstone Institute, are collecting quantitative information on divorce in a standard fashion and will use the method worked out by Barnes for presenting their results. We shall soon then be in a better position to test Gluckman's hypothesis, and to refine it (cf. p. 23).

I have suggested (1951) that population movements may be related to strains within the social structure, and have characterized the Plateau Tonga as highly mobile, i.e. as making frequent changes of residence from one village to another. Although, in the paper in which I put this forward, I gave a certain amount of information on the number of moves made by the people found in certain villages, the quantitative material is not expressed in a fashion which makes a direct comparison with other societies possible. For this it will be necessary to work out some method of computing a mobility rate. In any event, as matters stand, my assumption that the Tonga are highly mobile is only an assumption. When we have an adequate series of mobility rates for other societies, the Tonga may turn out to be unusually stable.

So far I have been speaking only of the utility of rates, and quantitative data in general, for cross-cultural comparisons. But they are equally useful to those who are concerned with a single society over a period of time. Even where a single anthropologist makes a return visit to a society which he studied ten to twenty years ago, he cannot be certain that the implicit standards against which his qualitative description was made have remained the same. The anthropologist who follows another into the same field has even more of a problem, unless his predecessor has made his yardstick explicit. Since anthropologists are today highly concerned with problems of culture change, some method of measuring trends must be developed, and I suspect that for this, quantitative information is again necessary. I have argued (1951) that as land shortage develops, the geographical mobility of the Tonga population will decline. I ought therefore to provide some measure of both land shortage and the rate of population mobility for the period when I worked with the Tonga so that anyone who works among the Tonga in the future will have a standard against which he can compare his own results.

Both the comparative method and the interest in problems of cultural or social change are therefore creating a new demand that the fieldworker should collect information on critical factors in such a way that direct comparisons may be possible.

How the information is to be collected remains the problem, which is more or less pressing according to the size of the unit with which the fieldworker is concerned and the time that he has at his disposal. Some collection of quantitative data has long been part of the standard schedule of fieldwork, and various suggestions for appropriate techniques have been made. Audrey Richards (1935) in the middle thirties recommended the adoption of the village census as a means of having some check upon the fieldworker's impressions. The census as a tool is admittedly most useful to the anthropologist working in an extant society, but Gifford (1926) has shown its possibilities even in situations where one is attempting to reconstruct a society with the aid of informants. Other survey techniques have also been used, and Streib (1952) has argued for their utility in studies of semi-literate societies, instancing his own work among the Navaho. Some form of census work is probably by now a standard technique among fieldworkers, at least among those who are dealing with extant societies.

The real argument lies not with regard to the use of the census, but how it shall be used, to what units it shall be applied, and how it can be combined with other field techniques to produce the most adequate description of the society which is to be studied. The anthropologist who works within a restricted geographical area and with a population numbering only some hundreds, or at the most several thousand, can afford to ignore sampling problems. Since he can collect his information for every man, woman, and child in the universe with which he deals, the question of the representativeness of his material does not arise. Moreover, he can combine his census work with a close observation of the members of the society which he is studying, and this gives him a valuable cross-check upon the accuracy of the information supplied to the census questionnaire. The material derived from the census, from any other survey technique employed, and from detailed observations, combines into a unified picture of a single entity at the end of his study.

Most anthropologists today find themselves in a very different situation, even when they are still working with what may be termed pre-literate societies. Those of us who have worked in Africa are usually faced with the problem of studying a unit whose population may be less than a hundred thousand, but is very frequently on the scale of several millions. This population may be a highly differentiated one, showing both social stratification and geographical or local variations. Frequently no very obvious boundary distinguishes it from its neighbours. Instead there may be gradual changes in language and customs over a tract of several hundred miles. At either extreme, the people may be very different, but at no one point would it be possible to say that one was now dealing with a different population, or a different society, or a different culture. Sheer size of population, sheer extent of geographical space, sheer degree of cultural differentiation, combine to make it impossible for the anthropologist to study and describe such a society in the same way as he does the small-scale societies with which most early fieldworkers were concerned.

In these circumstances it has frequently been argued that the census has little utility, since it is impossible to obtain a representative sample for the entire community which is to be studied, and that one must therefore confine oneself to qualitative descriptions of the way in which the society functions or of the different aspects of its culture. Attempts have been made to meet the objections on the score of representativeness, either through the use of a random sample or through some form of stratified sample. Neither one is particularly satisfactory.

Usually we have insufficient information about the universe from which the sample is to be drawn to allow us to apply sample techniques that would meet the standards set up for statistical analysis. In Central Africa, for instance, we usually lack even that vital necessity, an accurate estimate of the total size of the population with which we are to work. In 1946, when I began work with the Plateau Tonga, official estimates of their population varied between 80,000 and 120,000. Information on the distribution of the population was no better. In 1946 I could find no maps that would give me the location of villages. Maps were available giving some rough indication of the roads, but I was told that I could not expect to find a road where one was indicated and that I might well find roads where none was shown upon the map. The official estimates of the population of the various chieftaincies into which Tonga country is divided for administrative convenience were no better than the estimates for the total population. Official records showed the theoretical size of each village, but these were admittedly very far from indicating the true state of affairs. The records also listed by name all adult male taxpayers residing in each village, but a man listed officially under a village might be living anywhere else within Tonga country, or he might have gone away to work in the industrial areas, or he might be dead. Information on differences in custom, on the degree of missionary and other European influence, or on any other significant variables upon which a stratified sample might have been constructed was lacking, except for figures giving the amount of maize sold by each producer during the previous year. After several years in Tonga country, spent in touring from one area to another collecting survey material, I might have been in a position to consider the possibility of obtaining a not too unrepresentative sample for census purposes, but this was only after I had completed most of my fieldwork. My colleagues of the Rhodes–Livingstone Institute who went to other peoples in the region found themselves in much the same situation.

We also had to face another problem in deciding upon the utility of a census technique, and that was whether or not we should be able to collect a sufficient number of cases in the time at our disposal to make the technique worth using. If we had to spend a good proportion of our time in moving from place to place and in discovering appropriate people to question, it was obvious that at the end we should probably have little to show for our efforts. Though we could count on two tours, of approximately twelve months each, time was still limited. Furthermore, each of us had only the assistance of a clerk–interpreter in making the study. These men were of varying abilities, but none was trained as a research assistant. As time went on and the anthropologist became fluent in the language of the area while the assistant came to know his job, it became possible to divide the work somewhat, and thus to increase the amount of information that could be collected. My own assistant became invaluable, and in the end was doing a good deal of census work independently, with an occasional check by myself so that I could be certain of his accuracy in recording. (Eventually funds were obtained to employ and train a team of African assistants, to be attached to the various anthropologists working in the field and to collect quantitative information of various types under their guidance. But this occurred only after my own fieldwork was completed and I had left Central Africa.)

All these considerations forced us to consider carefully just what we were doing, and the units to which our final studies were to apply. We agreed that we ought to be able to compare our results, and this meant that we were to collect information on the same problems, and to present this information in as standard a fashion as possible. But we also felt that we had to relate our material to a given body of people. In a sense the result was that we tended to re-create the situation of the anthropologist who works within a small-scale society. We artificially delimited a unit for study, roughly a small geographical area containing a number of villages. Here we made the majority of our observations, and here we collected our quantitative material on a systematic basis. Or rather, we selected two or three such units, and cross-checked the information for each one against the other. Each unit was treated as a universe, within which we made no attempt to sample. Instead we collected information for the census for each individual in the area, returning again and again until each person had been interviewed. This took a good deal of time, and, indeed, it sometimes took more time to track down the one or two persons missing during the main census period than it did to do a census of all the rest of a village. It was not, however, time completely wasted, for every visit to a village could be used to build up a picture of the general background of those living within it and to add to information on points not directly involved in the census.

Since we were taking our quantitative material from the people within a small geographical area, the census could be easily incorporated with a set of other field techniques – observation, collection of genealogies, discussions with informants about matters of custom or the ordinary flow of daily events, attendance at rituals, etc. The problems of rapport were less because we were working with people whom we knew and who knew us. Moreover, since all were being subjected to the same barrage of questions, they minded it less than if one or two from a village had been chosen at random and they had had to wonder why fate had brought this infliction upon them and not upon their neighbours. Information obtained in the general give-and-take of daily life or during sessions when other matters were to the fore frequently gave a good check upon the accuracy of the answers obtained to census questions. Census information from several individuals also gave us some cross-check, as when a woman was asked for information on her children and it corroborated information that one of her sons had given regarding his parents and siblings. After the information was collected, we were able to get the maximum use from it because it applied always to people whom we knew and who were in the same social group as others about whom we had similar information.

After our first six months of fieldwork, we arrived at a standard census form that could be used in all the areas we were working in and that contained questions directed at getting information we all agreed was essential. At the same time, there was sufficient space on the form for the individual fieldworker to include additional questions as he decided that particular matters relevant to his field of inquiry needed systematic checking. Thus the final census form that each fieldworker used was adjusted to the particular problems of the area in which he worked, but at the same time certain relevant information was being collected in each area, and the information was being collected in a similar fashion so that comparable rates could be obtained.

The final census form that I used among the Tonga covered the following information:

Information on Kinsmen

Parents: names, clan, and ethnic affiliation, birthplace, present residence if still alive, cross-reference to their census cards if they were in the census area.

Siblings: names, sex, residence if alive, final residence if dead, cross-reference to their cards if they lived within the census area, names and sex and residence of their children if not in the census.

Spouse: names, clan affiliation, previous kinship term used, approximate date of marriage; if terminated, manner and approximate date of termination; number of plural marriages; whether or not marriage represented inheritance of widow.

Children: names and sex of children by each spouse or by lover or mistress, approximate birth dates, residence if alive, approximate date of death if dead and place of final residence, cross-reference to their census cards if they were within the census area.

Personal Information

Name, alternative names, sex, place of birth, approximate data of birth, clan, and ethnic affiliation, where and by whom reared.

Place of residence: village, chieftaincy, number of hut against chart of village, kinship relation to the head of the household.

Physical defects.

Religious affiliation, amount of schooling, occupation or craft specialization, official status, any indications of economic status.

Previous places of residence, and their sequence; reason for present residence.

Marriage payments, amount and from whom assistance received; payments of damages for elopement or for the impregnation of an unmarried girl, whereabouts of child.

Details of puberty ceremony (from women only): length of seclusion, by whom secluded, number of animals killed at final ceremony and by whom provided, length of time elapsing between final ceremony and marriage.

Labour history (for men): place of work, type of work, manner of reaching work and how this was financed, wage earned, amount brought back to village and for what this was used, sequence of trips to work, reason for going (this last a fairly useless question).

Fields: number, how obtained, and from whom.

Crop sales: sales from the previous harvest of maize, beans, peanuts, and other saleable crops – amount sold and money received.

Succession: whether or not informant had ever succeeded to a position or inherited the name of a dead person, and, if so, the kinship relation of the two.

House dedication: kinship category of the ancestor to whom the household was dedicated.

Household: number of people living in the household, and their relationship to one another.

In addition, if the informant had a sibling, child, parent, or spouse who was away at work, I tried to obtain details of the absent worker's labour history, including the length of time he had been gone, his present place of work, and whether or not he was in touch with his relatives and either visited them or sent them gifts of goods or money from time to time.

This may seem a long list of questions to batter informants with, but at the end my chief regrets were that I had not included more questions in the systematic check, that I included some of the questions too late to have a complete coverage for all the people in the census, and that occasionally I had grown slipshod and omitted a question or two during an interview. Some of the questions have little significance in themselves, but in combination with others on the schedule they may be used to throw light on a variety of problems.

In addition to the information about the individuals in the census area, further information about each village was included in the file containing the cards for each village. The headman and other adults in the village were interviewed to obtain the history of the village: the approximate date of its founding, if this had occurred within living memory, its previous locations, the succession to the headmanship, and the relationship of the successor to his predecessor. By the use of genealogies I attempted to discover how each person in the village was related to all others resident there. A numbered hut chart was drawn showing the physical layout of the village at the time of the census.

Other information collected about the inhabitants of the villages was on a cumulative basis. Villages in the two areas chosen for intensive study were watched over a four-year period, and I recorded births, puberty ceremonies, marriages, divorces, deaths, trips away to work, return of labour migrants, changes in hut sites, and changes in residence, throughout the four years. After the harvest and the sale of crops had been completed, we collected information each year on the amount that had been sold by each household. This material was either recorded on the census card or a cross reference was made to the place where it could be found in the file of other field notes.

During my first field tour I worked in four different areas, and planned to make these my unit of observation. In three I took censuses during that first year. Later it became necessary to reduce the number of areas to only two, and I chose one that was close to the belt of European farms and the railway line and one that was back in the reserve on the edge of the hills of the escarpment country. The two were contrasts in various ways: one was under Roman Catholic influence, the other under Seventh Day Adventist. One had only a small cash income from the sale of crops, the other had a much higher average income from crop sales and included a number of relatively wealthy progressive farmers. One was dominated by a government-appointed chief who lived in one of the villages, the other had no chief resident within it. One owed allegiance to a rain shrine or set of shrines, and there was community-wide participation in the rain and harvest rites, while in the other few concerned themselves with the local rain shrine or with the rites connected with it. One was considered by the Tonga to be a conservative area where old customs were still followed, the other was considered to be a progressive area where the people were trying to be like Europeans. The two areas lay about thirteen miles apart, and many of the people in the progressive area had originally come from the conservative one.

I re-did the census for these two areas in 1948, during my second tour, and thereafter kept it up to date by constant visits. In addition to the information that I had for these two areas, I also had incomplete census data from a third area studied in 1947, and I supplemented this with further material drawn from a census, carried out by my clerk in 1949–1950, of villages which lay in an intermediate zone between the progressive and conservative areas. In analysing the data, I have first compiled the material by area, compared the figures for the four, and, if no significant differences appear, then I have treated the material as a single body of data and indicated that it relates to all four different Tonga areas to which the census was applied. If significant differences appear, then the material for each area is handled separately, and I am concerned to find why the differences should appear and what factors are involved.

My knowledge of the area visited only in 1947, and of the intermediate area added in 1949–1950, is much less than it is for the two areas of intensive work, though even here the census material pertains to known groups, of a known size, and to all the people within the given areas. But I have made my formulation of problems and my analysis on the basis of my work in the two intensive areas and have used the material drawn from the other two only to test the wider applicability of the analysis.

The following discussion will show some of the uses to which the census information can be put. I would suggest that cross-cousin marriages are of most importance among the Tonga where people are most dependent upon mutual assistance, and where they are least affected by the market economy and the possibility of developing ties with the strangers who work along the railway line. When I analysed the crop sales for the three areas, I found that Area I (the progressive area) had the largest average income from this source; Area II (the intermediate area) had a significantly lower income; Area III (the conservative area) had the lowest income. The three areas are in the same order with respect to proximity to the railway line, Area II being only slightly farther removed from the railway than Area I. From all the marriages of informants in each area, I extracted the number of cross-cousin marriages and show it as a percentage of the total number of marriages. The results are given below:

	Area I	*Area II*	*Area III*	*Total*
Cross-cousin marriages shown as a percentage of all extant marriages	18·56	17·69	33·63	23·43

There is a real difference between Area I and Area III in line with my original argument, but Area II seems contradictory, at least if crop sales are any indication of the influence of impersonal market relationships upon a people.

Material derived from the census is also useful for checking general impressions, and frequently a check of the data indicates a trend very different from that which has been assumed. I originally assumed that the period of seclusion for girls at puberty had been progressively diminished by mission and school influence. When I compiled material on the length of the seclusion, classifying the material according to the decade in which the woman had been born, I found that there had actually been a progressive increase in the length of time of seclusion in all areas, but that this trend had been reversed for the last group of women to reach puberty. I now suspect that the increased prosperity of the Tonga, due to the development of a market for their crops and the introduction of tools allowing a larger area to be cultivated, enabled more families to indulge in the status-producing practice of lengthy seclusion, which indicated that the family had sufficient food and to spare. In early years, when the Tonga seem to have faced a hunger period as an annual event, since they did not produce enough grain to last from one harvest to the next, few families could reach the ideal length of seclusion.

Again, from the statements of informants, I believed that formerly Tonga women married much earlier than they do today and that girls were frequently married immediately after their puberty ceremony. Again, when the material on the length of time between the puberty seclusion and the marriage was analysed according to the decade in which the woman was born, the facts were directly contrary to popular belief and my understanding of the situation. Today I find that when I make a statement about the Tonga I am inclined first to check it against the material drawn from the census to see whether or not I am coming anywhere near the facts of the case. Impressions can be thoroughly wrong; so can the statements of informants. Getting out the material to check one's statements from the census forms may consume a good deal of time, but it also gives one some assurance that the statement is reasonably accurate, at least for the particular small group with which one has been dealing.

Whether or not my material for the areas studied is in any way representative of the Tonga people as a whole, I do not know. This is a problem which may be of some concern to the administration and to the technical assistants who are trying to deal with the Tonga as though they were a single unit. I do not think it is a problem that need concern the anthropologist who is trying to make a study of the interrelation of social factors in a single social system. After all, each area studied does represent a unit in which the people are in close social relations with one another. The factors that exist within that set of relations can be dealt with as though one were dealing with an isolated society. The anthropologist certainly has a duty to outline his method and the area to which his information applies, and furthermore he ought to be able to give some indication of variations over the general area that might affect his analysis and make it inapplicable or applicable elsewhere. This seems to be about the limit to which he can go, with the time, the assistance, and the resources at his disposal. I see no reason why information collected on particular small units within a larger area that bears the same 'tribal' name should not be used for comparison with information drawn from similar small units within other large areas that bear different 'tribal' names. The result of the intensive study of small units may not make for the best description in the style of a standard ethnography, but it is most likely to provide us with the type of information we need for testing hypotheses and for formulating new research into the relation between various social factors.

J. CLYDE MITCHELL

On Quantification in Social Anthropology[1]

QUANTIFICATION AND THE ANTHROPOLOGICAL APPROACH

THE methods of social anthropological study are frequently contrasted with those in the other social sciences. Traditionally anthropologists have pursued their studies among peoples whose languages, customs, and social institutions have differed sharply from their own. In this situation, according to some, their task has been primarily to translate the cultures of these peoples into the idiom of the anthropologists' own culture. Here the anthropologist cannot depend upon quantitative data derived from sample surveys which sociologists typically collect in their field studies, but has to rely mainly upon intimate knowledge arising out of a long-standing acquaintance with a few informants. Accordingly, the 'anthropological method' has tended to be taken as synonymous with the intensive study of small communities through participant observation without the use of quantitative methods. By contrast, sociological methods are assumed to involve schedules, questionnaires, and statistical procedures (see, for example, Katz, 1953; Kroeber, 1954, p. 290). The result has been an increase in quantitative material and statistical analysis in sociology and the other social sciences, but a rudimentary development of these methods in social anthropology. 'The anthropologists,' Nadel comments (1951, p. 6), 'have tended to become the biographers of single societies; often they chose small groups, where the intensive studies could be more adequately applied; always they had to exclude, or to use merely in an approximate fashion, that most valuable tool of modern sociology—statistics.' In 1953 Driver discerned some softening in the situation for he was able to write

[1] Some of the points in this paper were originally published in my paper 'Quantitative Methods and Statistical Reasoning in Social Anthropology' in *Sudan Society* II (1963b) 1–23. I am grateful to the Editor for allowing me to incorporate parts of that paper here. It would be an onerous task to review the use of quantitative material in the whole field of recent publications in social anthropology. I have restricted myself mainly, therefore, to the field I know best: Central and South Africa.

that statistics are 'still generally avoided to-day like the mother-in-law [though] the attitude towards [them] is gradually shifting from one of hostility towards one of respect' (1953, p. 54). But McEwen, writing a decade later (1963, p. 161), was constrained to observe that, in spite of recent developments in the use of statistical methods among anthropologists, 'traditional scepticism of formal methods still appears dominant'.

The collection of quantitative material in anthropological fieldwork has increased considerably during the last twenty years but its origins go back farther. In so far as British anthropology is concerned, the main stimulus probably came from Malinowski, though Rivers in 1900 had published a pioneering paper on quantifying sociological data available in genealogies. Malinowski advocated the use of quantitative methods as part of the process of his detailed 'concrete documentation'. Kaberry (1957, p. 80) says that Malinowski maintained that the anthropologist should 'measure, weigh and count everything that could legitimately be measured, weighed or counted', but he himself was never very systematic at this.

Malinowski's pupils, and those whom he influenced, however, were able to put his injunctions into effect with important results. It is quite clear that Firth in his fieldwork in 1929 for *We The Tikopia* had collected data in a form that was amenable to quantification but he presented it only in connexion with the demographic problem. But in his subsequent study, *Social Change in Tikopia*, he was able to make excellent use of a wide range of social facts collected in 1929 by comparing them with those in 1952 in thirteen tables – in itself an interesting comment on the increasing acceptance of quantitative presentations in modern anthropological monographs. Similarly, in his study of Malay Fishermen (1946), he was able to make extensive use of quantitative data. Richards, in her account of Bemba economy in 1933, presented quantitative material particularly on the labour input of women (1939, p. 104) and men (1939, pp. 396–397) and of men and women (1939, p. 387). Subsequently (1940), she presented some of the earliest quantitative data we have in the anthropological literature on marriage and divorce. Read at about the same time was making studies among the Ngoni of Nyasaland for which she was able to present some of her material in quantitative form (1942). In 1938 Schapera had pointed out that quantified data were useful in assessing the validity of statements and observations which informants professed to be of general relevance (1938, p. 30). Subsequently he made extensive use of quantitative data in his study of land tenure (1943), of labour migration (1947), and of marriage among kinsmen (1950).

It is clear that the necessity of presenting information in quantitative form where possible had become accepted before the 1939–1945 war. After the war a strong stimulus was given by the work done under the aegis of the Rhodes–Livingstone Institute. We have already noted Richards's pioneering use of quantitative methods in her studies of the economy of the Bemba peoples and of marriage. Godfrey Wilson, the first Director of the Institute, set the tone thereafter to be followed by making extensive use of quantitative data in his study of Broken Hill in 1939–1940 (1941–1942). Subsequently, Gluckman, and the agriculturists who worked among the Plateau Tonga of Mazabuka, quantified their analysis of land-holding and usage (Allan *et al.*, 1948). The practice of gathering full data in quantifiable form was established particularly in a field-training trip to the Lamba near Ndola (Mitchell and Barnes, 1950), where quantitative information was collected on population characteristics, kinship and clan composition of villages, marriage and divorce, labour migration, and family income and expenditure. This practice was continued in later studies conducted by Barnes in his study of marriage (1951) and divorce (1949), my own work on the Yao (1956), Colson's on the Plateau Tonga (1958), Watson's on the Mambwe (1958), Turner's among the Ndembu (1957), and Garbett's among the Shona (1960).

Statistical methods have not been unpopular in all fields of anthropological inquiry, for there is a long and respectable tradition dating from Tylor's classic paper in 1889 of using quantitative methods to demonstrate the association among cultural traits in different societies. This tradition has persisted in social anthropology in spite of trenchant criticisms of the basis and logic of the procedures involved. It finds modern expression in the numerous works based on the Human Relations Area Files (see Köbben, 1952). These works are primarily concerned with certain universals of social behaviour: they are concerned more with 'society' than with 'societies'. They seek to establish from an examination of the characteristics of many hundreds of societies certain regularities and to interpret these in terms of some theoretical proposition.

The use of quantitative methods where they are potentially more useful, that is in the analysis of field data, is much less common. There appear to be several reasons why this is so. It is partly due to the sort of societies in which anthropologists have worked and hence the way in which anthropologists have by custom pursued their fieldwork. It is partly due also to a possible reluctance to use methods based on material that has been collected in a way that violates the theoretical assumptions underlying random sampling and the mathematical procedures derived from them; and partly from misgivings about the appropriateness of quantitative and statistical methods to the sort of material with which anthropologists are normally dealing. This latter point of view is held by those who define social anthropology as the study of cultural phenomena or of the cultural aspects of social phenomena. Leach has pointed out that certain facts, such as legal rules, can hardly be stated in quantitative terms. Thus he observes that it is either true or not true that the English permit marriage with a deceased wife's sister (1963, p. 175). Fortes advanced the same point of view some years earlier when he argued that social facts viewed as cultural phenomena, 'can only be dealt with by direct observation and qualitative description and that quantitative methods therefore are inapplicable to them' (1949a, p. 57). This type of social fact refers to the norms and ideals of a people. If we accept this definition of the subject-matter of anthropology then clearly statistical methods are inappropriate.

But few social anthropologists would hold that norms and ideals alone are the data with which they are concerned. They are interested also in actual behaviour in the light of these norms and beliefs. For example, the amount of bridewealth actually paid, as against what should be paid, may tell us more about marriage arrangements than the fact that bridewealth must be paid and how it should be paid. Quantitative description and statistical analysis is, as Fortes points out, quite appropriate to this type of fact.

There is in fact no dichotomy of methods of research between those in social anthropology and those in the other branches of sociology. The social anthropologist seeks to establish the regularities between one observed fact and another and to relate them to each other in a logical way. The essential propositions in this process must be stated verbally: the art of fieldwork and the techniques of analysis cannot be reduced to mere mathematical manipulations. At the same time, the more detailed knowledge which quantitative methods allow and the correlations between phenomena which statistical reasoning can educe should be the essential foundation on which anthropologists start to erect their generalizations about the social behaviour of the people they study. Quantitative methods are essentially aids to description. They help to bring out in detail the regularities in the data the fieldworker has collected. Means, ratios, and percentages are ways of summarizing the features and relationships in data. Statistical measures based on the theory of probability go beyond the mere quantitative data and use devices to bring out the association between the various social facts the observer has collected. These are essentially analytical procedures and, as Fortes puts it, 'are nothing more than a refinement of the crude methods of comparison and induction commonly used' (1949a, p. 59).

THE ROLE OF QUANTIFICATION

The value of systematic quantification is that it ensures that the 'negative' cases, which are important in any analysis, are not overlooked. If, for example, a fieldworker is interested in the association between wealth and village headmanship, it is clearly important to record the wealth of those who are not village headmen as well as the wealth of those who are, and this is best done as part of a routine inquiry. As Richards comments in the use of census forms in anthropological inquiry: 'Information collected on a regular form of this sort is, owing to the frailty of the observer, always more complete. I found in practice that I nearly doubled the information I had previously obtained by the more pious resolution to "ask as many people as I could". The blank column stares at the anthropologist accusingly' (Richards, 1938, p. 54).

Systematic inquiry of this sort is no more than an aid to good ethnography. An example of the effective use of quantitative material in this way is provided by the work of Watson and Turner. Watson sets out to examine the way in which the social system has adapted itself particularly to the economic changes which were afoot when he made his study. To do this it was necessary for him to present an accurate description of the social attributes of Mambwe labour migrants and the population out of which they had come. In a set of nine tables he presents detailed information on the age and marital status of migrants in wage-earning employment, where they were working, and how long they had been away. These basic facts provide the support for Watson's description of the pattern of wage-earning in the population and how it relates to the social structure.

Quantification, however, while it is an important method of data collection, should be an aid to, and not the purpose of, fieldwork. Just what should be counted and how far the counting should be taken should be dictated by the sort of theoretical propositions the anthropologist is trying to establish. Theory should determine his use of statistics: his statistics should not delimit his theory. The survey of the Lamba villages conducted as an exercise in fieldwork training for a set of neophyte anthropologists provides an example of where quantification went beyond the requirements of the conceptual framework of the study. So assiduously were the quantitative data pursued that Gluckman was led to exclaim in the introduction: 'This report also seems to me to show that quantitative calculations alone are unsatisfactory. They show us the trees, but not the wood and this is my general impression of the report. As Bergson said on examining a spider's foot through the microscope, "we see very well, but we don't know what we are looking at." They have concentrated so much on numerical calculations that we do not learn what the social structure is' (Mitchell and Barnes, 1950, p. 18).

Turner's analysis of the social structure of the Ndembu (1957) provides a good example of the nice balance between quantitative data and structural analysis. Turner presents us with a meticulous analysis of the structure of Ndembu villages and supports his analysis with twenty-three tables showing the mobility of persons through villages, the social composition of the villages, and the age and conjugal status of the people in the villages. Here the quantitative data are used descriptively in order to show the general regularity in the material being presented. It is against this regularity that specific variations may be assessed, for as Turner points out in connexion with village fission: 'Numerical analysis tends to ignore as irrelevant the unique features of each instance of fission and to stress regularities, the statistically normative pattern' (1957, p. 239). But departures from these regularities pose problems for further examination and 'apparent exceptions to statistical regularities obtained from genealogical data on village fission prove to be themselves regularities within a wider system of social relationships' (1957, p. 232). Here Turner illustrates the fruitful interaction between quantitative description and case analysis.

The presentation of data in quantitative form in fact imparts a discipline to description which it otherwise might not have. This is illustrated in Cunnison's report on local organization on the Luapula (1950). In this report Cunnison says that there is a preference for the marriage of a man to his father's sister's daughter (*mufyala*). 'The mother's brother's daughter,' he continues, 'is also *mufyala* but marriage here is theoretically forbidden because a man may take the place of his mother's brother and even before he does so he may call his mother's brother's daughter simply "daughter"' (1950, p. 20). A diagram depicting the marriage rules shows that the marriage with mother's brother's daughter is in the prohibited category. Later Cunnison records the proportion among 166 marriages of men with different kinds of kinswomen. We learn that of the 166 marriages, seven (or 4·6 per cent) were with real or classificatory father's sister's daughters, while nine (or 5·6 per cent) were with the real or classificatory mother's brother's daughter (1950, p. 21). Thus, in spite of the rule, supported by cogent rationalization, that a man ought not to marry his mother's brother's daughter, in fact such marriages are at least as frequent as those of the enjoined type. This discrepancy between actual behaviour and the norm poses a new problem of analysis.

It is not essential that quantitative methods should have been used to reveal the discrepancies between the ideal rules or the informants' conceptions of behaviour and actual behaviour: it could be argued that accurate observation would also have shown up the inconsistency. This may be so, but the collection of the data in a form suited to quantitative presentation requires the fieldworker to work to a routine and provides the opportunity of his discovering facts of which he may not have previously been aware.

Quantification of certain aspects of social structure may also play an important role in elaborating and refining hypotheses. We can illustrate this by referring to Gluckman's well-known hypothesis linking high marriage stability with patriliny and low stability with matriliny and bilaterality (Gluckman, 1950). When Gluckman wrote he was not able to test his hypothesis against quantitative data: he had to rely on statements that the divorce rate was 'high' or 'low' in different societies. Unfortunately, not all anthropologists express divorce frequencies in comparable form, so it is difficult to test hypotheses such as Gluckman's. However, in the last decade there have been several studies which have expressed divorce frequencies by means of comparable measures. *Table 1* sets out some of these for Bantu peoples.

TABLE I DIVORCE RATIOS AMONG BANTU PEOPLES

	Ratio A	*Ratio B*	*Ratio C*	*Mode of Descent*
Kgatla	3·5	a	a	Patrilineal
Shona	9·4	32·6	11·3	Patrilineal
Tonga (Gwembe)	19·3	42·0	26·3	Matrilineal
Ganda	24·3	68·0	27·4	Patrilineal
Mambwe	19·8	40·8	27·9	Patrilineal
Yao	30·7	70·1	35·3	Matrilineal
Ngoni	28·5	55·8	36·9	Omnilateral
Tonga (Plateau)	29·8	57·1	28·4	Matrilineal
Herero	29·5	53·1	39·8	Double unilineal
Bemba	33·2	a	a	Matrilineal
Lamba	33·1	61·3	41·8	Matrilineal
Soga	37·8	a	a	Patrilineal
Luvale	39·0	70·0	45·0	Matrilineal
Ndembu	52·7	80·1	61·4	Matrilineal

a. Details not available.

Ratio $A - \frac{\text{Total number of marriages dissolved by divorce}}{\text{Total number of marriages ever contracted}}$

Ratio $B - \frac{\text{Total number of marriages dissolved by divorce}}{\text{Total number of marriages dissolved by both divorce and death}}$

Ratio $C - \frac{\text{Total number of marriages dissolved by divorce}}{\text{Total number of marriages contracted excluding those ended by death of a spouse}}$

Sources: For the Luvale, White (1960, p. 40); for the others, Mitchell (1963a).

An examination of these ratios shows that Gluckman was both right and wrong. In general his hypothesis has been upheld in that on the average the patrilineal people in this table have lower divorce ratios than the matrilineal. But the table also shows that some patrilineal peoples have divorce ratios which are as high as some matrilineal peoples and some matrilineal peoples have ratios as low as some patrilineal. These findings lead to the conclusion that the hypothesis as it stands needs some refinement, and the table of divorce ratios suggests that one way of approaching this would be to examine the social structure of the patrilineal peoples with a low ratio against those with a high ratio and to do the same with the matrilineal peoples. In this way we might be able to discover the factors which give rise to the difference in the divorce ratios.

Quantitative data have proved particularly useful in the study of social change. It is difficult to say whether the frequency of marriage between people of different social classes or different ethnic groups or religious affiliations has changed between one period and another unless the comparative frequency of such marriages have been previously determined. Firth, for example, has used quantitative data to good effect in the study of change in Tikopia (1959, pp. 191–212). In 1929 he had recorded data on the continuity of names and sites of residence, on household composition, on the social origin of marriage partners, and so on. In 1952 he was able to compare these findings with those of 1929 and draw conclusions about the slow rate of change. Of particular interest here was the decline in the opinion that members of the chief's lineage should marry only members of the lineage of other chiefs. Firth's statistics (1959, p. 208) show, however, that as between 1929 and 1952 the proportion of marriages between members of chief's lineages and commoners had remained virtually constant.

Quantitative data have also been used by Garbett (1960) in a study of changes in some Shona villages over a ten-year period. Garbett was able to carry out a survey of a group of five Shona villages in 1958 in exactly the same way as they had been surveyed by Bernardi in 1948. Among a number of aspects of change, Garbett considers he is able to show that, while the overall rate of labour migration had doubled, the village structure in terms of the proportion of kinsmen of various kinds present in them had not altered appreciably. This conclusion was possible only because Bernardi had published his data in a quantifiable form and Garbett was able to prepare tables that could allow the data compiled at the two different times to be compared.

A third way in which quantitative data have been used is to bring out the significant relationships between categories of social phenomena. One of the classical analyses of this sort is that of Fortes of the relationship between lineage organization and household composition among the Ashanti (1949). He reports the results of a survey of household composition in two Ashanti settlements and is able to show by using simple percentages how the composition of households differs through the operation of the divergent principles of matriliny and conjugality, according to local conditions and to the sex and age of the head of the household. Fortes concludes: 'Our investigation shows how elementary statistical procedures reduce apparently discrete "types" or "forms" of domestic organization in Ashanti life to the differential effects of identical principles in varying local contexts' (Fortes, 1949, p. 84).

Spindler and Goldschmidt (1952, p. 81) are so convinced of the value of supplementing traditional methods of anthropological inquiry in the study of culture change that they write: 'Traditional ethnographic methods would not have yielded useful conclusions to the problem of cultural change that we set ourselves. It is doubtful if we could have arrived at the proper acculturational groups without the use of a schedule and sample data; it is certain that their use could not have been validated without such data, and obvious that the social involvements of these group differentiations could never have been understood.'

Social phenomena are complex. One of the advantages of collecting material in quantitative form is that statistical procedures have been developed to disentangle the effects of several causative factors lying behind observed phenomena. This is the purpose behind the detailed analyses of the factors underlying the prestige of village headmen among the Yao (Mitchell, 1956, pp. 76–107). A detailed analysis of the social characteristics of 424 Administrative village headmen in relationship to the marks of rank which they possessed showed that several factors played an important role in the struggle for prestige of village headmen. Among these were the kinship of the village headman with the chief, the size of the village he controlled, and the history of the village. The tribe and religion of the headman proved to have little effect. These correlations had emerged from direct observation in the course of ordinary fieldwork – in fact the characteristics to quantify were determined by direct observation – but quantification enabled the generality of the relationship between the social characteristics of village headmen and their social prestige to be demonstrated, and also enabled us to determine which social characteristics were most important.

TYPES OF QUANTITATIVE DATA

The fieldwork data, quantitative or qualitative, which social anthropologists use to base their conclusions on are all derived ultimately from observation. From this point of view there is no essential difference in the two types of data. Quantification has no magical property to confer accuracy on the data: if the basic observations are inaccurate or incomplete, statistics derived from them will assuredly also reflect these weaknesses. What quantification achieves is a condensation of facts so that the regularities and patterns in them are more easily discernible. It follows that the quantification must be made in terms of categories of classification that are meaningful for the purposes the observer has in mind. The difficulty with many statistics collected for official use is that frequently they have been assembled on a basis which is irrelevant for sociological purposes, and they are, for that reason, correspondingly less useful to research workers. There would be little point, for example, for an official census to record whether Yao headmen were of Invader stock or not, but this is very important in the analysis of the position of headmen in the social structure.

In general, therefore, the social anthropologist must collect his own quantitative material, for only he is able to say what categories of data are likely to be relevant to his analysis. This does not mean that he is always unable to use official statistics. Clearly, official census figures, for example, or records of maize, cattle, cotton, or tobacco sales may be of immediate and direct interest to a social anthropologist. It means rather that official statistics can provide useful if not essential background information for the social anthropologist. But almost invariably he finds it necessary to collect the material he needs for his analysis himself.

Sociological data may be collected by a variety of field techniques, ranging in intimacy of social contact from the intensity of participant observation on the one hand, to the transiency of contact in formal social surveys on the other. The social anthropologist usually prefers to work towards the 'participant observation' end of the continuum. This does not mean that the data he collects by these techniques are of necessity not quantifiable. Characteristics of units which can be isolated such as individual households, marriages, office holders, lineages, villages, or even larger units may be classified and counted however the material has been collected. The real process of abstraction lies in the classification not in the enumeration. An anthropologist may go through his notebooks after he has left the field and classify the material into categories that are relevant for his analysis. But he can do this only if his material has been collected systematically enough for him to categorize his cases accurately – and of course if he has a set of meaningful categories to put his cases into.

It is because of the necessity of collecting material systematically that schedules have come to be used more and more in fieldwork.[1] Obviously it is impossible to lay down hard and fast rules about the content and design of schedules for use in anthropological fieldwork. The sort of information the fieldworker wants to record, the physical conditions under which he is working, how he goes about his fieldwork, whether he is to complete the schedule himself or have interviewers do it for him, all affect the design, layout, and character of the schedule. Some interviewers prefer to use a schedule printed on stiff card in which the material is recorded in abbreviated or code form. Others are not embarrassed by large double foolscap census sheets and the awkwardness of handling these in windy or rainy circumstances where tables and chairs are rare. Some fieldworkers may wish to record data on particular aspects of the life of the people they are studying, as, for example, economic data or psychological data. Clearly they will need special schedules for these data. Others may wish to collect a few basic demographic and social facts which are of the most general relevance and utility. All fieldworkers will want to fill the margins and backs of their schedules with on-the-spot observations and comments that they will wish to follow up at some future opportunity.

In general there are certain types of information that most fieldworkers will probably find useful and even important when they come to analyse their material. Basic genealogical and demographic data are of this sort. In addition to this basic information there may be other material that is significant for the particular study the fieldworker is engaged upon but will not necessarily be relevant in other studies. Whether an informant is 'Red' or 'School', for example, will be highly significant in the Eastern Cape of South Africa but hardly anywhere else.

A few schedules used by anthropologists have been published, but it is by no means the practice among anthropologists as it is among sociologists to let their readers see what sort of information they have sought to collect. Richards, in her early article on the place of the village census in anthropological fieldwork, published the schedule she herself had used (Richards, 1938, p. 55). Colson lists the types of information she collected on her census schedules when she was working among the Plateau Tonga (see above, pp. 11–12, and Appendix). Types of schedule used in urban areas are available in Reader (1961, pp. 171–172), McCulloch (1956, pp. 84–85), and Pons (1956, p. 272).

As in all schedules the greatest danger lies in attempting to exploit the opportunity to collect information and therefore to ask too many questions

[1] I distinguish between 'questionnaires', which are completed by the respondent himself, and 'schedules', which are completed by an interviewer. Schwab (1954) discusses different types of schedule that might be used in anthropological studies.

about too many things. This is perhaps less of a danger where the anthropologist himself collects the information. First, this type of data collection usually comes at a phase of fieldwork when the anthropologist has had time to decide what the important questions are that he has to ask. Second, as Colson describes, the schedule is completed in the course of general fieldwork during which constant visits are common and the urgency for making the most of the opportunity of collecting a wide variety of items of information is reduced. Third, of course, since the anthropologist will be collecting the information himself, he will quickly appreciate how easily hostility and resentment can develop if a schedule seems interminably long and pointless to the respondent.

The information to be collected by means of schedules and formal interviews should be trimmed down to what the fieldworker feels is absolutely essential for his purposes. Frequently the fieldworker is in no position to make the judgement of what is and what is not essential until his researches are quite well advanced. If he is not clear about this even after extended fieldwork, then it is clear that he is not yet ready to try to quantify his material.

One type of basic information which most anthropologists find it essential to collect, regardless of their theoretical orientations, is demographic information. It is usually necessary to say how many people constitute the community that is being studied. But relatively few anthropologists have collected the requisite information to enable them to make an assessment of population growth or have not tried to present the material if they have collected it. Thus one of the points in Turner's analysis, for example, is that fission of villages is only partly related to population growth. Yet he does not present data to show how fast the population is increasing though clearly he must have collected the requisite information. On the other hand, there have been several studies that have shown how material collected in the course of anthropological fieldwork can be used to estimate population growth (e.g. Ardener, 1962; Culwicks, 1938, 1939; Fortes, 1943; Mitchell, 1949a). Most of these studies have used the net reproduction rate to assess population growth but some simpler, if cruder, measures such as fertility ratios have not been used to the extent to which they could be.[1]

Demographic measures of this sort may be important in posing theoretical problems. Lineages, for example, cannot continue to manifest their

[1] Barnes (1947, p. 53) has reminded us that Kuczynski pointed out that the minimum of information required to gauge population trends is (i) sex, (ii) whether past puberty or not, and in the case of women, (iii) the number of children born alive, (iv) the number of children still alive. One way in which this information can be used to estimate population trends is given in Myburgh (1956). The reader is also referred to MacArthur's book *Introducing Population Statistics*, which is particularly useful for anthropologists.

segmentation in viable social groups unless the population is expanding. Conversely, it would be expected that a low rate of reproduction would affect the type of settlement pattern and kinship differentiation which a society shows. An interesting illustration of this comes from the Luvale of north-west Zambia. White reports that the reproductive performance of the Luvale, as estimated by several measures, is low. The number of living children under the age of 5 years per 1,000 women aged 15 to 50 (i.e. the fertility ratio) is only 269 as against 738 for the Yao or 820 for the Plateau Tonga. The net reproduction rate has been estimated at 0·89 but was probably slightly higher, i.e. just at replacement level (White, 1959, p. 54). The causes of this low fertility, which incidentally is also shown by Luvale women in town, are not known, but some interesting sociological consequences appear to flow from it. In marked contrast to the neighbouring Ndembu and other Central African matrilineal peoples, Luvale lineages are of considerable depth. They are internally segmented and form the nuclei of village communities, but their villages do not break up as frequently as those, say, of the Ndembu or the Bemba. Instead the Luvale are able to keep their gardens going for considerable periods. This is partly because they are a cassava-growing people which means that they can use their soils for longer periods than if they grew millet, but also presumably because the population does not press on resources so quickly. It is interesting to note that where there is a rapid division of villages we find positional succession linking the parts of a divided village subsequently into formal relationships. There is no positional succession among the Luvale (White, 1960, p. 13). Clearly there are a series of problems of social organization here which may possibly be related back to a low rate of reproduction.

Other types of demographic measure may also be important for anthropological analysis. One of these, for example, is the sex ratio in relation to polygyny. Anthropologists are sometimes led into making false inferences about the influence of demographic factors in this connexion. For example, some conclude that if there are many polygynous marriages then this must be because there are more adult females than adult males in the population. It has long been known, however, though possibly not yet fully appreciated, that the polygyny rate is also a function of the difference of age at first marriage between men and women. If men marry on the average much later than women the total number of years the women are able to spend in marriage is more than that of the men even if the sex ratio is equal. This discrepancy can only be explained by the fact that some of the marriage-years experienced by the women are shared by one man, i.e. in polygyny. Gibson (1958) has provided good data for the Herero and has analysed it in a sophisticated way. He shows that men on the average are eleven years older than their wives on first marriage and that the mean difference in age at marriage increases in the second, third, and subsequent marriages of men (i.e. they marry younger wives). Correspondingly the mean difference for women *decreases* with successive marriages, i.e. women contract second and subsequent marriages to older men. Thus, while there is a relatively high rate of polygyny among the Herero, this occurs without a marked discrepancy in the sex ratio.

These examples illustrate the way in which quantitative material may be used to pose problems in research or to provide solutions to problems already posed. The presentation of basic demographic data such as age and sex distributions, measures of population trends, tabulations of conjugal status by age, is becoming standard in anthropological monographs. Some advance has also been made in presenting village structure in standard form (e.g. Turner, 1957; Watson, 1958; Colson, 1958; Garbett, 1960) and in presenting marriage and divorce statistics in a form that allows them to be used in comparative analysis (see below, pp. 61–64). In time, it is hoped, no student of social anthropology will be considered prepared for fieldwork until he knows how to present relevant types of basic information in standard quantitative form.

SAMPLING

If we may assume that the type of information that needs to be collected is known, we are faced with two fieldwork problems: from whom are we going to collect the information and how are we going to go about collecting it? The first problem concerns sampling, and the second fieldwork methods.

Sampling has presented a difficult problem to anthropologists. The customary procedures of moving into a community and of building up social relationships within it by participating in the activities as much as possible has made the willingness of the people to accept a stranger in their midst a most important consideration in the anthropologist's choice of his venue of study. It is true that most anthropologists also attempt to take a number of other factors into account in deciding where they will settle. Questions of accessibility, how 'typical' the community is of the people the anthropologist is interested in, how much affected they are by urban influences or contact with other peoples, or even the extent to which communities are 'atypical' and have special characteristics which may contribute more to the understanding of the social system of the community than 'typical' units, all play a part. Probably in most cases the anthropologist uses some existing relationship with a person he already knows to gain entry into the community. This is particularly true when the anthropologist begins to move about outside the community of first entry. These adventitious factors conspire, however, to make the anthropologist's sample what the social surveyors call a 'purposive' sample rather than a truly random one. This carries with it serious limitations to the validity of drawing inferences about the universe of which the community is assumed to be representative.

The difficulties are not merely those of finding a community in which the anthropologist will be able to work in the way that his profession has decreed to be necessary. Even if he wishes to draw a type of sample that would satisfy the statisticians, formidable difficulties still arise. One of these is that if a suitable sample is to be drawn then the research worker must be able to define the universe adequately. This means that every unit in the universe he wants to study should be open to selection with a known degree of probability. In the sort of societies that anthropologists study, however, the kind of records that would provide an adequate frame for sampling seldom exists. To select a random sample of villages in a given area we would need to be sure that every village is known and identifiable. The sample when drawn from these villages and if selected by a truly random method will be representative of these villages within a calculable degree of probability. If the records are incomplete, however, the sample is not a truly random one and it is erroneous to treat it as if it were.

Even if it is technically possible to draw a truly random sample, or to use some method of systematic sampling which does not call for a specification of the universe, the anthropologist faces difficult problems in using this sample. In the first place the units are likely to be scattered geographically and involve expensive and time-consuming travel. But a more serious difficulty is that the method of inquiry that the anthropologist uses, i.e. long periods of residence in one area, prevents him from working in more than two or three different areas in one field tour.

It is technically incorrect to use statistical measures based on probability theory to make inferences about the population at large from a sample unless that sample is a truly random one. Even if anthropologists may not have taken a random sample, however, they may still claim that their samples are representative of the communities they are studying because their data are 'typical' (see Ardener, 1962, pp. 1–9). This point is also raised by Barnes (p. 60), who argues that in collecting divorce statistics even though we cannot draw a random sample of villages to survey we can try to ensure that the villages are 'typical' in respect of say, kinship, history, structure, and apparent wealth and then assume that they are also typical in respect of marriage stability. This, however, is a dubious assumption and purposive selection of this sort cannot be a substitute for random sampling.

One of the assumptions of taking a random sample is that the various factors associated with marriage stability, which differ among themselves, will offset each other over the whole sample and so minimize bias. But at the same time they should provide sufficient variation among themselves to enable the variation of marriage stability to be analysed in terms of these factors.

Sampling in anthropological fieldwork is complicated also by considerations concerning the nature of the universe of events out of which the anthropologist wishes to draw his sample. The assumptions which underlie sampling are that the sampling units in the population are accessible, distinguishable, and independent of each other. For demographic purposes the unit of analysis is the cluster of individuals such as a household or a village. But if individuals are sampled they can be chosen quite independently of other individuals.

In social anthropology, however, the unit of analysis is not the individual but the social relationships in which he is involved. This introduces some knotty problems. One of these refers to the fact that a social relationship is essentially an abstraction from behaviour and as such is not a separable, isolated, and immediately perceptible phenomenon available for random selection. Let us consider as an example an attempt to assess the frequency of accusation of witchcraft between two categories of kinsmen in order to test the hypothesis that witchcraft accusations occur in those relationships in which there is likely to be hostility but no socially approved way of expressing hostility. Let us suppose that we have found in our study that there are a large number of accusations between brothers. To assess the significance of our data we must relate the number of witchcraft accusations to the number of brother–brother relationships. If we were designing a statistical study to test the hypothesis we would need to draw a random sample of brother–brother relationships and then examine them to see in a given period how many accusations of witchcraft are made between the two. Unfortunately brother–brother relationships are not concrete and thus cannot be selected for sample. We could, however, select some men at random and find out how many brothers they have. The assumption here would be that the social relationships of any individual selected at random would be representative of the social relationships which all individuals like him are involved in. Even if we accept this we are still left with the problem of deciding whether merely being a brother is a 'relationship' in terms of the hypothesis. The two men, for example, may hardly see each other from one year's end to the other, so that from the point of view of the hypothesis their relationship can hardly be considered to be the equivalent of an intimate relationship between two brothers who see each other every day (Marwick, 1952, and below, pp. 242–243).

Another problem arises from one of the fundamental assumptions in social anthropology: that social relationships between people in a community constitute a *system*. This means that the relationships linking the people in a community an anthropologist studies are not independent of one another. Strictly speaking we cannot take a sample of brother–brother relationships because they do not form a separate and independent phenomenon which can be considered apart from all other relationships in which an individual is involved. The starting-point in sampling for most statistical work in social anthropology must usually be the individual. For example, in computing divorce ratios the unit of analysis is the marriage but the sampling-unit is the individual. Since there seems to be no way of sampling marriages directly, the only method open to us is to sample individuals. This may involve us in difficulties. In the first place two individuals, if they are a man and a woman, may be involved in the same marriage. In the second place where an individual has, or has had, a number of marriages, his selection in a sample may introduce a bias analogous to that in cluster sampling due to an undue weighting in the sample of elements that are in some way alike.

It is obviously an advantage when collecting quantitative data to work with a representative sample if this is at all possible, and perhaps anthropologists should put more effort into sampling, which in practical terms implies trying to overcome the resistance of informants who have been selected on a basis other than their willingness to co-operate with the anthropologist. Specific sampling procedures will need to be adopted to suit individual fieldwork situations. It is unlikely that a suitable sampling frame will be available for the drawing by random numbers or some other means of a simple sample of individuals, families, villagers, or other units of inquiry. Systematic sampling, whereby every '*n*'th sampling unit – individual, family, village, etc. – is chosen in turn as it is encountered in the field, may appear to obviate the need for an accurate sampling frame since this is created, as it were, as the study proceeds. But this is not likely to be true since in order to be effective, all the sampling-units in the community must be exposed to the possibility of selection. Because anthropological fieldwork is so time-consuming and the number of units that can be covered in a normal field trip so limited, the sampling fraction must be set in advance so as to include the whole of the community in the possibility of being selected for investigation. This implies an adequate knowledge of the universe of units to be sampled and this is, as I have said, normally not easily obtainable.

In order to avoid some of the disadvantages of simple sampling, recourse might be had to stratified or multi-stage sampling. Normally in stratified sampling different proportions of cases are drawn from significant categories of the population to ensure that sufficient cases of each are included to enable a satisfactory statistical analysis to be made. In so far as anthropological studies are concerned, regional areas might be taken as the strata and units within these selected for study, thus avoiding some of the geographical scatter that is likely to arise out of simple sampling.

Multi-stage sampling can achieve the same effect. Here a number of group units such as, for example, wards or villages in a chiefdom are selected by some random method. Then specific sub-units such as household or individuals are selected by a random method from *within* the groups for interview. These methods of selecting units for study avoid some but not all of the disadvantages outlined earlier in connexion with sampling for anthropological fieldwork.

But anthropologists are likely to raise objections on the grounds that units selected for study at random, especially if they are individuals or simple families, will be torn out of their social context and cannot be examined in an anthropological framework which sees these units as part of a larger embracing social system. To some extent this objection may be met by what is known as 'cluster sampling'. Here the sampling-units may be fairly large, as, for example, villages or even wards. The units of study are randomly selected from a list of known units but the whole unit is studied. Adopting this procedure involves some difficulties in the calculation of certain types of statistical measure such as standard errors when they apply to the elements of the unit, as, for example, individuals in a village where the village is the sampling-unit. But the awkwardness of computation is outweighed by the advantage of working with a unit which is a 'community' in itself.

The inadequate sampling procedures normally used by anthropologists impose serious restrictions on their use of statistical measures particularly if they wish to extrapolate from the samples to the whole populations of which their samples purport to be representative. Statistics are usually used in other social sciences in order to generalize about some larger universe, but anthropological fieldwork has usually involved intense and intimate knowledge of a relatively restricted segment of a society, and, usually, anthropologists have been prepared to generalize about the society as a whole from this restricted experience.

This is not as unjustified as it may seem for much depends upon what features of the sample we wish to generalize about. If we are referring to certain measurable characteristics of the sample, as for instance its age and sex structure, or the number of divorces its people on the average have experienced, we may only assume that these characteristics are general for the whole population if the sample is a truly random one. But an anthropologist is usually aiming rather at stating the *logical* connexions between social facts, as for example the necessary pattern of relationships between a mother's brother and a sister's son in a patrilineal society. If he has been able to establish this in one segment of the society it is probable, because of the intrinsic nature of the connexion, that it is general for other segments in the same type of society.

Statistical measures, therefore, may be used in two different ways. They may be used either to estimate the limits within which some characteristic measured in the sample is likely to fall in the parent population, or they may be used to make relationships among data *within* the sample explicit. If it is relevant the anthropologist may prepare cross-tabulations of age and village headmanship, for example, and possibly show that there is an unmistakable relationship between them as measured by ratios or correlation coefficients. He could apply a chi-square test to this cross-tabulation and so determine the independence, or otherwise, of the characteristics he is considering. But he may not argue from the data, unless he has taken a truly random sample, that the correlation between the two phenomena in the population at large is likely to fall within certain specified limits. His statement is confined to the data he is handling and they may not be applicable to the whole population. This is because the correlation at this stage is a *surface* one. If he is now able to demonstrate that the correlation is also a *logical* one then his justification for considering it general for the whole society is much greater.

DATA COLLECTION

Even if the sample drawn is impeccable from the statistical point of view, the anthropologist is still faced with the difficulties in the collection of his data. Perhaps the most important of these lies, as Nadel suggests (1951, p. 6 ff.) in the sort of fieldwork the social anthropologist has done traditionally. Since he is seldom buttressed by the authority of a government officer, he must rely on personal contact with his respondents to gain their co-operation. People living in isolated remote areas are usually suspicious of strangers, so it is seldom possible for a fieldworker to introduce a team of literate interviewers to conduct a social survey among them even if the interviewers are from the same ethnic group as he is studying. He must therefore collect the data himself and because this takes time it is not surprising that many social anthropologists are unable to assemble enough quantitative data to justify their using sophisticated statistical procedures on them.

The difficulties of collecting quantitative data in anthropolitical fieldwork are exacerbated by the fact that the peoples among whom an anthropologist works do not usually think in quantitative terms in the same way as do people who live in industrial or commercial societies. The ages of people involved in social situations, for example, are significant for many of the problems the anthropologist wishes to analyse, but it is unusual for the people to reckon their ages in years. It is consequently extremely difficult and time-consuming for the anthropologist to record ages accurately.

As Colson has pointed out, however, these difficulties need not constitute an insuperable barrier to the collection of quantitative data. In the first place, as she observes, if the circumstances in the field allow of it, census-taking can become a routine activity for the anthropologist. In this way the anthropologist systematically visits every individual or household in the community and ensures that a certain basic set of information is recorded for each. The people of the community will probably know the anthropologist and since everyone is subjected to the same inquiry, this sort of activity comes to define the role of the anthropologist. Even if the situation in the field precludes this, data can be built up systematically over time as points crop up in conversation, in the settlement of disputes, on ritual occasions, or in any other way in the normal course of social interaction in the community. But if sufficient quantitative material for detailed statistical analysis is to be collected in the short time normally available for fieldwork, the anthropologist must rely on additional interviewers to collect it for him. It has become customary in many field studies for anthropologists to employ at least one assistant who comes from among the people he is studying. This assistant serves as an interpreter and general informant in the early stages of the fieldwork while the anthropologist is learning the language and becoming familiar with the way of life of the people. Later, when the anthropologist is able to work on his own, the assistant is able, as Colson points out, to work on his own to collect standard types of information which may be used in quantitative analyses later.

This procedure may be extended and several interviewers used, so some of the techniques of the social survey now become applicable. But the use of numbers of interviewers introduces problems of its own. First of all, a certain minimum level of education is needed in order that the interviewers should have the standard of literacy to be able to record information accurately and to understand the questions. Experience in Central Africa suggests that interviewers who have ten years of education are immeasurably better than those who have eight: those who have twelve years are slightly better than those who have ten. But if interviewers have more than this, unless they are exceptionally suitable on personal grounds, they do not do as well as those with less education. This is probably because the gap in education between the interviewers and the respondents, most of whom are illiterate cultivators, becomes too great and the task becomes too monotonous for them. Interviewers with this level of education who are also fluent in the language of the people of the area being surveyed, however, are usually in short supply and there may be real difficulties in finding them (see Schwab, 1954; Streib, 1952).

The use of interviewers with relatively low education presupposes that the data they are capable of collecting is limited to straightforward demographic and personal information of the type called for on the Census Form that appears in the Appendix (p. 247). But even this calls for some training in the filling out of the schedule, and in the techniques of age estimation, cross-checking the reliability of responses, and the other skills that make for successful survey interviewing. For this reason it is often not feasible to use part-time interviewers such as school-teachers, university students, or high-school scholars on vacation, unless the inquiry is of the simplest type.

The whole question of rapport is also raised by the introduction of interviewers who are strangers into a remote tribal area. The respondents in areas such as these may be more hostile to interviewers than to the anthropologist himself. This is borne out by the use of a team of interviewers in the fieldwork of the anthropologists of the Rhodes–Livingstone Institute. While Watson was able successfully to use interviewers among the Mambwe in Northern Rhodesia, van Velsen at the same time found that this was impossible in Nyasaland (1964, p. xx). Many different factors seem to have operated here, among which was the intensity of political resentment in Nyasaland against people from outside Nyasaland at the particular time of the fieldwork; the problems arising out of ethnic animosities and the particular difficulty of strangers in Lakeside Tonga society which derives from the nature of their social system; and possibly also the position of the interviewers, who felt insecure in an environment which was unfamiliar linguistically and culturally and hostile to boot.

Teams of interviewers have been used most extensively in 'social survey' type studies in towns and peri-urban areas, where the information called for has been of a fairly straightforward demographic kind. Here, perhaps, the short, focused interview is more appropriate than the rather more leisurely, rambling interview typical in rural fieldwork.

If the information called for goes beyond the straightforward demographic data, serious difficulties arising out of interview bias may ensue. Marwick provides an interesting discussion of the problems relating to this in his paper dealing with an attitude survey in a rural area in Northern

Rhodesia (Marwick, 1956). Marwick found that in this sort of survey statistically significant differences in responses to questions were given when he was the interviewer as against his two African interviewers, and there were also significant differences between the interviewers themselves, who were dissimilar in temperament and social insight.

If the investigation is large enough to result in substantial numbers of interviews by each interviewer and there are an appreciable number of interviewers employed, it is possible to test the reliability of individual interviewers by allocating interpenetrating samples to them and testing the results obtained by individual interviewers against probability tests. Few anthropological surveys are likely to be large enough for this to be possible and the only recourse open to the anthropologist is to make occasional checks on the work of individual interviewers and to estimate their reliability in this way.

There is undoubtedly a difference in the quality of material collected by an anthropologist as against that collected by an assistant, however efficient the latter is. This difference arises out of the theoretical orientation of the anthropologist who is able, during the routine census-taking, to seize upon some reported irregularity or peculiarity in behaviour and use it to illuminate the operation of custom and thus deepen his understanding of the social system. Interviewers are auxiliaries and not substitutes in fieldwork.

DATA-PROCESSING

The processing of quantitative material once it has been collected often presents unexpected labour and chagrin to fieldworkers who are inexperienced in handling this sort of data. This is not only in respect of the computations to be performed on the data to bring out the required relationships, but also in the sheer mechanics of preparing suitable tabulations from the material.

Of course, to a considerable extent these problems beset any other social scientists with quantitative material to handle. The general problems, therefore, are described in any general textbook dealing with research methods such as those of Moser (1958), Goode and Hatt (1952), or Yates (1960). So far as the anthropologist is concerned, there are two aspects of his activities which present particular problems in his handling of quantitative data. The first of these relates to the circumstances under which the anthropologist does his fieldwork. In contrast to the urban sociologist who is conducting a social survey and who will probably have facilities available in the form of skilled punched-card services for the handling of his data immediately it is produced by the interviewers, the anthropologist must accumulate his material in the field and can only expect to convert it into more manipulable form when he comes out of the field. If he needs preliminary tabulations from his material, therefore, he must produce them manually. This implies that the data should preferably be recorded in a form that makes the abstraction of information easy.

Second, while the social surveyor is likely to collect comparatively little information for a large number of respondents, the anthropologist, accustomed to working intensively in small-scale communities, is likely to have extensive material on comparatively few respondents. This means that his schedules are likely to be complicated and that difficulties arise in reducing them to quantifiable generalizations.

Most anthropologists reduce the raw data in their schedules to tabulations by means of the basic pencil-and-paper 'bar-and-gate' counting. This is usually possible because the number of cross-tabulations required is small and the number of schedules to be thumbed through limited. This method quickly becomes tedious and inaccurate if either of these two conditions is changed. When this stage is reached most fieldworkers find it worth while to record all the relevant information concerning each unit on a slip of paper or a card and then to sort these cards into piles according to the tabulations wanted. For example, for the purposes of the detailed analysis of the 424 village headmen in Chapter IV of *The Yao Village*, I typed information about each village headman on a small slip of paper 1½ inches by 2½ inches in size. Where the category of classification was not immediately apparent as, for example, in regard to kinship with the chief, I marked the card with a distinctive symbol (e.g. a triangle, a square, or a circle for different kinds of kinship). These symbols were in different colours to denote whether the kinship was direct or by clan. In addition lines ruled across the card in different colours made classification into categories with different marks of prestige immediately apparent. It was not difficult then to sort these cards into piles each of which represented a cell in a cross-tabulation. This device reduced the tedium of tabulating the material but involved two difficulties. In the first instance where the category of classification of the headman was not immediately apparent the details had to be perused individually on each card and consciously reclassified each time a tabulation was made. This happened, for example, where tabulations involving the size of the villages in class intervals were concerned. Second, each pile had to be counted manually to get the cell totals. Where a mistake was made and the marginal totals from one table did not agree with another, the entire table had to be re-done.

The first of these difficulties can be overcome by using edge-punched cards known in British circles as Cope-Chat cards and in American as McBee Keysort Cards (Yates, 1960, pp. 110–111; Goode and Hatt, 1952, p. 318). Here the information referring to the unit in question is typed on to the card in the normal way. Each characteristic or attribute to be analysed is assigned a particular hole or set of holes along the margin of the card. For example, we might assign the top left thirteen holes to thirteen five-year age categories. The hole of the appropriate age category for the individual is now opened out to the edge of the card so that the card will fall off a thin knitting needle if it is passed through that hole and lifted. The method of use is now straightforward. The cards are stacked in a neat deck. A thin knitting needle is passed through the first of the holes denoting the first age category. If the deck of cards is now lifted by the needle all those which have had the first hole position opened out will fall out of the deck and may be piled ready for counting. The second age category is simply obtained by passing the needle through the second hole and lifting the bundle to allow those punched out to fall out. Mistaken sorts are immediately noticeable when the cards are stacked in their appropriate piles, since they should all have a wedge-shaped nick at the relevant hole for that pile.

In this system each unit – individual, household, village, lineage, or whatever it is – is represented by one card, so the number of units that can be handled is limited only by the ease with which the cards can be accommodated on the knitting needle. The size of the card determines the number of holes around the edge and hence the number of characteristics or attributes that might be handled. A card of dimensions 4 inches by 6 inches, which is a convenient size for ordinary purposes, would have 99 holes in it. (One corner is cut off at an angle to allow cards upside down or facing wrongly to be picked out immediately. The cut-off corner sacrifices one hole). The equipment needed apart from the cards is a ticket clipper with which to open out the appropriate holes and a 13-gauge knitting needle.

A newly introduced system of card-punching that is likely to be of considerable use to anthropologists is that known as the Brisch–Vistem System (Garbett, 1965). In this system each card represents a given characteristic or attribute, while each individual unit is assigned the same determinate position on each card. A card of dimensions 6 inches by 11 inches will accommodate 1,000 units. The technique here is to punch a hole for an individual possessing an attribute in the card representing that attribute but not in the cards denoting contrasting attributes. A hole is punched out on all the cards for the attributes the individual possesses. There may be twelve cards representing twelve age categories, two cards for sex, five cards for socio-economic status groups, and so on. The particular attribute cards say, for Individual No. 25, are selected, and a hole punched in position No. 25 in all of these cards. To count up the people of given age groups and socio-economic status categories, for example, two cards representing the intersection of a row and a column of a table are placed on top of each other. The positions in which holes coincide represent individuals possessing both characteristics. These may be counted very quickly and entered on a table. The striking advantage of the system is that provided the upper limit of the number of cases is known not to exceed the capacity of the card (i.e. 1,000 on a 6-inch by 11-inch card) then all the data can be accommodated on a relatively small number of cards represented by the number of categories of characteristics which are likely to be needed – usually not more than, say, 200.

The advantages of these two systems are that they are portable, may be used in the field, and are relatively inexpensive. But if the numbers involved become large and the analysis complicated, the physical labour of counting totals manually becomes arduous. It is here that mechanical processing becomes essential.

Mechanical processing may be performed on Hollerith cards or on magnetic tape if computers are being used. The underlying principles here are no different from those applying to hand-sorted cards. All the data must be translated into a numerical code. These code numbers are then punched into standard-size 8 inches by 3 inches Hollerith cards, which can accommodate ten normal punch positions and two over-punch positions in each of 80 columns across the card. Once the cards have been accurately punched they may be sorted and tabulated mechanically with suitable machinery, or used as data input into most computers. Mechanical processing relieves the fieldworker of an enormous amount of work but it imposes the responsibility upon him to prepare his data in a form that may easily be punched into the cards.

The most important step in this direction is in converting the material on the schedules into suitable numerical code form. If mechanical processing has been foreseen from the start the schedule may be designed to allow suitable space opposite items of information so that the code number may be written in opposite them in readiness for punching. If the known categories of classification of any characteristic are not likely to exceed twelve – or better ten, since it is unusual for the two over-punch positions to be printable – then a single column may be assigned to that characteristic. For example, we may decide on ten age groups and assign to the first age group the code number '0', to the second '1', and so on. The age of the person is coded into one of these single-digit codes and is punched into the appropriate column by the punch operator. More complicated data such as kinship, for example, will need more than one column to accommodate all the possible categories.[1] With two columns there are 100 possibilities (or 144 if the two over-punched positions are used as well).

Normally the schedules used by anthropologists will not have been designed with the intention of mechanical processing. In this case it is best to prepare a coding sheet that sets out the allocation of the columns of the card with appropriate spaces for writing the code figures in them. The fieldworker then completes a coding sheet for each schedule and the card is punched up from the coding sheet. An allocation of columns for an identification number is always essential so that the card can be traced back to the original schedule if queries arise.[2]

Coding is a tedious and demanding chore. The majority of schedules can be coded simply and directly but there are usually some difficult cases that can be coded only by the person who knows how the particular piece of information is to be used in subsequent analysis. In a sense, successful coding implies that the relevant categories of analysis have already been decided upon. Re-coding will sometimes be found necessary when the fieldworker has started working with a classification that subsequently turned out to be inappropriate for his purposes.

The tedium and time taken in coding have prompted some research workers to design schedules in which the interviewer in recording the information allocates it to a category that has already had a code number given to it (e.g. Reader, 1961, Appendix 2). There is obviously a great advantage in this procedure, but it demands accurate recording on the part of the interviewer, since coding cannot be checked, and it requires a good knowledge of what responses are likely to crop up so that code numbers may be allocated to them in advance.

There is no substantial difference in preparing material for processing on a computer as against a punched-card tabulator except that care must be taken in the former that no illegal characters are included through multiple

[1] Banton (1956) has suggested a 'logical' code for kinship relationships encountered in household analysis. This code is logical in that any type of relationship can be worked out and coded by this system. I have found that it is usually possible to include all relationships encountered in ordinary surveys within the hundred possibilities allowed for in two columns. This is not as neat as a fully flexible coding system but it is usually worth economizing on columns.

[2] The question must be decided what unit of analysis each card represents. Usually one card bearing personal details is punched for each individual. I have found it convenient, however, for some purposes to treat each marriage, or each birth, or each job as the unit of analysis, so a separate card is punched for each event. In this case the basic personal details for the individual are repeated on the card for each marriage or job. This allows greater flexibility of tabulation than if all the individual's marriages, births, or jobs are punched on to one card.

punching.[1] The particular layout and punching procedure to be used depends on the sort of equipment it is to be processed on. Fieldworkers who intend to use mechanical and electronic equipment for processing, therefore, should seek the advice of the operators before preparing their material for punching. Unfortunately the best way to learn this art is by making the mistakes, and it is becoming more and more desirable that all students who wish to do fieldwork should have the experience of preparing at least one set of quantitative data for mechanical or electronic processing as part of the fieldwork training programme.

METHODS OF ANALYSIS

I have suggested that quantitative data may be used in two different ways. First, they may be used to indicate the general features of a community as, for example, Turner uses the data about village composition in his description of Ndembu social structure. The various demographic measures such as birth rates, death rates, replacement rates, divorce frequencies, age distributions, tables of the frequencies of kinship categories found in villages, ownership of cattle, and income distribution, are measures of this kind. These the anthropologist uses as he thinks necessary to supplement his verbal descriptions. Quantitative data may also be used, however, to express the underlying relationship between phenomena either by assessing them against some theoretical model developed on the basis of probability theory or by computing one of the various measures of correlation or association. Examples of the former type of analysis are the various tests of significance of differences. But much may be done in a variety of problems by the much simpler procedures of comparing straightforward probability distributions against an observed distribution. Take, for example, the question whether or not men and women who belong to joking clans are likely to marry each other. It would be a simple matter to record the clans of the spouses currently married. If no selection of marriage partners in terms of clanship were exercised the number of marriages between the members of any two clans would be a simple function of the numbers of men and women in those clans. If we compare the actual number of marriages between members of different clans with the expected number on the assumption that *no* selection took place, we will soon see whether

[1] It is sometimes permissible to punch two or more holes in a column of a card when punch-card tabulators are being used. This is particularly useful in attitude studies, where two five-point scales and a 'don't know' response can be accommodated in the twelve positions of a Hollerith column. This means that twice the number of items may be included on a card than if each item were punched into its own column. This procedure may, however, bring difficulties in print-outs, controlling, and other tabulation processes.

there is more or less marriage than can be expected by chance.[1] This is not difficult to do and it can throw a good deal of light on inter-clan marriages. A good example of the use of this technique is provided by Ackerman's analysis of inter-clan marriage among the Purum where he shows by this method that the 'ideal' does not accord with practice. This enables him to throw a good deal of light on the debate about Purum kinship (Ackerman, 1964).

Examples of correlation analysis of fieldwork material in the broadest sense are not common in anthropological literature. The most sophisticated uses of statistical techniques have been made in connexion with 'cross-cultural' studies, where coefficients of correlation, chi-square tests, and even factor analysis have been used to show the relationship between features of cultures or to determine the extent to which cultural traits are characteristic of particular cultures. But these powerful analytical tools, in contrast to the practice in economics, psychology, and sociology, have not been used much to bring out the underlying relationships of observed regularities in anthropological data.

An attempt to use some of these techniques is to be found in Chapter IV of *The Yao Village*, where the relationship between the prestige of village headmen and various factors associated with it are elucidated by means of various tests of statistical significance. A difficulty in all attempts such as this, however, is that an underlying feature of a social system such as prestige, for example, will express itself in many different forms, so a relationship between any two observed aspects may only be a common expression of an underlying feature. If there is a correlation between being an Invader headman and having certain marks of prestige, is it because Invader headmen have larger villages and the prestige is really derived from the size of the village?

Analyses that set out to uncover the consistent relationships lying behind social phenomena must take cognizance of the multivariate nature of the material they are concerned with. For this purpose techniques such as the analysis of variance and covariance, the analysis of factorial arrangements, factor analysis, and latent-structure analysis are likely to prove particularly useful. An attempt to perform an analysis of this sort is provided in Appendix E of *The Yao Village*.[2] Earlier in the book it had been shown that the possession of marks of prestige by village headmen could be related to a number of their social characteristics. All these characteristics operate

[1] I have used this technique to show that there is a strong selection of spouses by tribe on the Copperbelt (Mitchell, 1957). In examining inter-clan marriages an allowance would have to be made for clan exogamy.

[2] This appears only in the second printing of the book.

simultaneously, so a correlation of any one of them with marks of prestige may only be an expression of some other factor with which the first is highly correlated. But through the analysis of the way in which the symbols of prestige are distributed among village headmen with varying *patterns* of social characteristics, it is possible to show that the size of the village and the headman's kinship with the chief are the main factors that influence the possession of marks of prestige.[1]

The amount of computation involved in multivariate analyses of various sorts has been a drawback to their use in the past. With the rapid expansion of the use of computers for all kinds of statistical analysis in the past decade, this difficulty has been greatly reduced. It is likely that over the next decade there will be rapid strides forward in the application of statistical methods to the solution of anthropological problems.[2]

It is undeniable that the significant advances in social anthropological thought over the last quarter-century have been made by people who have relied little on quantitative material to embellish their descriptions and used no statistical devices to point up their generalizations. It is debatable whether the leaders of social anthropological thought in the next twenty-five years will be able to follow suit. Statistical analysis is a powerful tool in the hands of the modern social scientist, and social anthropologists cannot afford to forgo the aid they can derive from using it. It should take – and is taking – its rightful place as one of the many techniques social anthropologists must use in their quest to document and understand man's infinite social variety.

[1] This is achieved by a 2^4 factorial arrangement where the origin, the size of the village, kinship with the chief, and the religion of the headman are reduced to dichotomies and the distribution of marks of prestige in sixteen different response patterns is analysed.

[2] I am here concerned only with quantitative methods in anthropology. The application of mathematical thinking such as graph theory, for example, to the analysis of networks of kinship systems holds out possibilities that have only recently begun to be explored.

is taken solely as a correlation of any one of them with marks of prestige may only be an expression of some other factor with which the first is highly correlated. Thus through the analysis of the way in which the principal features are distributed among whole lineages with varying degrees of [illegible] characteristics it is possible to show that the size of the village and the lineage's standing with the chief are the main factors that influence the possession of such prestige.[1]

The amount of computation involved in multivariate analyses of various sorts has been a drawback to their use in the past. With the rapid expansion of the use of computers for all kinds of statistical analysis in the past decade, this difficulty has been greatly reduced. It is likely that over the next decade there will be rapid strides forward in the application of statistical methods to the solution of anthropological problems.

It is undeniable that the significant advances in social anthropological thought over the last quarter century have been made by people who have used little or no quantitative material to substantiate their descriptions and used no statistical methods to point up their generalizations. It is debatable whether the leaders of social anthropological thought in the next quarter century will be able to ignore statistical analysis as a powerful tool in the hands of the modern anthropologist, and social anthropologists cannot afford to ignore this and they should learn to use it. It should take its rightful place as one of the many techniques social anthropologists must use in their attempt to document and understand man's complex social reality.

[1] [illegible]

J. A. BARNES

The Frequency of Divorce

I. THE NEED FOR MEASURES

As we accumulate more information on systems of kinship and marriage, so it becomes both necessary and possible to develop more precise and refined analytical tools with which to convert this information into an ordered body of knowledge. Some analytical concepts remain, and probably always will remain, intractably qualitative, and efforts to give them numerical or quantitative expression fail. Other concepts can be readily expressed quantitatively and can be given greater comparability, repeatability, and discriminatory power.

In this essay I discuss only one analytical concept, divorce frequency, and endeavour to show that this is better expressed quantitatively rather than qualitatively. I argue that, to be usable, quantitative expressions must be standardized and I suggest various standardized procedures to be followed. I am concerned only with divorce frequency, but I hope that my arguments may have wider application and that other writers may be encouraged to treat other concepts in the same way, as for example I have done elsewhere for inter-generational residential continuity (Barnes, 1960).

A great deal has been written on the frequency of divorce in modern societies (see Monahan, 1962 and references therein; Henry, 1952). By 'modern' I refer, for present purposes, to those societies where all births, deaths, marriages, and divorces are registered and where a central organization publishes limited statistical information derived from these registrations. The analytical problem is then how to extract as much understanding as possible from the published data. The modern demographer usually does not have direct access to the individual registrations themselves and can influence only partially both the range of information recorded at registration and the extent to which this information is made public. On the other hand, he can be confident that registration is reasonably complete and that all the information registered is taken into account in any published report.

By contrast, the ethnographer working in a tribal society usually finds that registrations of births and other demographic events are either non-existent or erratic and published information quite inadequate. His problem is therefore quite different from that of his metropolitan colleague. He has to devise the best way of collecting directly the information that would otherwise come from registrations, and he has to employ analytical procedures specifically appropriate to information collected in this way and directed towards his own research ends. For most purposes the conventional procedures of population analysis are inapplicable.

In the first place, registrations usually record contemporary events, and published information based on them is available relating to a long series of years. The ethnographer works in a community with at best only meagre written records from the past. His contemporary records are restricted to the period he spends in the field, and this is rarely longer than three years from initial contact to final departure. He therefore has to collect information retrospectively, and for many purposes is restricted to collecting this information from the individuals directly concerned with these events who happen to be still alive and present at the time of the ethnographer's visit. Memory is a poor substitute for contemporary documentation. Second, the size of the unit he analyses is significantly different. The demographer deals with information giving an average or cumulative account of a large population of maybe many millions, and is constantly concerned with reducing the size of the units he examines so that each may be as homogeneous as possible. The ethnographer, because his resources for collecting information directly are limited, deals with quite a small population, and often seeks to extend the applicability of his findings to as wide an area as possible. Third, the demographer is more often than not concerned with establishing a local secular trend and is therefore particularly interested in comparing conditions prevailing at two or more points in time. He notes, for example, that the proportion of children in some locality under the age of fifteen was much higher in 1963 than it was in 1903. The ethnographer may eventually aim at making similar comparisons, but his first task is not to compare a society at two points of time. It is rather to compare one society with others. He first has to ask whether divorce is rare or frequent before he can go on to inquire whether divorce is less frequent than it used to be. In other words, his first model is static or eternal, and only as a second step can this be refined by introducing secular trends. Even then, his comparison is likely to be fairly broad, between the experience of one generation and that of the next, rather than one year and the next. Fourth, in some tribal societies the frequency of divorce is much greater than in any modern society, and in many tribal societies mortality is also much higher. The ethnographer has therefore to consider in his calculations the influence of mortality on the frequency of divorce, a complication the demographer can usually ignore (see Jacobson, 1949).

For these reasons, and no doubt there are others, the ethnographer has to construct his own tools for use in the bush. However, even those who work in highly documented communities may sometimes find it expedient to follow the example of their colleagues on the frontier. Difficulties of direct access to registrations, limitations on the information recorded on them, and the inadequacy of published reports may make it worth while for the inquirer who is primarily concerned with a small community to collect his own information on marriage, divorce, and other events even when effective registration exists. In particular, it is difficult and most laborious to build up the genealogical structure of a community from the information contained in registers of births and marriages, however accurate these may be. It is usually simpler to proceed by direct inquiry. Information about marriage and divorce can then be collected economically as part of a genealogical inquiry.

In this essay I am concerned with procedures for calculating numerical indices. I therefore ride roughshod over many important and intriguing problems: what constitutes a marriage; what is the difference between estrangement, separation, and divorce; at what point in time during a protracted process is the transition made from one state to another; what relation is there between conjugal happiness and the absence of divorce? For our present restricted purposes these questions are irrelevant. For purposes of calculation, I assume that anyone at any time is either married or not; and that a marriage can end only by divorce or by the death of one or other partner. There are many societies where these assumptions are inapplicable and for them some modification of the methods I outline may be necessary. But for many more societies these assumptions do not do too much injustice to the facts.

Nor can I discuss here in any systematic way the sociological significance of the differences between one society and another as revealed by the various measures of divorce frequency. I am not directly concerned therefore with whether or not spouses live together, or are faithful to each other, or love one another; nor am I concerned with whether or not a low divorce frequency is determined by a particular method of tracing descent or by a specific mode of economic production. I restrict myself to the limited technical problem of how to indicate divorce frequency, and most of my discussion is a consideration of how one measure of frequency differs from another.

Several writers have written on marriage in various societies and have said nothing about divorce. We may infer that divorce in these societies is at least not so rampant as to force itself on the attention of these writers, but this is an unsure inference and not very informative.

Many writers have given qualitative statements about the frequency of divorce in the societies they describe. I have collected about sixty different forms of statement, varying from 'divorce was never practised' to 'divorce was a common event', through such phrases as 'people think carefully before divorce', 'marriage stability is remarkably high', 'the instability of marriage is striking', and 'divorce is . . . almost an annual event'. These phrases are better than nothing, but they are of very limited comparative utility. What is 'striking' or 'remarkable' to one observer may well seem commonplace to another, and what seems to be a 'very high divorce rate' to one writer may seem 'normal' to another. Part of the difficulty in interpreting these statements comparatively is common to any attempt to use qualitative adjectives to describe a quantitative phenomenon, but with divorce frequency there is a special difficulty that with very few exceptions divorce is nowhere positively valued. We do not find earnest efforts being made to increase the divorce rate, and although divorce may be tolerated, it is very rarely acclaimed. Hence *any* divorce rate is likely to be called 'high' (see Murdock, 1950, p. 201 on the Crow). So when a writer describes divorce as 'frequent' we do not know what kind of comparison he has in mind and we have no way of telling if 'frequent' divorce implies approximately equal frequencies in two societies. At best, these qualitative statements enable us to group societies into two broad categories, those with 'rare divorce' and those with 'frequent divorce', with many societies left indeterminate, e.g. those where 'marriage is fairly permanent', or where 'divorce is not a rare occurrence'.

It is difficult to use these descriptive phrases for ranking societies in precise order of divorce frequency, though for gross comparison they may be adequate. Thus, for example, if we wish to contrast the frequency of divorce among the Zulu and the Nyasaland Yao, or in the Irish Republic and the State of Nevada, it may be sufficient to say that divorce is rare in one system and frequent in the other. If, however, we wish to compare societies that in this respect are not so different from one another, these descriptions are inadequate and we have to use measures of frequency that are more precise and more objective. Divorce may be said to be common in two societies that have in fact quite different divorce frequencies, and two observers may report on the same society in conflicting terms. For example, the Fort Jameson Ngoni, when I worked among them in 1946–1949, considered that divorce was rife in their society, while the administration considered that it was not very frequent. The Ngoni took their standards from their own past, while the Administration's standard was based on contemporary conditions among the neighbouring matrilineal tribes. Gluckman's discussion of the frequency of divorce among the Southern Bantu (1950, p. 204) illustrates the difficulty of collating the qualitative comments of a variety of writers.

Many ethnographers have sought to give greater precision to their reports by publishing numerical indices of divorce frequency. Unfortunately, these indices have been calculated in several different ways and it is sometimes difficult to compare data from different societies.

The measures used are of four kinds. First, there are those referring to the present marital state of a population, and in particular to the number of people in the population who have been divorced, who are still alive, and who have not yet married again. Second, we have those referring to the cumulative marital experience of a population, indicating how many times persons have been married and divorced. These two kinds of measure are discussed in section 2. Measures in the third group indicate in various ways what proportion of marriages eventually end in divorce while the fourth group comprises those measures that indicate how many divorces occur within a delimited period of time. These last two kinds of measure are discussed in sections 4 to 10.

In modern societies, as defined above, all marriages and divorces are registered with some central organization, and demographic tools are designed to make the best use of information already collected. Hence the commonest measures are rates relating the number of divorces granted during a year or a decade to the number of marriages taking place during the same period or to the mean number of married couples in the population. These rates have their inherent limitations and in addition are difficult to determine in simple societies where the total population is usually unknown and where the registration of marriages and divorces is at best only partial. It might be possible in a simple society to observe a restricted population and record all the marriages and divorces occurring within it during the period of observation, and thus to construct a divorce rate; but the small size of the population that can be handled by one observer, or even by a small field team, would make this an inefficient way of working. We have to rely on the testimony of informants for information about marriages and divorces we cannot observe, and we assume that our informants can give us better information about past events in their own lives than about contemporary events in the lives of others. Hence we extend our sample backwards in time rather than outwards in space. In a rapidly changing society this procedure has its hazards but, with proper precautions, it can be used to give an indication of the magnitude of the changes taking place.

The various measures of divorce frequency do not all deal with precisely the same social facts and the particular measure we utilize in analytical and comparative work will depend on the purpose we have in mind and on the availability of the information. For instance, we may be concerned with the stability of first marriages only and need an index that omits second and higher-order marriages. We may be interested in the relative frequency of death and divorce as modes of ending marriage and then do not need an index of divorce frequency from which the effects of mortality have been eliminated. In general we cannot make special inquiries among a variety of societies on the matters we are concerned with, and in any comparative study we have to rely on such information as others have thought worth publishing in tribal monographs and descriptive articles. Therefore it is important that there should be sufficient standardization in the presentation of data to enable valid comparisons to be made. It is also important that certain basic material should be published whether or not the author has any particular comparative inquiry in mind. For at first glance it may not appear significant in, for example, a discussion of Lamba society to note that 119 in a sample of 194 marriages ended in divorce. Yet these data can become of interest when we discover how the sample of marriages was collected and what happened to those that did not end in divorce, for then we can compare this proportion with similar measures collected in the same way from other societies. We may then be able not only to make general observations about all the societies compared but also to add to our understanding of Lamba society itself.

The more precisely we define divorce frequency, the more necessary it is to state exactly what we mean by marriage and divorce in any one society. If we vary our definitions we are likely to vary our frequency. For example, in his discussion of marriage stability among the Tallensi, Fortes (1949b, p. 85 f.n. 1) specifically excludes from his statistics short-lived marriages in which no bridewealth was paid and no children born. Had he not made this exclusion his measure of Tallensi divorce frequency would have been much greater. Among the Fort Jameson Ngoni bridewealth is paid in only 4 per cent of marriages, and had I restricted my divorce calculations to marriages with bridewealth, my measures of frequency would have been very different from those I calculated on the basis of all marriages. Just as it is sometimes difficult to decide when a valid marriage has been entered into, so it may be difficult to distinguish divorce from separation. These important problems have to be tackled, but I am not concerned with them here. I merely stress the need to state for each society what definitions have been used for statistical purposes.

Societies vary not only in frequency of divorce but also in the facility with which divorce can be obtained. Divorce is sometimes said to be 'rare and difficult' or 'frequent and easy' and, even though these two aspects may be interrelated, it is important in analysis to keep them separate. 'Difficult' and 'easy' describe the obstacles, legal and social, in the way of divorce and do not automatically indicate its frequency. In some studies we are told only that divorce is easy to obtain and we may be tempted to assume that divorce is therefore frequent. Yet this inference may be false. For example, in the community I studied in western Norway during 1952–1953, divorce has been possible by mutual consent and on other grounds under a divorce law that had been in force substantially unchanged for over forty years and that has been considered to be one of the most liberal in Europe. Yet in my inquiry into marriage and divorce, in a sample of over a hundred marriages, I encountered only one instance of divorce; and this case had occurred while the couple concerned were domiciled in the United States of America and subject to its laws. Granqvist (1931, p. 164 ff. and 1935, p. 257 ff.) has described another society in which divorce is easy and yet infrequent. We may expect to find occasionally a society in which divorce is comparatively difficult and yet frequent. It might be possible to construct an index of the facility with which divorce can be obtained in a specified society, but clearly we would then have to deal with phenomena quite different from those that are our present concern (see Goode, 1962).

2. PRESENT MARITAL STATUS AND CUMULATIVE MARITAL EXPERIENCE

The ***present marital status*** of a population indicates how many people at a particular moment have never been married (or are unwedded; see Mitchell and Barnes, 1950, p. 22), are currently married, widowed, or divorced. This information is usually easy to obtain but tells us little about the frequency of divorce. If divorce is swiftly followed by remarriage, then, however frequent divorce may be, at any one time there will be few divorced persons in the population. The status of divorced person is transitional between one married state and the next, and though many may pass through it few may be in it. In a polygynous society a man who divorces his wife may never appear as divorced, for he may still be married to another wife, although his former wife may be classified as divorced.

Since divorce is a possibility only after marriage, it is preferable to relate the number of divorced persons to the wedded or ever-married population (i.e. all those who have ever been married) rather than to the total population including never-married persons. Men and women should be shown separately.

The *cumulative marital experience* shows the number of times to date that members of a population have been married, divorced, or left as widowers or widows. In an open community, where some members take spouses from outside, the experiences of men and women may differ, and everywhere we may expect differences with respect to age. Alterations in the age composition of a sample population may affect the average number of marriages and divorces experienced by persons of each sex. An age-specific analysis may show that change has occurred in marriage patterns. For example, if we see that men in their thirties have on the average experienced twice as many divorces as men now in their forties, it is likely that the expectation of divorce at ages below forty has risen during the last two decades. It is often difficult to get accurate information about the ages of tribal informants and hence many ethnographers have been unable to divide their informants into age categories. Yet data on cumulative marital experience, as indeed on any cumulative social characteristics, are directly affected by the age composition of the population from which they are drawn. In general, the older the informant the more times he will have been married, the more times he will have experienced divorce and widowhood. Hence the difference between two samples may be due as much to differences in age composition as to differences in patterns of marriage and divorce. A recent analysis of cumulative divorce experience, specific for age and sex, has been given by Cohen (1961, p. 1242) for a Kanuri sample.

Some writers indicate merely the mean number of marriages and divorces per head, but it is preferable to show the number of persons who have experienced 0, 1, 2, . . . marriages, so that median and modal values can be calculated.

Data on present marital status and cumulative marital experience from three societies are shown below in *Table 1*.

3. MARRIAGE SAMPLES

The computation of present marital status and cumulative marital experience is based on a sample of individuals of varying present status and past experience. It is relatively easy even under field conditions to select a sample of individuals so that the grosser biases of sampling are avoided. The rest of the measures discussed in this paper are constructed not from samples of individuals but from samples of marriages, and in the special conditions of fieldwork in simple societies an unbiased sample of marriages is much harder to select.

One commonly used method of sample collection is through genealogical inquiry. An informant is asked about his kinsfolk and affines in some systematic way, and the marital history of each of his relatives is noted. The effectiveness of this method varies, for in some societies where marriages are not very stable the chance that a marriage will be remembered is greater if it lasted a long time and gave rise to many live children (each of whom is a potential informant) than if it was childless and of short duration. Everywhere there are childless couples, but no one has them as his parents. Hence any probing into the unrecorded past by the genealogical method will tend to give a sample of marriages which, at least in the earlier years, is biased in favour of long and fertile marriages. These are less likely to have ended in divorce than are short infertile marriages, and the divorce frequency in the sample may therefore be lower than in the population as a whole. This type of systematic forgetting, analagous to 'structural amnesia' (Barnes, 1947, p. 52), occurs widely and can have sociological significance (see Kuczynski, 1944, p. 25 f.), but in this context it is merely another hazard. On the other hand, if divorce is rare, it is possible that marriages ending in divorce may be remembered for their notoriety. Schapera (1940, p. 294) has made inquiries into divorce by the genealogical method among the Tswana, where divorce is rare.

An informant who has been married many times may forget some of his (or her) own marriages, particularly if these were childless, shortlived, or unhappy. But in general an informant is likely to be more accurate in reporting his own marriages than in recollecting those of other people. An alternative method of inquiry, therefore, is to examine all the marriages ever experienced by a selected body of (say) male informants and to classify these by the way in which they were terminated, how long they lasted, and whether or not they are still extant. The most serious objection to this procedure is that the universe sampled is not related in any simple way to the total number of marriages that have occurred within a given time in a society. In modern societies we examine all the marriages that have taken place and divide up this universe by isolating the marriages taking place in each year. Most of the men involved in these marriages in recent years are still alive, but as we go back in time so a larger and larger proportion of the men marrying in each year has died. In a closed simple society, if we would examine all the marriages experienced by all living men we would be dealing with almost all the marriages that had taken place in the society in recent years, but owing to mortality we would include only a smaller proportion of marriages from each of the earlier years. Without full information on male mortality and on the ages at which men married, we cannot accurately relate our findings to those from modern society. If we make the assumption that our closed simple society is also static, with no changes taking place, we can overlook this dispersal of our sample through the years and then make a direct comparison, but this assumption is often difficult to defend. We may abandon the assumption and still claim fairly enough that our sample reflects what had been happening within the last generation or so and compare it with other samples derived in the same way, but we must realize that some differences may be due solely to different mortality or to differences in age of marriage. It would be possible to follow a procedure analogous to that used in computing the net reproduction rate to overcome some of these difficulties. We can calculate the frequency of divorce for sub-samples of men in each age group and these can then be applied to a constructed population with a standard age distribution, but this procedure is useful only if we can assume that no secular changes have occurred.

A further objection to assembling a sample of marriages from the experience of informants is that the sample may then contain some marriages that took place outside the territory associated with the society we are studying and that would therefore not be included if we had been able to derive a sample from marriage registrations. For example, some of the male informants may have been labour migrants and have married foreign women while they were away working. Here a contrast in interest becomes apparent. In a modern society, we usually study an ecclesiastical, civil, or legal system that grants marriages and divorces to individuals who supplicate for them; the focus of study is generally the system rather than the individuals. In a simple society, we often find that individuals can get married or become divorced in a variety of ways and under a variety of jurisdictions, and our focus of study is then the individuals themselves. Marriages and divorces experienced in distant places and with foreign spouses are properly regarded as part of the marital experience of our informants and appropriately included in our sample.

Despite its shortcomings, the examination of all the marriages experienced by a selected body of informants is the commonest basis for computing divorce frequency; we must therefore examine its implications. Any sample drawn from men should be checked against a sample drawn from a similarly selected body of women. Women may be more, or less, reticent about their marital histories than men, and there may be differences in their histories as actually experienced. Thus if men move about the country more than women and contract marriages while working in the towns, their marital histories may show a larger average number of marriages and divorces than those of rural women. In an increasing or decreasing population, with men making their first marriage at a later age than women, the number of marriages, and hence the number of divorces, per head in each age group will differ for men and women (Hajnal, 1950b,

p. 317). Women may conceal their divorces more carefully than men, as among the Tallensi and Plateau Tonga.

If men and women can both be interviewed and all their marriages collected, then in general some of the marriages experienced by the men will also have been experienced by some of the women. Thus if we take all the men and women in some residential unit, for example a village, we shall learn about those marriages linking each married couple living in the village from the women as well as from their husbands. The testimony of a woman may not be identical with that of her husband, and in general the histories of man and wife will overlap in only one of their several marriages. It is not often that a man marries the same woman twice, although it seems that in at least one society, the Bemba, this is a recognized procedure (Richards, 1940, p. 100 and White Fathers, 1954, s.v. *uku-bwekeshanya*). The simplest way of indicating the overlap between the experiences of male and female informants is to divide the material collected into three parts, as follows:

1. Marriages for which both partners were informants.
2. Marriages for which the only informants were men.
3. Marriages for which the only informants were women.

By comparing the accounts of part 1 given by men and by women, we can gain some idea of the relative reliability of their information, and by careful inquiry we can hope to guess at what actually happened in these marriages. Armed with this estimate of the reliability of men as informants, we can look at part 2, and can estimate the reliability and possible bias of the information there. After similarly weighing the evidence of part 3, we are in a better position to decide whether or not any differences there may be between parts 2 and 3 are due to differences in actual experience or merely to differences in reporting that experience.

Even with completely reliable informants and a completely closed and homogeneous community, part 1 is likely to differ from the other two parts. This arises from the way in which we choose our group of informants. Often the most convenient method of sampling is to use all the wedded (i.e. ever-married) inhabitants of a village as informants. In this way an inquiry into divorce can be conveniently combined with a large number of other inquiries into such topics as kinship, co-residence, economic co-operation, and the like. Using this method, a marriage in which at the time of the inquiry the partners are living in different villages is twice as likely to be included in the sample as a marriage in which they are living in the same village. Suppose, for example, there are 300 villages in the society we are studying and we decide to make our inquiry in one of these villages selected arbitrarily. If a man X and his wife, or former wife, Y are both living in P village, then if we select P village we include X–Y marriage in our sample, and if we select any other village we exclude it. Hence there is one chance in three hundred that their marriage be chosen. On the other hand, suppose that Z lives in P village and his wife, or former wife, T lives in Q village. Their marriage will be included in our sample if we choose either P or Q village, and hence they have two chances in three hundred of being selected. In this way our sample, whichever village we select, contains a higher proportion of marriages like Z–T than it would had we drawn our sample from the whole of the society studied. Hence our calculations derived from the sample are biased in favour of marriages like Z–T and against those like X–Y. If there was no significant difference between these two kinds of marriage, this would not matter. If men and women take spouses indiscriminately from within and from outside their own villages and also maintain separate households after marriage, then there may be no bias in the sample. But in most societies this is not so. Most of the marriages in which both spouses are to be found in the same village are extant, although we may occasionally find a woman living in the same village as a man from whom she has been divorced. Most of the marriages in which spouses are found in different villages have been terminated in divorce, although we may also find a few marriages in which for some reason or other, such as the demands of co-wives, or the exigencies of employment, husband and wife are living apart. In general, then, the bias in our sample in favour of marriages with spatially separated spouses is a bias in favour of marriages ending in divorce.

Bias of this kind is greatest when the sampling unit is completely exogamous. If there is village exogamy and husband and wife live together, there is only a small chance that a woman will be living in the same village as her divorced husband. If she subsequently married another man in her former husband's village, or if he has married another women in hers, the former couple may be found in one village. Most divorced couples are found living apart, and under these conditions almost all extant marriages have a single chance of selection and almost all marriages ending in divorce a double chance. Bias will be least when the sampling unit is endogamous, for all marriages in which both partners are alive then have equal chances of selection, whether they are extant or have ended in divorce. It seems probable that in general the smaller the residential unit the greater the proportion of marriages contracted with spouses outside the unit, so the smaller our sample the greater the danger of this kind of bias.

This bias applies to the whole sample of all marriages in which at least one partner is resident in some unit such as a village and is therefore included as an informant. The bias does not apply equally to the three parts of this sample, as defined above. Part 1 consists of marriages in which both partners live in the village and therefore consists largely of extant marriages. Marriages ended in divorce appear in part 1 only if former spouses continue to live in the same village after divorce or if they both happen to have moved independently to some other village. Most marriages ending in divorce fall into parts 2 and 3.

A possible correction for this bias which suggests itself is to weight the parts of the sample so that marriages in part 1 have twice the weight of those in parts 2 and 3. Unfortunately there are objections to this.

In the first place, some of the marriages in parts 2 and 3 may involve spouses or former spouses who live outside the area being studied. For example, if T lives not in Q village but in some other society the chance that her marriage with Z is in the sample is reduced to one in three hundred, for she herself cannot be an informant whatever village we select. Therefore her marriage ought to receive the same weight as those in part 1. The same argument applies if X or Z is a labour migrant. If the society concerned is relatively isolated we may perhaps ignore this complication. If it lacks clear social boundaries, either because it is stateless or because many of its members are temporary migrants, or if it is one in which there is frequent marriage with foreigners, we must take this complication into account. A man whose marriage has ended in divorce may be more likely to emigrate than his happily married neighbour, while a woman may be more likely to divorce her husband if he stays away at work for years than if he lives with her in the village.

A second objection to this suggested weighting is that it overlooks the effect of mortality. In general, part 1 does not contain any marriages ended by death. Yet in our example, even if T did live in a village which we can select, she cannot be an informant if she is now dead. By this reckoning all marriages in which one spouse is dead ought to be weighted as if they were in part 1. If only marriages ended by death were involved we could easily isolate them in parts 2 and 3 and weight them accordingly. Even if our attention is restricted to divorce and we are not interested in mortality, we still cannot neglect marriages ended by death for, as will be shown later, we need to correct our first estimates of divorce rates by allowing for mortality. We have also to consider the effect of death for another reason. In some marriages ended in divorce one spouse is alive and the other dead. These marriages appear in parts 2 and 3 but, like marriages ended by death, they have only a single chance of selection and should therefore be weighted as though they were in part 1. Our revised weighting procedure is then as follows. We sub-divide part 2 of our sample into parts 2*a* and 2*b*. Marriages in which the non-informing spouse is dead or living outside the society studied fall into part 2*a*, and those in which the non-informing spouse is alive and would have been interviewed if we had selected some other village fall into part 2*b*. Part 3 is sub-divided in the same way. We then give parts 1, 2*a*, and 3*a* a double weight in our final sample and parts 2*b* and 3*b* a single weight.

It will be seen that correction by weighting is not a simple matter. To apply this correction we must inquire into the whereabouts of our informants' former spouses and ascertain whether they are alive or dead. If this can be done easily and accurately the way is open for applying this correction. If it is impossible to get reliable information about former spouses it is perhaps safer to use an unweighted sample, giving details of how it is divided among its three parts, rather than to attempt a correction on an unsatisfactory basis.

Samples based on the experience of men alone contain the equivalent of parts 1 and 2, and those based on women's experience contain parts 1 and 3. For convenience we may refer to samples of this kind as men's and women's samples. If we add together men's and women's samples drawn from the same residential unit without making any allowance for overlap, we then have a sample made up of part 1 twice and parts 2 and 3 once. This is merely our original sample corrected by giving part 1 double weight.

An illustration of the different values obtained for divorce ratios by changing the basis of sampling is given in section 5.

The sample village should be selected carefully so that it may be representative of the society being studied. Since usually among simple societies very little is known in advance about the population, and since it is usually quite impracticable to select villages at random, this is not easy. What can be done is to compare the village selected with a large number of other villages in respect of criteria which do not require lengthy investigation. Thus we may not be able to repeat a divorce inquiry in many villages in order to see if our first inquiry gave typical results. But we can compare the village in which, for better or worse, the detailed inquiry was made with many others for readily discoverable characteristics such as size, history, kinship structure, apparent wealth, and external contacts, and so verify that in these respects our sample village is typical of its area. In the absence of any better information we then make the assumption that our divorce data are also typical for a larger population. This is an assumption, but it is no less defensible than, for example, many of the assumptions we have to make about village homogeneity and comparability before we can apply the usual statistical formulae for margins of error. We can also increase the size of our sample by adding together data from several villages.

Even if the sample village is found by this rough test not to be typical it is worth while pursuing inquiries, providing that the fact of atypicality is always emphasized. We cannot explain away social phenomena by merely noting that other people behave differently. If inquiries have reached an advanced stage it may not be worth while shifting from a well-tried and well-known set of informants, however atypical they may be, to a typical but untried and unknown set somewhere else. It is surely better to have good information about atypical communities than meagre information about typical ones.

4. DIVORCE RATIOS

Marriages can be classified by age and status of spouses, year of commencement, duration, termination, and a great variety of other characteristics. The simplest measures of divorce frequency that are related to marriages rather than to individuals take into account only the method of termination of marriages and ignore all other characteristics. The usual ethnographic statement is that among some designated group of people such and such a percentage of marriages end in divorce. Unless further information is given, this statement may refer to any one of the following three ratios (see Mitchell and Barnes, 1950, p. 16):

A. The number of marriages ended in divorce expressed as a percentage of all the marriages in the sample.

B. The number of marriages ended in divorce expressed as a percentage of all marriages in the sample that have been completed by death or divorce.

C. The number of marriages ended in divorce expressed as a percentage of all marriages except those that have ended by death.

In general, for any one society these three ratios will all be different, and if we do not know which ratio is intended, the statement that a certain percentage of marriages end in divorce is not very informative. Ratio *B* measures the relative frequency with which marriages end in divorce rather than in the death of one or other spouse. Hence differences in the value of this index between two societies, or between the same society at two points in time, may be due to changes in mortality rather than to changes in the propensity to divorce. When married people live together, they are exposed to the risk of divorce for longer and, other things being equal, more marriages end in divorce. If mortality rises, some married people who would have become divorced had they lived will die before they can take this step, and the percentage of marriages ending in divorce therefore falls.

If we are looking for an index that will measure divorce propensity without reference to mortality, this dependence on mortality is a weakness in ratio *B*; but ratios *A* and *B* are even more fallible. *A* and *C* have meaning only in relation to a sample drawn from a live population, for it is only from live informants that we collect extant marriages. These ratios are therefore affected by mortality and migration as they show themselves in the age composition of the population, the sex ratio, and so on. If we turn from *A* and *C* and use only *B*, with completed marriages only, our sample contains marriages that on the whole are less recent than those used with *A* and *C*. In addition, if our marriages have been collected from living people in the manner discussed in section 3, ratio *B* will be biased in favour of short-lived marriages. The longer a marriage has persisted, the shorter the period that will remain after it has been terminated during which one or both of the spouses will be still alive and able to give us information. To give an extreme case, suppose hypothetically that in a certain society most couples live together to a ripe old age and then die of grief within a few days of each other. Any analysis of marriage in this society based only on the completed marriages experienced by living people would exclude the bulk of these long-lived marriages and would deal mainly with the marriages of couples who had deviated from the common pattern. Yet if we attempt to overcome these shortcomings by including marriages experienced by dead people we encounter the bias due to selective forgetting mentioned earlier. In modern societies where calculations are based on all registered marriages, deaths, and divorces, and are not restricted to marriages experienced by living people, these objections to ratio *B* do not apply.

Ratio *C* is less strongly affected by mortality than *A* and it seems likely that *C* is the most satisfactory of these indices for comparisons of divorce frequency among simple societies. Measures of divorce frequency in modern societies are usually expressed in the form

$$1. \quad \frac{\text{number of divorces occurring in a given period of time}}{\text{number of weddings occurring in the same period of time}}$$

or

$$2. \quad \frac{\text{number of divorces occurring in a given period of time}}{\text{mean number of marriages extant during the same period of time}}$$

The latter is clearly the better measure. Neither corresponds to any of our three ratios. However, it is sometimes said with reference to a modern society that some specified percentage of marriages end in divorce, and something like ratio *B* is then intended. Hence it may be desirable to calculate *B* as well as *C* and to publish them both. If necessary, *A* can then be derived from *B* and *C* by the formula:

$$1/B + 1/C = 1 + 1/A$$

The Frequency of Divorce

Divorce ratios have been published for several societies. Information available in 1950 is given by Barnes (1949, p. 45, *Table 3*) and more recent ratios for Bantu Africa have been collected by Mitchell (see above, p. 23, *Table 1*).

TABLE I PRESENT MARITAL STATUS, CUMULATIVE MARITAL EXPERIENCE, AND DIVORCE RATIOS : ARABS, NGONI, AND LAMBA

	Palestinian Arabs	*Fort Jameson Ngoni*	*Lamba*
Present marital status			
Men:			
number in sample	105	116	133
percentage divorced	0	6·0	2·3
Women:			
number in sample	148	223	195
percentage divorced	0	6·4	11·3
Cumulative marital experience			
Men:			
number in sample	105	104	125
percentage ever divorced	5·7	39·4	
mean number divorces per head	0·06	0·49	0·41
Women			
number in sample		210	177
percentage ever divorced		23	
mean number divorces per head		0·30	0·36
Divorce ratios			
Number of divorces in sample	11	115	119
Ratios:			
A	4·3	28·5	33·1
B	7·7	55·8	61·3
C	8·7	36·9	41·8

Sources: Arabs: Granqvist (1931, 157 ff. and 1935, 269). Granqvist includes betrothed men, but I have excluded them, and have used only her live male informants to calculate the divorce ratios.
Ngoni: Barnes (1951, Tables III, IV, IX, X, and XI).
Lamba: Mitchell and Barnes (1950, pp. 46–48).

Given information on present marital status, cumulative marital experience, and divorce ratios, we can begin to determine whether divorce is, in some unqualified sense, more frequent in one society than another. This information for Palestinian Arabs, Fort Jameson Ngoni, and Lamba is given in *Table 1*.

Table 1 shows that we can state confidently that divorce is more frequent among the Fort Jameson Ngoni than among the Palestinian Arabs, for by every index that we can calculate from the available data, Ngoni divorce frequency exceeds that of the Arabs. But can we say that divorce is more frequent among the Lamba than among the Fort Jameson Ngoni? All three Lamba divorce ratios are higher than the corresponding Ngoni ratios, more Lamba women are currently divorced, and they have been divorced more often. On the other hand, more Ngoni men are divorced and they have been divorced more often. The two patterns of divorce cannot be explained without an examination of such factors as the incidence of polygyny, the speed of remarriage, and the extent of male labour migration, as found in the two societies. No simple answer placing one society above or below the other can be expected. Furthermore, the differences in the three divorce ratios though consistent are small and may not necessarily be of sociological significance. We can examine in the usual way the possibility that the difference between the divorce ratios of the Fort Jameson Ngoni and Lamba may have arisen by chance, in a statistical sense. The calculations necessary are set out in *Table 2*.

TABLE 2 FORT JAMESON NGONI AND LAMBA DIVORCE RATIOS

	Society					
Ratio	*Lamba*		*Fort Jameson Ngoni*		χ^2	p
A	33·1%	(119/360)	28·5%	(115/403)	1·83	$0{\cdot}1 < p < 0{\cdot}2$
B	61·3%	(119/194)	55·8%	(115/206)	1·79	$0{\cdot}1 < p < 0{\cdot}2$
C	41·8%	(119/285)	36·9%	(115/312)	1·50	$0{\cdot}2 < p < 0{\cdot}3$

Sources: Lamba: Mitchell and Barnes (1950, p. 47).
Ngoni: Barnes (1951, p. 53).

Table 2 shows that the differences between the Fort Jameson Ngoni and Lamba divorce ratios, as shown by these samples, are not statistically significant, though these figures suggest that larger samples might yield statistically significant differences. We should require further information before we could attach any sociological importance to the fact that the Lamba ratios are slightly higher than the Ngoni.

5. SAMPLES DRAWN FROM THE EXPERIENCE OF ONE SEX: AN ILLUSTRATION

We can use ratios *B* and *C* to illustrate the arguments put forward in section 3 for separating marriages for which both partners are informants from those for which only one partner is an informant. Our data refer to the Fort Jameson Ngoni.

Information was collected about all marriages experienced by ever-married men and women in six villages. One village, yielding 107 informants, was twenty-five miles away and in a different county (see Barnes, 1954, p. 117) from another village yielding 55 informants. These two villages were selected for me to live in by the county chiefs concerned. The remaining four villages, yielding 173 informants between them, were close together but in a third county and twenty miles away from the other two. They were villages accessible from my base camp, built at a site chosen by the administration. I was able to compare these six villages with many others; in size, ethnic composition, wealth, history, and kinship structure they are fairly typical Ngoni villages. Together they constitute about one per cent of the Fort Jameson Ngoni population.

I endeavoured to include all ever-married people as informants but failed to do so. A few people were always away from home, as for example a brickmaker who worked long hours every day at a Mission and who went off drinking every weekend. A few people who were interviewed were excluded from the sample since their histories as given to me were either grossly truncated, internally inconsistent, or patently untrue. I amended the histories related by a few other informants in the light of information received from their neighbours and kinsfolk. Whenever possible I returned to the informants concerned and checked the emendations with them. Even after this process I occasionally had reliable information on one or more marriages experienced by an informant but inadequate information on others known or thought to have been experienced by him (or her). In these circumstances I rejected his entire history, excluding from my sample even his adequately recorded marriages except where his spouses were also informants. Some of these rejected informants told me of their more respectable marriages and concealed marriages that had ended unhappily. Had I included their partial histories I would have introduced bias in favour of long and happy marriages.

In all, 117 men and 222 women were interviewed and their marital histories utilized to form the sample. The preponderance of women is due to the high degree of male labour migration from the area. The informants constituted 86 per cent of the ever-married men and 88 per cent of the ever-married women whose principal domicile was in these six villages during 1946–1949. The men and women in the sample had experienced 403 marriages. Both man and wife were interviewed in 111 marriages, while in the remaining 292 marriages only one partner was interviewed. In the course of this and other inquiries information was acquired about many other marriages, of both living and dead people. For reasons discussed in section 3, this additional information was not used at all in making calculations.

All marriages collected in this way were divided into four categories, *E, D, H, and W*, as follows.

- *E* Marriages extant at the end of the inquiry (1948 in one village and 1949 in the other five) including marriages in which the spouses were separated but not divorced.
- *D* Marriages ended in divorce.
- *H* Marriages ended by death of the man.
- *W* Marriages ended by death of the woman.

The sample was also divided into three parts, as described above in section 3. Divorce ratios were calculated for each part separately and for the whole (unweighted) sample.

Had I conducted my inquiries through men only, I would have collected only parts 1 and 2 of this sample. Divorce ratios were calculated for these two parts taken together, and for the similar women's sample formed by adding parts 1 and 3. The distribution of marriages in four categories and three parts, and divorce ratios *B* and *C* for these different samples, are set out in *Table 3.*

The distribution of marriages in the three parts is much as might have been expected. The large number of extant marriages for which women were the only informants was due to labour migration, where men had gone away and left their wives behind. Some of the extant marriages for which men were the only informants were polygynous marriages in which the couples lived in separate villages.

The divorce ratios for part 1 differ widely from the rest, as could be expected. Ratio *B*, the simple measure of the relative frequency of death and divorce as a method of terminating marriage, does not vary widely between the other five possible samples, with a minimum value of 50·8 per cent for part 3 and a maximum of 64·5 per cent for the men's sample. Since part 3 contains all, except one, of the marriages terminated by death of the man, the lower value of *B* for part 3 is a reflection of the fact that marriages are more likely to end by death of the man than of the woman. Ratio *C* shows a greater range of variation, from 25·8 per cent for the women's sample to 65·6 per cent for part 2. The unweighted sample gives a higher *C* than either the men's or the women's sample, for, as we have discussed earlier, an unweighted sample is likely to be biased in favour of marriages ended in divorce. We may perhaps regard the figure of 36·9 per cent for the unweighted sample as an upper limit of the true value of *C*.

Unfortunately I did not systematically collect information about the whereabouts of former spouses, although I did ascertain that in many instances informants did not know where their former spouses were living

TABLE 3 FORT JAMESON NGONI DIVORCE RATIOS, DISTINGUISHING BETWEEN MALE AND FEMALE EXPERIENCE

Basis of calculation	*Marriages in each category*					*Divorce ratios*			
	E	*D*	*H*	*W*	*Total*	*B*		*C*	
1. Marriages for which both partners were informants	103	7	1(*a*)	0	111	87·5%	(7/8)	6·4%	(7/110)
2. Marriages for which men were the only informants	22	42	0	26	90	61·8%	(42/68)	65·6%	(42/64)
3. Marriages for which women were the only informants	72	66	63	1(*b*)	202	50·8%	(66/130)	47·8%	(66/138)
TOTAL	197	115	64	27	403	55·8%	(115/206)	36·9%	(115/312)
All marriages for which men were informants	125	49	1	26	201	64·5%	(49/76)	28·2%	(49/174)
All marriages for which women were informants	175	73	64	1	313	53·0%	(73/138)	29·4%	(73/248)

Notes (*a*) After I had collected the marital histories of man and wife in this marriage, and before I had finished the inquiry, the man died.
(*b*) I interviewed this woman before she died. I also interviewed her husband, but since I could not get adequate information on some of his other marriages, he was not used as an informant in this sample.

Source: Unpublished field notes, 1946–1949.

or whether they were alive or dead. A division of parts 2 and 3 into *2a*, *2b*, *3a*, and *3b* therefore cannot be undertaken. I have used the unweighted sample, with a certain amount of misgiving, in all subsequent calculations.

6. MARRIAGES CLASSIFIED BY DURATION

A more elaborate method of analysis depends on knowing how long each marriage lasts. With this additional information we can calculate the probability that a marriage will end in divorce or death within a given time and hence compute the mean expectation of married life at the beginning of a marriage. We can provide a fuller picture of marriage and divorce than is possible by means of a single ratio and we can separate more rigorously the effects of mortality from divorce. Roughly comparable calculations for divorce in the United States of America have been made by Cahen (1932), Monahan (1940), Jacobson (1950), and others, but the methods they use are not directly applicable to data from simple societies. The method set out here is specifically designed for use by the ethnographer who has to collect all his own field data from living informants. It was first published, albeit in a slightly more complicated and less logical form, more than a dozen years ago and I regret that it has scarcely been used; I know of only two other published studies (Mitchell, 1961 and 1963a) that utilize similar methods. Nevertheless, there is nothing intrinsically difficult in the method and it provides a more reliable index of divorce frequency than any other method so far available.

Our procedure is analogous to that followed in the construction of a life table. The marriages in a sample are treated as a cohort exposed to the risks of divorce and mortality, risks that vary in intensity with the duration of the marriage. Special calculations are made to allow for the fact that many of the marriages in the sample are extant, and we do not know how or when they will end. Other calculations enable us to separate the effects of divorce from those of mortality.

Instead of presenting a purely algebraic exposition of the method of calculation, I make use of the sample of marriages described in section 5 to illustrate the steps to be followed. I provide an algebraic justification for the method but also set out in detail the arithmetical operations that are entailed, in the hope that even those who are not interested in the argument may be able to apply the method mechanically. I am well aware that the obviously inadequate empirical data used here scarcely deserve the protracted treatment I give them. When I collected these data I did not have the present analysis in mind. But despite the small size, manifest inaccuracy, and significant bias of this sample, it will serve my present purpose, which is to demonstrate a method of analysis rather than to discuss the characteristics of Ngoni social life. The imperfections of the illustrative data do not impair the validity of the analytical method.

I made an estimate of how long each completed marriage in the Ngoni sample lasted and, for each marriage that was extant at the time of my survey, how long it had lasted so far. This length of time I refer to as the completed duration of the marriage or its duration-so-far, as the case may be. The shortest duration in the sample was one week and the longest fifty-three years. The marriages were divided into four categories, *E*, *D*, *H*, and *W*, defined earlier in section 5 in connexion with divorce ratios, and were also classified according to durations, calculated to the nearest whole year. These nominal durations range from zero to fifty-three years, and for purposes of calculation marriages with the same nominal duration and belonging to the same category are treated as identical. Thus in this context we ignore the fact that the marriages began at a wide range of points in historical time and for purposes of calculation treat them as if they all began simultaneously. For we are concerned here only with the magnitude of the time that has elapsed in each instance from the beginning of the marriage and not at all with whether the marriage began many years ago or quite recently. We group together events occurring at the same point of developmental time (see Fortes, 1958, pp. 4–5) with reference to marriage, irrespective of their location in historical time. In other words, we ignore any changes that may have taken place in the society during the last few decades and seek only to present a picture that will be approximately true throughout that period. This limitation can be overcome by, for example, comparing a sample of recent marriages with a sample drawn from the experience of an earlier generation, treating each of these as a separate cohort, but the calculations for each sample will then follow steps similar to those described here for a combined sample.

The marriages grouped together as having the same nominal duration may have exact durations that vary within certain limits. It was possible to obtain accurate information on some marriages from contemporary Mission records, and a few informants could state the calendar year in which they had been married, divorced, or left a widow or widower. For the rest, my estimates were based on the number of years that had elapsed since the event I sought to date and on its relation to events in the life of the informant, to datable historical events, and to the present age of children born of the marriage. In many instances I was able to estimate the calendar year in which the event had happened but could not tell at what point in the year the event had probably occurred. My estimates of marriage durations were arrived at in one of two ways, directly or indirectly. In some instances

I was able to ascertain directly that the marriage lasted, say, ten years. In order to make other sociological analyses not discussed here, I then made as good an estimate as I could of the calendar years in which the marriage began and ended. In other instances I proceeded indirectly. I was able to establish that a marriage had begun in such-and-such a year, and had ended in some other year, but I could not tell whether these events had occurred at the beginning, middle, or end of the years concerned. If the arithmetic difference between the dates is ten years, the marriage is included in a ten-year cell.

In fact the duration of such a marriage may have been anything between just over nine years to just under eleven years. This variation in possible actual duration applies in every year in the table, so that those marriages included in the eleven-year cells may have lasted anything between just over ten years to just under twelve years. Each cell has thus a potential span of two years, one year on either side of its nominal duration, and there is an overlap of a year in the coverage of successive rows of cells. For purposes of calculation we make the assumption that the coverage of each cell is only one year, half a year on either side of its nominal duration, thereby eliminating overlap. Thus we assume, for example, that all marriages in the ten-year cells have exact durations lying between nine years and a half and ten years and a half, and this period we refer to as the ten-year interval. This assumption is justified for those marriages whose lengths were estimated directly and does not introduce any great error when applied to indirectly derived durations. We make the further assumption that in each cell exact marriage durations are distributed uniformly throughout the period of a year covered by the cell.

Marriages with durations of less than six months are classified as having a nominal duration of zero to the nearest whole year. We assume that exact durations in the zero cells are uniformly distributed between nothing and six months, and that therefore the mean value of the durations is three months. The durations of all marriages in the zero cells were estimated directly. The period from the beginning of marriage and six months later we refer to as the zero-year interval.

We refer to the number of marriages in the sample that are extant and which have a nominal duration-so-far of i years as E_i, where i stands for zero or any positive integer. The number of marriages of completed duration of i years ending in divorce is referred to as D_i, and similarly with H_i and W_i for marriages ending in the death of the husband and of the wife respectively. The variables j and x are used interchangeably with i.

The number of marriages for each year of nominal duration and for each of the four categories is set out for the Ngoni sample in *Table 4*.

TABLE 4 NGONI MARRIAGE SAMPLE; DISTRIBUTION BY DURATION AND CATEGORY

1 *i* *Nominal duration*	2 E_i *Extant marriages*	3 D_i *Marriages ended in divorce*	4 H_i *Marriages ended by husband's death*	5 W_i *Marriages ended by wife's death*
0	16	9	0	0
1	9	10	0	1
2	19	8	1	4
3	13	11	2	0
4	12	13	6	0
5	11	13	2	1
6	5	10	2	2
7	5	2	5	2
8	5	10	7	1
9	11	2	4	0
10	6	5	4	3
11	4	4	2	0
12	4	5	2	0
13	5	1	3	1
14	4	2	0	2
15	4	0	0	3
16	1	3	2	0
17	7	2	0	0
18	0	0	2	0
19	2	1	0	1
20	4	0	4	0
21	2	0	0	1
22	3	0	2	0
23	3	1	0	0
24	5	0	3	0
25	3	0	0	0
26	2	0	0	0
27	3	1	0	0
28	1	1	1	1
29	4	0	2	0
30	0	0	1	1
31	2	0	3	0
32	2	1	0	0
33	0	0	0	0
34	0	0	0	0
35	3	0	0	0
36	3	0	1	0
37	1	0	0	1
38	2	0	0	0
39	2	0	0	1
40	0	0	0	0
41	1	0	0	0
42	1	0	0	0
43	1	0	0	0

TABLE 4 *(contd.)*

1 i *Nominal duration*	2 E_i *Extant marriages*	3 D_i *Marriages ended in divorce*	4 H_i *Marriages ended by husband's death*	5 W_i *Marriages ended by wife's death*
44	3	0	1	1
45	0	0	0	0
46	0	0	1	0
47	0	0	0	0
48	0	0	0	0
49	2	0	0	0
50	1	0	0	0
51	0	0	0	0
52	0	0	0	0
53	0	0	1	0
Σ	197	115	64	27

All the information we shall use in our subsequent calculations is contained in *Table 4*. The rest of this analysis is devoted to manipulating the figures in this table.

If the data are good enough we can proceed in our analysis to treat each year of duration separately. Our calculations are then simplified, and we obtain results that are specific for single years. This procedure is to be preferred, but it is misleading if applied to empirical data that are not sufficiently numerous and accurate. The distribution of Ngoni marriages by duration set out in *Table 4* clearly fails this test. There are too few marriages in the later rows to give reliable averages, and in the earlier rows, where there are more marriages, the distribution of durations is often uneven and erratic. We are forced therefore to group rows together so as to remove most if not all of the irregularities of distribution likely to be due to inaccurate estimation of durations. Grouping of rows complicates our calculations, but gives more reliable results. From inspection of *Table 4* it seems appropriate to group together the first ten rows into five pairs of adjacent rows, so that the zero row and the first-year row are taken together, likewise the second- and third-year rows, and so on. From the tenth-year row onwards, rows are grouped into fives, so that we take together the tenth-year to the fourteenth-year rows, the fifteenth-year to the nineteenth-year rows, and so on. The resulting grouped distribution of marriages classified by duration and category is shown in *Table 5*, columns 3, 7, 8, and 9.

For convenience we adopt a double suffix convention, whereby for example $D_{i,j}$ indicates the sum of the number of marriages ending in divorce with durations ranging from i to j years inclusive. The span of exact durations covered by the $D_{i,j}$ cell is therefore from $i - \frac{1}{2}$ years to $j + \frac{1}{2}$ years. If however $i = 0$, then $D_{0,j}$ indicates the sum of divorces at durations ranging from zero to j years, and the exact span of the cell is from zero to $j + \frac{1}{2}$ years. We shall apply this double suffix convention to all appropriate parameters used in our analysis, and shall refer to the period of duration covered by the i, j cells as the (i, j) interval. As far as possible, the letter i will be used to denote the beginning-point of an interval, and j the end-point. When we need to indicate the exact coverage of an interval we shall use a prefix-suffix convention, whereby exceptionally, ${}_0D_{1\frac{1}{2}}$ stands for $D_{0,1}$, and in general ${}_{i-\frac{1}{2}}D_{j+\frac{1}{2}}$ stands for $D_{i,j}$. Since no marriage lasts for ever, many parameters have a constant value for all intervals beyond the last interval in which marriages are recorded. These limiting values we refer to by using the symbol for infinity, ∞. Thus for example $D_{0,j}$, the number of marriages ending in divorce at durations ranging from zero to $j + \frac{1}{2}$ years, reaches a maximum value as j increases, and then does not increase further. We therefore refer to the total number of divorces in the sample as $D_{0,\infty}$.

7. CONVERTING EXTANT TO COMPLETED MARRIAGES

We have in *Table 5*, columns 3, 7, 8, and 9, a sample of marriages classified by duration and by mode of termination, if any. Unfortunately we cannot proceed directly to construct the history of a cohort of marriages, for we have to treat separately the two types of duration used in the classification. Usually the distribution of durations-so-far of the extant marriages will be quite different from the distributions of completed durations of the marriages ended in divorce or death. To overcome the shortcomings of using a sample of completed marriages only, as discussed in section 3, we have to make use of the evidence provided by the extant marriages; yet we cannot treat the durations-so-far as if they were even approximately the same as completed durations. On the other hand, the extant marriages do not provide sufficient information to enable us to distinguish between the risks of termination by divorce and by death. We have therefore to make use of both extant and completed marriages, but we must treat them differently.

The difference between the distributions of durations-so-far and completed durations may be demonstrated by a hypothetical example. Suppose that in a community there are 50 new marriages each year and that of these, 2 last for exactly one year, 2 for exactly two years, 2 for three years and so on; the two longest marriages last for twenty-five years. The distribution of completed durations is then quite uniform for each year from one to

TABLE 5 NGONI MARRIAGE SAMPLE: SURVIVAL TABLE

1 i	2 j	3 $E_{i,j}$	4 $e_{i,j}$	5 $G_{i,j}$	6 $M_{i,j}$	7 $D_{i,j}$	8 $H_{i,j}$	9 $W_{i,j}$	10 $F_{i,j}$	11 $t_{i,j}$	12 $D'_{i,j}$	13 $H'_{i,j}$	14 $W'_{i,j}$	15 $F'_{i,j}$	16 R_i	17 $R_i + R_{j+1}$	18 $L_{i,j}$
0	1	25		0·57143	6·64045	19	0	1	20	0·33202	25·3084	0	1·3320	26·6404	403	779·3596	584·5197
2	3	32		2·63095	30·57373	19	3	4	26	1·17591	41·3423	6·5278	8·7036	56·5737	376·3596	696·1455	696·1455
4	5	23	22	5·5	63·91432	26	8	1	35	1·82612	73·4791	22·6090	2·8261	98·9142	319·7859	540·6576	540·6576
6	7	10	7	1·75	20·33638	12	7	4	23	0·88419	22·6103	13·1893	7·5368	43·3364	220·8717	398·4070	398·4070
8	9	16	0	0	0	12	11	1	24	0	12	11	1	24	177·5353	331·0706	331·0706
10	14	23		2·8	32·53820	17	11	6	34	0·95701	33·2692	21·5271	11·7421	66·5383	153·5353	240·5323	601·3308
15	19	14	6	0·6	6·97247	6	4	4	14	0·49803	8·9882	5·9921	5·9921	20·9724	86·9970	153·0215	382·5538
20	24	17	1	0·1	1·16208	1	9	1	11	0·10564	1·1056	9·9508	1·1056	12·1620	66·0246	119·8871	299·7177
25	29	13	13	1·3	15·10702	2	3	1	6	2·51784	7·0357	10·5535	3·5178	21·1070	53·8625	86·6180	216·5450
30	34	4	2	0·2	2·32416	1	4	1	6	0·38736	1·3874	5·5494	1·3874	8·3242	32·7555	57·1868	142·9670
35	39	11	−2	−0·2	−2·32416	0	1	2	3	0·77472	0	0·2253	0·4506	0·6758	24·4313	48·1868	120·4670
40	44	6	9	0·9	10·45871	0	1	1	2	5·22935	0	6·2294	6·2294	12·4587	23·7555	35·0523	87·6307
45	49	2	5	0·5	5·81039	0	1	0	1	5·81039	0	6·8104	0	6·8104	11·2968	15·7832	39·4579
50	54	1		0·3	3·48624	0	1	0	1	3·48624	0	4·4862	0	4·4862	4·4864	4·4864	11·2160
55	59	0		0	0	0	0	0	0		0	0	0	0	0	0	0
Σ		197		16·95238	197	115	64	27	206		226·5261	124·6502	51·8235	403			4452·6962
·10	11	10															

$N = 403 \quad b = 11{\cdot}620786 \quad b' = L_{0,\infty}/N = 11{\cdot}0489$

twenty-five years' duration. It is easy to show that in this community there are at any time 650 (= 25 × 26) marriages extant and that of these there are 25 with durations-so-far of zero, to the nearest whole year, 49 marriages with nominal durations-so-far of one year, 47 with two years, 45 with three years, and so on; there is one marriage with duration-so-far of twenty-five years. The distribution of nominal durations-so-far is thus not uniform and does not follow the distribution of completed durations.

In general, the distribution of durations-so-far approximates to the survival curve for marriages, whereas the distribution of completed durations follows the first differential of this curve, multiplied by minus one.

Our procedure is then to replace the extant marriages in the sample by an equal number of hypothetical completed marriages, with durations distributed so that, if applied to a constant number of marriages beginning each year, they would yield at any point in time the observed distribution of durations-so-far. Before we can do this, we must examine in detail the relationship between durations-so-far and completed durations in a community where there is a constant stream of new marriages coming into being, and where the proportion of marriages surviving after any specified length of time remains constant. This examination will give us equations we can use in the sample to convert from real extant marriages to hypothetical completed marriages.

For suppose that new marriages come into being at a constant rate of n marriages each year, and that the chance that a marriage will be extant x years after it has begun is $S(x)$. Then $S(o) = 1$ and $S(x)$ is some monotonically decreasing function of x.

Then at any time the number of marriages extant with exact (not nominal) durations-so-far of x years is proportional to $S(x)$. In particular, if u and v are any positive numbers, with v not less than u, and ${}_uE_v$ is the number of extant marriages with exact durations-so-far lying between u and v years, then

$$ {}_uE_v = n\int_u^v S(x)\,dx \tag{1} $$

The number of completed marriages with exact durations of x years is proportional to

$$ -dS(x)/dx $$

and if ${}_uG_v$ is the number of marriages with completed durations lying between u and v years that begin, or that end, each year, then

$$ {}_uG_v = n[S(u) - S(v)] \tag{2} $$

We observe E, and our task is to calculate G in terms of E when the connexion between them is defined by equations (1) and (2). Since we have grouped our rows into pairs and into fives, we have in *Table 5*, column 3, the values of $E_{0,1}$, $E_{2,3}$, . . ., and $E_{10,14}$, $E_{15,19}$, . . ., and it is in terms of these values that we have to find $G_{1,2}$, $G_{3,4}$, . . . and $G_{10,14}$, $G_{15,19}$, ...

Now from equation (1) we have that

$$E_{0,1} = {}_0E_{1\frac{1}{2}} = n\int_0^{1\frac{1}{2}} S(x)\,dx$$

and

$$E_{2,3} = {}_{1\frac{1}{2}}E_{3\frac{1}{2}} = n\int_{1\frac{1}{2}}^{3\frac{1}{2}} S(x)\,dx$$

As a first approximation, we assume that $S(x)$ is lineal between 0 and $1\frac{1}{2}$, and between $1\frac{1}{2}$ and $3\frac{1}{2}$. Then

$$E_{0,1} = 3nS(\tfrac{3}{4})/2 \tag{3}$$

and

$$E_{2,3} = 2nS(2\tfrac{1}{2}) \tag{4}$$

In general, for $i = 2, 3, 4, \ldots$, assuming $S(x)$ lineal between $i - \frac{1}{2}$ and $i + 1\frac{1}{2}$, or between $i - \frac{1}{2}$ and $i + 4\frac{1}{2}$, as the case may be, then

$$E_{i,i+1} = 2nS(i + \tfrac{1}{2}) \tag{5}$$

and

$$E_{i,i+4} = 5nS(i + 2) \tag{6}$$

Now, from equation(2) we have that

$$G_{0,1} = n[S(0) - S(1\tfrac{1}{2})]$$

$$G_{2,3} = n[S(1\tfrac{1}{2}) - S(3\tfrac{1}{2})]$$

and in general, for $i = 2, 4, 6, 8, 10, 15, 20, \ldots$

$$G_{i,i+1} = n[S(\mathrm{i} - \tfrac{1}{2}) - S(i + 1\tfrac{1}{2})]$$

$$G_{i,i+4} = n[S(i - \tfrac{1}{2}) - S(i + 4\tfrac{1}{2})]$$

To find n, we now assume that $S(x)$ is lineal between 0 and $2\frac{1}{2}$. An alternative assumption will be examined later. Then

$$\begin{aligned} n = nS(0) &= nS(\tfrac{3}{4}) + 3n[S(\tfrac{3}{4}) - S(2\tfrac{1}{2})]/7 \\ &= 10nS(\tfrac{3}{4})/7 - 3nS(2\tfrac{1}{2})/7 \\ &= 20E_{0,1}/21 - 3E_{2,3}/14 \end{aligned} \tag{7}$$

Likewise

$$\begin{aligned} nS(1\tfrac{1}{2}) &= 4nS(\tfrac{3}{4})/7 + 3nS(2\tfrac{1}{2})/7 \\ &= 8E_{0,1}/21 + 3E_{2,3}/14 \end{aligned}$$

Therefore

$$G_{0,1} = nS(0) - nS(1\tfrac{1}{2}) = 4E_{0,1}/7 - 3E_{2,3}/7 \qquad (8)$$

Next, to find $S(3\frac{1}{2})$, we assume that $S(x)$ is lineal between $2\frac{1}{2}$ and $4\frac{1}{2}$, so that

$$S(3\tfrac{1}{2}) = [S(2\tfrac{1}{2}) + S(4\tfrac{1}{2})]/2$$

Hence

$$\begin{aligned} G_{2,3} &= nS(1\tfrac{1}{2}) - nS(3\tfrac{1}{2}) \\ &= 8E_{0,1}/21 + 3E_{2,3}/14 - E_{2,3}/4 - E_{4,5}/4 \\ &= 8E_{0,1}/21 - E_{2,3}/28 - E_{4,5}/4 \qquad (9) \end{aligned}$$

For

$$i = 4, 6, 8$$

$$\begin{aligned} G_{i,i+1} &= nS(i - \tfrac{1}{2}) - nS(i + 1\tfrac{1}{2}) \\ &= [nS(i - 1\tfrac{1}{2}) + nS(i + \tfrac{1}{2}) - nS(i + \tfrac{1}{2}) - S(i + 2\tfrac{1}{2})]/2 \\ &= E_{i-2,i-1}/4 - E_{i+2,i+3}/4 \qquad (10) \end{aligned}$$

Similarly, for $i = 15, 20, 25, \ldots$

$$G_{i,i+4} = E_{i-5,i-1}/10 - E_{i+5,i+9}/10 \qquad (11)$$

To calculate $G_{8,9}$ from equation (10) we need to know $E_{10,11}$. This is found from E_{10} and E_{11} in *Table 4*, column 2, and is shown separately in an additional row of *Table 5*, column 3. Likewise, to find $G_{10,14}$, rather than use equation (11), we make a better approximation by using $S(9\frac{1}{2})$.

For

$$nS(9\tfrac{1}{2}) = nS(8\tfrac{1}{2})/2 + nS(10\tfrac{1}{2})/2$$

$$nS(14\tfrac{1}{2}) = nS(12\tfrac{1}{2})/2 + nS(17)/2$$

Hence

$$G_{10,14} = E_{8,9}/4 + E_{10,11}/4 - E_{10,14}/10 - E_{15,19}/10 \qquad (12)$$

A special approximation may be made when $S(x) = 0$. Suppose that there is no extant marriage with a duration of more than $5y + 4$ years, so that the interval $(5y, 5y + 4)$ is the last for which $E_{i,j} \neq 0$. Then $S(5y + 2)$ is positive, whereas $S(5y + 7) = S(5y + 12) = 0$. If we follow the normal assumption about the lineality of $S(x)$, we then have that $S(5y + 4\frac{1}{2})$ is positive, and hence that $G_{5y+5,5y+9}$ is positive. In other words, the effect of these assumptions about lineality is to add an additional interval to the total range of durations for which there are marriages in the sample. Thus, in the Ngoni sample, the longest extant marriage had lasted fifty years, and hence, in *Table 5*, the interval (50, 54) is the last for which there are any extant marriages. If we followed equation 11 in calculating $G_{50,54}$, we would also have some hypothetical completed marriages in the interval (55, 59).

If there are real completed marriages in the sample with durations in that interval, no special calculation is called for. If, however, there are neither real completed nor extant marriages in that interval, it seems better to adopt a formula that gives $S(x) = 0$ for all x greater than the end of the last interval that contains marriages. Thus if $(5y, 5y + 4)$ is the last interval with any real marriages, we make $S(x) = 0$ for all $x \geqslant 5y + 4\frac{1}{2}$. We then have $G_{5y+5,\,5y+9} = 0$. If we follow this convention, then for the last interval containing marriages we have the equation

$$\begin{aligned} G_{5y,\,5y+4} &= nS(5y - \tfrac{1}{2}) - nS(5y + 4\tfrac{1}{2}) \\ &= nS(5y - 3)/2 + nS(5y + 2)/2 \\ &= E_{5y-5,\,5y-1}/10 + E_{5y,\,5y+4}/10 \end{aligned} \qquad (13)$$

For the next interval, we take

$$G_{5y+5,\,5y+9} = 0$$

A similar set of equations can be worked out for use when the empirical data are good enough to permit a year-by-year analysis. It can be shown that

$$n = 8E_0/3 - E_1/3 \qquad (14)$$

$$G_0 = 4E_0/3 - 2E_1/3 \qquad (15)$$

$$G_1 = 4E_0/3 - E_1/6 - E_2/2 \qquad (16)$$

and for $i = 2, 3, 4, \ldots$

$$G_i = E_{i-1}/2 - E_{i+1}/2 \qquad (17)$$

If the last cell to contain marriages is the yth-year cell, then we take

$$G_y = E_{y-1}/2 + E_y/2 \qquad (18)$$

Under some conditions, the assumption that $S(x)$ is lineal throughout the first interval can be improved. If the number of marriages that end in death during the first half of the first interval is negligible, and if a divorce takes more than this length of time to arrange, then it is better to assume that $S(x) = 1$ at the midpoint of the first interval, and that all marriages ending within the first interval end during the second half of the interval.

If we are working with two-year intervals so that the first interval is (0, 1), then its midpoint is at three quarters of a year, and we assume that

$$S(3/4) = S(0) = 1$$

but that $S(x)$ is lineal between 3/4 and the midpoint of the next interval, $2\frac{1}{2}$.

Then

$$E_{0,1} = {}_0E_{1\frac{1}{2}} = {}_0E_{3/4} + {}_{3/4}E_{1\frac{1}{2}}$$
$$= 3nS(0)/4 + 3nS(9/8)/4$$
$$= 3nS(15/16)/2$$

That is, $nS(15/16) = 2E_{0,1}/3$
As before

$$nS(2\tfrac{1}{2}) = E_{2,3}/2$$

Then

$$n = nS(3/4) = nS(15/16) + 3n[S(15/16) - S(2\tfrac{1}{2})]/25$$
$$= 28nS(15/16)/25 - 3nS(2\tfrac{1}{2})/25$$
$$= 56E_{0,1}/75 - 3E_{2,3}/50 \qquad (19)$$

and $\quad nS(1\frac{1}{2}) = [9nS(15/16) + 16nS(2\frac{1}{2})]/25$
Therefore

$$G_{0,1} = nS(0) - nS(1\tfrac{1}{2})$$
$$= 28nS(15/16)/25 - 3nS(2\tfrac{1}{2})/25 - 9nS(15/16)/25 - 16nS(2\tfrac{1}{2})/25$$
$$= 19nS(15/16)/25 - 19nS(2\tfrac{1}{2})/25$$
$$= 38E_{0,1}/75 - 19E_{2,3}/50 \qquad (20)$$

and

$$G_{2,3} = 9nS(15/16)/25 + 16nS(2\tfrac{1}{2})/25 - nS(2\tfrac{1}{2})/2 - nS(4\tfrac{1}{2})/2$$
$$= 9nS(15/16)/25 + 7nS(2\tfrac{1}{2})/50 - nS(4\tfrac{1}{2})/2$$
$$= 6E_{0,1}/25 + 7E_{2,3}/100 - E_{4,5}/4 \qquad (21)$$

Equations (20) and (21) are thus alternatives for use in place of equations (8) and (9).

The same alternative assumption can be made, if appropriate, when making a year-by-year analysis. A similar line of reasoning gives us

$$n = 24E_0/11 - E_1/11 \qquad (22)$$
$$G_0 = 8E_0/11 - 4E_1/11 \qquad (23)$$

and $\quad G_1 = 16E_0/11 - 5E_1/22 - E_2/2 \qquad (24)$

Equations (22), (23), and (24) are alternative to equations (14), (15), and (16) respectively.

We may check the accuracy of these equations by reference to the illustrative example mentioned earlier, of a community with fifty new marriages each year, having completed durations ranging uniformly from one to twenty-five years. As noted above, under these conditions we have

$$E_0 = 25 \quad E_1 = 49 \quad E_2 = 47 \quad E_3 = 45 \ldots$$

$$E_{23} = 5 \quad E_{24} = 3 \quad E_{25} = 1 \quad E_{26} = 0 \ldots$$

Using equations (17), (18), (22), (23), and (24), we have

$$\begin{aligned} n &= 50{\cdot}091 \quad [50] \\ G_0 &= 0{\cdot}364 \quad [0] \\ G_1 &= 1{\cdot}727 \quad [2] \\ G_2 &= 2 \quad [2] \\ &\ldots \\ G_{24} &= 2 \quad [2] \\ G_{25} &= 2 \quad [2] \\ G_{26} &= 0 \quad [0] \end{aligned}$$

The values shown in square brackets are those given by the distribution of real completed marriages, and it will be seen that the hypothetical distribution given by our equations is identical with it except for the first two intervals, where there is a small discrepancy. We cannot expect to get so close a fit as this from our equations in all instances.

We can now apply the equations to the Ngoni marriage sample. The distribution of durations-so-far of extant marriages, $E_{i,j}$, is shown in *Table 5*, column 3. Among the Ngoni, divorce sometimes does occur within the first few months after marriage, and hence our alternative assumption is inappropriate. We apply equations (8), (9), (10), (11), (12), and (13) to give us $G_{i,j}$. $G_{0,i}$, $G_{2,3}$, $G_{10,14}$, and $G_{50,54}$ are calculated individually. For the other values, we first calculate $e_{i,j}$, shown in column 4, where

$$e_{i,j} = E_{i-2,j-2} - E_{i+2,j+2} \tag{25}$$

for the two-year intervals, and

$$e_{i,j} = E_{i-5,j-5} - E_{i+5,j+5} \tag{26}$$

for the five-year intervals. Values of $e_{i,j}$ are found by subtracting the term in column 3 in the row below from the term in the row above. For the two-year intervals,

$$G_{i,j} = e_{i,j}/4 \tag{27}$$

and for the five-year intervals

$$G_{i,j} = e_{i,j}/10 \tag{28}$$

It will be seen that, in the Ngoni sample used as illustration, $G_{i,j}$ is negative for one interval. This is due to unevenness in the distribution of durations-so-far in the sample. This may be caused in part by inaccurate estimation of marriage durations, but it is also due to limitations in our theoretical model. In our discussion we began by considering a marriage survival curve which, by definition, must be monotonically decreasing, so that its differential is never positive. G_i is therefore zero or positive for all values of i. But we had to assume that the rate at which new marriages begin is constant, and that all marriages, whenever begun, are governed by the same survival curve. In practice, the rate at which new marriages begin varies, and there are variations over the years in the intensity of the risks of divorce and death. Married couples move in and out of the area under study, so that the extant marriages in a sample include only some of the surviving marriages from earlier years. But to reach an approximate result we proceed as if these assumptions were true, even though, as in the Ngoni illustration, this leads to one negative value of $G_{i,j}$, and hence of some other parameters calculated from it. Had we followed a year-by-year analysis, several values of G_i would have been found to be negative.

The distribution of hypothetical durations given by $G_{i,j}$ indicates only the required ratios and not necessarily the number of hypothetical completed marriages we need at each interval. We have to ensure that the real extant marriages in the sample are replaced by an equal number of hypothetical completed marriages. In all there are $E_{0,\infty}$ extant marriages. Hence the required number of hypothetical completed marriages in the (i, j) interval is $M_{i,j}$, where

$$M_{i,j} = bG_{i,j} \tag{29}$$

and

$$b = E_{0,\infty}/G_{0,\infty} \tag{30}$$

But

$$\begin{aligned} G_{0,\infty} &= G_{0,1} + G_{2,3} + \ldots + G_{8,9} + G_{10,14} + G_{15,19} + \ldots \\ &= nS(0) - nS(1\tfrac{1}{2}) + nS(1\tfrac{1}{2}) - nS(3\tfrac{1}{2}) + \ldots \\ &\quad + nS(7\tfrac{1}{2}) - nS(9\tfrac{1}{2}) + nS(9\tfrac{1}{2}) - nS(14\tfrac{1}{2}) + \ldots \end{aligned}$$

But $S(x) = 0$ for all x greater than some x_0.
Therefore

$$G_{0,\infty} = nS(0) = n \tag{31}$$

and, using equation (7),

$$G_{0,\infty} = 20E_{0,1}/21 - 3E_{2,3}/14 \tag{32}$$

It will be noted that equation (31) holds only if the special formula given in equation (12) is used for calculating $G_{10,14}$. In general, if there is a change in the length of intervals midway in the table, care must be taken that $S(x)$ is given the same value at the change-over point when calculating $G_{i,j}$ for the intervals immediately before and immediately after this point.

$E_{0,\infty}$ is calculated by summing the values of $E_{i,j}$ given in *Table 5*, column 3. n is calculated from the values of $E_{0,1}$ and $E_{2,3}$ in the same column, and hence we obtain the value of b.

For the Ngoni sample, $E_{0,\infty} = 197$

$$n = 20 \times 25/21 - 3 \times 32/14 = 356/21$$

and hence
$$b = 11{\cdot}621$$

If the alternative assumption about the lineality of $S(x)$ during the first interval has been made, or if a year-by-year analysis is being undertaken, then the formula for n given in equation (14), (19), or (22), chosen as appropriate, must replace that from equation (7) used above.

Knowing the value of b, we multiply the values of $G_{i,j}$ shown in *Table 5*, column 5, by the constant factor b to obtain $M_{i,j}$, shown in column 6.

The next step is to divide the hypothetical completed marriages into those ended by divorce and those ended by death. The distribution of durations-so-far of extant marriages contains no clue to the likely mode of their termination and we have to turn to the real completed marriages for information about the appropriate allocation to make. We assume that at each duration the hypothetical marriages are divided between the three modes of termination in the same ratio as are the completed marriages.

There are $F_{i,j}$ real marriages with completed durations lying between $i - \frac{1}{2}$ and $j + \frac{1}{2}$ years, where

$$F_{i,j} = D_{i,j} + H_{i,j} + W_{i,j} \qquad (33)$$

There are $M_{i,j}$ hypothetical completed marriages at that duration. Hence of these we assign $D''_{i,j}$ to end in divorce, where

$$D''_{i,j} = t_{i,j} D_{i,j} \qquad (34)$$

and
$$t_{i,j} = M_{i,j}/F_{i,j} \qquad (35)$$

If we now combine real and hypothetical marriages, we have in the adjusted sample, during the (i, j) interval, $D'_{i,j}$ marriages ending in divorce, where

$$D'_{i,j} = D_{i,j} + D''_{i,j} = D_{i,j}(1 + t_{i,j}) \qquad (36)$$

Similarly,

$$H'_{i,j} = H_{i,j}(1 + t_{i,j}) \qquad (37)$$

$$W'_{i,j} = W_{i,j}(1 + t_{i,j}) \qquad (38)$$

and
$$F'_{i,j} = F_{i,j}(1 + t_{i,j}) \qquad (39)$$

where $H'_{i,j}$ and $W'_{i,j}$ are the numbers of marriages in the adjusted sample ending in the death of the husband and of the wife respectively during the (i, j) interval, and $F'_{i,j}$ is the total number of marriages in that interval.

$D_{i,j}$, $H_{i,j}$ and $W_{i,j}$ are derived directly from empirical data, via *Table 4*, and their values are shown in columns 7, 8, and 9 of *Table 5*. $F_{i,j}$ is given in column 10 and is found by adding corresponding terms in columns 7, 8, and 9. In column 11 we have $t_{i,j}$, obtained by dividing terms in column 6 by corresponding terms in column 10. $D'_{i,j}$ is given in column 12 and is obtained by adding unity to each term in column 11 and multiplying by corresponding terms in column 7. $H'_{i,j}$ and $W'_{i,j}$ are calculated in a similar way and are shown in columns 13 and 14. Finally, $F'_{i,j}$ is given in column 15 and is obtained either in a similar manner or by adding corresponding terms in columns 12, 13, and 14.

There is no need to calculate $H'_{i,j}$ and $W'_{i,j}$ if our attention is confined to divorce alone. These values are required if we wish to consider separately the chances of a marriage ending in the death of the husband and in the death of the wife.

In the Ngoni sample, it will be noted that although $t_{35,39}$ is negative, $1 + t_{35,39}$ is positive, and hence conveniently we are not dealing with any negative numbers of marriages in our adjusted sample. If the empirical data were such that our calculations gave negative numbers in the adjusted sample, then we would have either to work with longer intervals to overcome inaccuracies of estimation, or else to construct a more complicated model, appropriate to local conditions in the field, for converting extant into completed marriages.

8. MEAN AND MEDIAN MARRIAGE DURATION

The assemblage of completed marriages, distributed among different durations and different modes of termination according to the values of $D'_{i,j}$, $H'_{i,j}$ and $W'_{i,j}$ given by equations (36), (37), and (38), we refer to as our adjusted sample. We now use it to determine the history of a cohort of marriages exposed to the same risks of termination by death and divorce as in the adjusted sample.

We treat all the marriages in the sample as though they constituted a cohort, all starting at the same moment of time, and we examine how many of them are still extant at some later moment. In all there are N marriages in the sample, where

$$N = F'_{0,\infty} = E_{0,\infty} + F_{0,\infty} \qquad (40)$$

During the first eighteen months, $F'_{0,1}$ marriages end and there are then $N - F'_{0,1}$ marriages still surviving. During the next two years, the period covered by the (2, 3) interval, a further $F'_{2,3}$ marriages end, and there are then $N - (F'_{0,1} + F'_{2,3})$, i.e. $N - F'_{0,3}$ left. In general, after $i - \frac{1}{2}$ years, at the beginning of the (i, j) interval, there are R_i marriages surviving, where

$$R_i = N - F'_{0,i-1} \quad \text{for } i = 2, 4, 6, 8, 10, 15, \ldots \tag{41}$$

and $\quad R_0 = N$

The value of N is found by summing the terms of *Table 5*, column 15. By successively subtracting terms of column 15 from N we obtain R_i, shown in column 16.

The mean length of a completed marriage is found by calculating the number of marriage-years experienced by the cohort. Consider, for example, the (20, 24) interval. At the beginning of the interval R_{20} marriages survive. By the end of the interval, the number of survivors has been reduced to R_{25}. Assuming uniform distribution of durations during this interval, the mean number of marriages extant during the interval is

$$(R_{20} + R_{25})/2$$

and since the interval lasts five years, the number of marriage-years experienced by the cohort during this interval is

$$5(R_{20} + R_{25})/2$$

This argument can be applied to every interval, and in general we have that the total number of marriage-years experienced by the cohort is $L_{0,\infty}$, where

$$L_{0,1} = 3(R_0 + R_2)/4 \tag{42}$$

$$L_{i,i+1} = R_i + R_{i+2} \quad \text{for } i = 2, 4, 6, 8 \tag{43}$$

$$L_{i,i+4} = 5(R_i + R_{i+5})/2 \quad \text{for } i = 10, 15, 20, \ldots \tag{44}$$

In *Table 5*, column 17 we have values of $R_i + R_{j+1}$ obtained by adding pairs of adjacent terms in column 16. $L_{i,j}$ is shown in column 18 and is found by multiplying the corresponding term in column 17 by 3/4, unity, or 5/2 as appropriate. Summing the terms of column 18, we get $L_{0,\infty}$.

There are N marriages in the cohort and between them they experience $L_{0,\infty}$ marriage-years. Therefore the mean duration of marriage is b' years, where

$$b' = L_{0,\infty}/N \tag{45}$$

In the Ngoni sample, $N = 403$, $L_{0,\infty} = 4452{\cdot}70$ and hence $b' = 11{\cdot}05$.

The median length of marriage is obtained by inspection from *Table 5*, column 16, by noting at what duration half of the marriages, $N/2$, survive.

For the Ngoni sample, $N/2 = 201{\cdot}5$. By inspection we find that

$$R_6 = 220{\cdot}9$$

and

$$R_8 = 177{\cdot}5$$

Hence the median length of marriage is 6 to 7 years.

Data on mean and median marriage durations for the Ngoni and some other societies are given in *Table 7*.

9. RISK OF DIVORCE

After $j + \frac{1}{2}$ years, a total of $D'_{0,j}$ marriages in the cohort have ended in divorce. Therefore we may say that the chance, at the time of marriage, that divorce will occur within $j + \frac{1}{2}$ years is Q_j, where

$$Q_j = D'_{0,j}/N \tag{46}$$

In the Ngoni sample, $D'_{i,j} = 0$ for all $i \geqslant 35$, and hence in our analysis we shall not require further computations for values of $i \geqslant 35$. Instead of adding further columns to *Table 5*, where there are fifteen rows, it is more convenient to begin a separate divorce risk table, where only eleven rows are needed.

Values of $D'_{i,j}$, taken from *Table 5*, column 12, are repeated in *Table 6*, column 3. By successive addition of terms in column 3 we obtain $D'_{0,j}$, shown in column 4. The terms of column 4 are then divided by N to give Q_j in column 5.

In *Table 7* data on the probability of divorce occurring within a specified time after marriage are given for the Ngoni and for the Northern Rhodesia Copperbelt, the United States of America, and England and Wales. These data are expressed with reference to 100 marriages contracted, so that for the Ngoni $100Q_j$ is shown. Q_j is the chance of divorce occurring within $j + \frac{1}{2}$ years after marriage and for simplicity this is shown in the table as the chance of divorce within j years.

Next we contrast the mean and median duration of all marriages, as already calculated, with the mean and median duration of marriages ending in divorce. During the (20, 24) interval, for example, $D'_{20,24}$ of the cohort marriages end in divorce. Assuming uniform distribution of durations through the interval the mean duration of these marriages is twenty-two years and they therefore contribute $22D'_{20,24}$ marriage-years to the total experienced by the cohort. Similar arguments can be applied to every

TABLE 6 NGONI MARRIAGE SAMPLE: DIVORCE RISK TABLE

1 i	2 j	3 $D'_{i,j}$	4 $D'_{o,j}$	5 Q_j	6 $Z_{i,j}$	7 R_i	8 $q_{i,j}$	9 $p_{i,j}$	10 T_i	11 $L_{i,j}$	12 $a_{i,j}$
0	1	25·3084	25·3084	0·062800	18·9813	403	0·062800	0·937200	100	584·5197	0·0433
2	3	41·3423	66·6507	0·165386	103·3557	376·3596	0·109848	0·890152	93·7200	696·1454	0·0594
4	5	73·4791	140·1298	0·347717	330·6560	319·7859	0·229776	0·770224	83·4251	540·6576	0·1359
6	7	22·6103	162·7401	0·403822	146·9668	220·8717	0·102368	0·897632	64·2560	398·4170	0·0568
8	9	12	174·7401	0·433598	102	177·5353	0·067592	0·932408	57·6782	331·0706	0·0362
10	14	33·2692	208·0092	0·516152	399·2300	153·5353	0·216687	0·783313	53·7796	601·3308	0·0553
15	19	8·9882	216·9974	0·538455	152·7991	86·9970	0·103316	0·896684	42·1262	382·5538	0·0235
20	24	1·1056	218·1031	0·541199	24·3241	66·0246	0·016746	0·983254	37·7739	299·7177	0·0037
25	29	7·0357	225·1387	0·558657	189·9634	53·8625	0·130623	0·869377	37·1414	216·5450	0·0325
30	34	1·3874	226·5261	0·562100	44·3955	32·7555	0·042355	0·957645	32·2899	142·9670	0·0097
35	39	0	226·5261	0·562100	0	24·4313	0	1	30·9222	120·4670	0
	Σ	226·5261			1512·6719						

$K_{0,\infty} = 100 - T_{\infty} = 69{\cdot}0778$ $\qquad c = Z_{0,\infty}/D'_{0,\infty} = 6{\cdot}6777$

TABLE 7 DIVORCES, PER 100 MARRIAGES CONTRACTED, WITHIN SPECIFIED TIME AFTER MARRIAGE: NGONI, COPPERBELT, U.S.A. 1955, AND ENGLAND AND WALES 1939

	Divorces per 100 marriages contracted			
Nominal duration	*Fort Jameson Ngoni*	*Northern Rhodesia Copperbelt*	*U.S.A. 1955*	*England and Wales 1939*
0		2·36	1·810	0·01
1	6·280	5·53	4·262	0·01
2		8·18	6·669	
3	16·539	10·90	8·699	
4		13·19	10·379	0·2
5	34·772	16·14	11·766	
6		17·69	12·952	
7	40·382	19·93	13·998	
8		21·44	14·927	
9	43·360	21·94	15·808	0·9
10		22·75	16·570	
11		24·94	17·211	
12		25·58	17·788	
13			18·319	
14	51·615		18·812	
15			19·284	
16			19·734	
17			20·163	
18			20·571	
19	53·846		20·959	2·0
20			21·334	
21			21·688	
22			22·022	
23			22·330	
24	54·120		22·613	
25			22·865	
26			23·094	
27			23·300	
28			23·484	
29	55·866		23·652	2·6
30			23·800	
31			23·933	
32			24·052	
33			24·158	
34	56·201		24·251	
50	56·201		24·841	2·9

Sources: Ngoni: $100Q_j$ from *Table 6*, column 5, giving number of divorces within $j + \frac{1}{2}$ years.

Copperbelt: Mitchell (1961a, p. 19). Values in column xii, subtracted from 10,000. Intertribal first marriages contracted rurally, 1942–1954.

U.S.A. 1955: Jacobson (1959, p. 145). *Table 71*, column 5, values added cumulatively.

England and Wales 1939: Hajnal (1950a, p. 182). *Table 3*, column 6, values added cumulatively.

interval, and the total number of marriage-years experienced by those marriages in the cohort that end in divorce is $Z_{0,\infty}$ where

$$Z_{0,1} = 3D'_{0,1}/4 \tag{47}$$

$$Z_{i,i+1} = (i + \tfrac{1}{2})D'_{i,i+1} \quad \text{for } i = 2, 4, 6, 8 \tag{48}$$

and

$$Z_{i,i+4} = (i + 2)D'_{i,i+4} \quad \text{for } i = 10, 15, 20, \ldots \tag{49}$$

Values of $i + \frac{1}{2}$ and $i + 2$ are found by inspection from columns 1 and 2 of *Table 6* and are used to multiply corresponding terms in column 3 to give values of $Z_{i,j}$, shown in column 6. By adding the terms of column 6, we obtain $Z_{0,\infty}$, shown at the foot of the column.

The total number of marriages ending in divorce, $D'_{0,\infty}$, is given by the last term in column 4. The mean duration of marriages ending in divorce is then c years, where

$$c = Z_{0,\infty}/D'_{0,\infty} \tag{50}$$

For the Ngoni cohort, c has the value 1512·7/226·5, i.e. 6·68.

The median duration of marriages ending in divorce is found from inspection of *Table 6*, column 4. We find the duration at which $D'_{0,j} = D'_{0,\infty}/2$, for at that duration half of the divorces that occur will have taken place.

If required, the mean and median duration of marriages ending in death can be found in similar fashion.

For the Ngoni, $D'_{0,\infty}/2 = 113{\cdot}3$ and we find by inspection that $D'_{0,3} = 66{\cdot}7$ and $D'_{0,5} = 140{\cdot}1$. The median duration of marriages ending in divorce is from 4 to 5 years.

Data on the mean and median duration of marriage for the Ngoni and for the U.S.A. and England and Wales are given in *Table 8*.

TABLE 8 MEAN AND MEDIAN MARRIAGE DURATION: NGONI, U.S.A., AND ENGLAND AND WALES

	Duration in years		
Marriage type	*Fort Jameson Ngoni*	*U.S.A. 1955*	*England and Wales 1938–1939*
All marriages:			
Mean	11·05	31·5	36·03
Median	6–7	33·3	37·9
Marriages ending in divorce only:			
Mean	6·68		14·1
Median	4–5	6	10–19

Sources: Ngoni: *Table 5*, columns 16 and 18; *Table 6*, columns 4 and 6.
U.S.A.: Jacobson (1959, p. 145, *Table 71*, columns 6 and 9, and p. 149).
England and Wales: Hajnal (1950a, p. 182, *Table 3*, and p. 185, *Table 5*).

From this table it is clear that marriages last a shorter time among the Ngoni than they do in America or Britain. This is due partly to the higher frequency of divorce and partly to a higher mortality. As we would expect, in all three societies marriages ending in divorce tend to be shorter than the average for all marriages.

10. DIVORCE WITHOUT MORTALITY

So far we have considered only the probability that divorce will occur within a specified time after marriage. We now turn to examine the probability that divorce will occur within a specified interval. Consider for example the (20, 24) interval. R_{20} of the marriages in the cohort survive until the beginning of the interval, and of these $D'_{20,24}$ end in divorce at some point within the interval. Hence as a first approximation we may say that the probability, at the beginning of the interval, that divorce will occur before the end of the interval is $q_{20,24}$, where

$$q_{i,j} = D'_{i,j}/R_i \tag{51}$$

But this statement is only approximately true, for the R_{20} marriages are exposed not only to the risk of divorce but to the risk of termination by death as well. We treat these risks as causally independent but, as observed, they are mutually exclusive. We have to assume that there are some marriages that would have ended in divorce within the interval had not one or other of the spouses died before divorce could occur. Thus the number of divorces observed is less than it would have been if there had been no deaths.

The relationship between the theoretical probability of divorce in the absence of mortality and the observed probability is given by the equations

$$m_{i,j} = (H'_{i,j} + W'_{i,j})/R_i \tag{52}$$

$$q_{i,j} = q'_{i,j}(1 - \tfrac{1}{2}m'_{i,j}) \tag{53}$$

and

$$m_{i,j} = m'_{i,j}(1 - \tfrac{1}{2}q'_{i,j}) \tag{54}$$

where $q_{i,j}$ and $m_{i,j}$ are the observed probabilities of termination by divorce and by death, and $q'_{i,j}$ and $m'_{i,j}$ are the theoretical probabilities that would operate if one risk were present and the other absent. When, as in the present calculation, $m_{i,j}$ and $m'_{i,j}$ are probabilities of death occurring within an interval lasting not longer than five years, they are likely to be comparatively small, so that the error in assuming that

$$q_{i,j} = q'_{i,j}$$

can be neglected in an approximate analysis. If longer time intervals are used, $m_{i,j}$ and $m'_{i,j}$ become larger and it may be necessary to calculate $q'_{i,j}$

from the observed values of $q_{i,j}$ and $m_{i,j}$. When $m'_{i,j}$ is eliminated, equations (53) and (54) give

$$q'_{i,j} = \tfrac{1}{2}[2 + q_{i,j} - m_{i,j} - \sqrt{(4 + q^2_{i,j} + m^2_{i,j} - 4q_{i,j} - 4m_{i,j} - 2m_{i,j}q_{i,j})}] \quad (55)$$

If we take the probability of divorce occurring within the (i, j) interval as $q_{i,j}$, the theoretical probability of surviving the risk of divorce during the same interval is $p_{i,j}$, where

$$p_{i,j} = 1 - q_{i,j} \quad (56)$$

Since in reality mortality is always present as a risk, this survival probability does not correspond directly to any observed survival fraction. However we can construct a survival curve based on these probabilities which provides a useful measure of divorce frequency that is largely free from the influence of mortality. It is therefore of particular interest in studies of tribal societies where the cumulative effects of mortality are likely to differ substantially from those experienced in modern societies.

We consider the hypothetical history of a cohort of 100 marriages exposed to the same risks of divorce at each duration as observed in the sample of marriage but not subject to mortality. Then after a year and a half, $100p_{0,1}$ marriages survive. After $3\frac{1}{2}$ years, $100p_{0,1}p_{2,3}$ survive, and so on. In general, after $i - \frac{1}{2}$ years, T marriages survive, where

$$T_i = 100p_{0,i-1} = 100p_{0,1}p_{2,3} \ldots p_{i-2,i-1} \quad (57)$$
$$\text{for } i = 2, 4, 6, 8, 10$$

and

$$T_i = 100p_{0,i-1} = 100p_{0,1}p_{2,3} \ldots p_{i-5,i-1} \quad (58)$$
$$\text{for } i = 15, 20, 25, \ldots$$

We take

$$T_0 = 100$$

In *Table 6*, column 7, we have values of R_i taken from *Table 5*, column 16. We divide terms in column 3, $D'_{i,j}$, by corresponding terms in column 7 to obtain $q_{i,j}$, shown in column 8. These values are subtracted from unity to give $p_{i,j}$, shown in column 9. By multiplying 100 successively by terms in column 9 we obtain T_i, shown one row below in column 10.

The number of marriages in this hypothetical mortality-free cohort that end in divorce during the (i, j) interval is $K_{i,j}$, where

$$K_{i,j} = T_i - T_{j+1} = T_i(1 - p_{i,j}) = T_i q_{i,j} \quad (59)$$

and the total number of marriages ending in divorce is $K_{0,\infty}$ where

$$K_{0,\infty} = T_0 - T_\infty \quad (60)$$

T_∞ being the final value of T_i as i increases. This is given by the last row of *Table 6*, column 10. By subtracting this value from 100 we obtain $K_{0,\infty}$.

The most satisfactory single index of the magnitude of divorce risk in a society where the effects of mortality are too large to be overlooked would seem to be $K_{0,\infty}$. This is the percentage of marriages that, sooner or later, would end in divorce if there were no mortality.

For the Ngoni sample, $K_{0,\infty}$ is 100 − 30·9, i.e. 69·1.

A roughly comparable statistic for divorce frequency in Australia has been calculated by Day. At the duration-specific rates prevailing in 1954, 11·2 per cent of Australian marriages would end in divorce within 40 years if there were no mortality (Day, 1963b, p. 141, *Table 6*).

The observed percentage of Ngoni marriages eventually ending in divorce is $100Q_\infty$ and this will always be less than $K_{0,\infty}$. The difference between these two parameters is due to the effect of mortality on divorce frequency, and as a single index of the magnitude of this effect we may take

$$K_{0,\infty} - 100Q_\infty$$

For the Ngoni, $K_{0,\infty} = 69{\cdot}1$ and $100Q_\infty = 56{\cdot}2$.
Hence $K_{0,\infty} - 100Q_\infty = 12{\cdot}9$. In this sense, we may say that if it were not for mortality, 12·9 per cent more of Ngoni marriages would end in divorce.

II. DIVORCE RATES

In addition to calculating in various ways the cumulative effect of exposure to the risks of divorce and mortality over the years, we can compute the magnitude of divorce frequency at any given marriage duration. We relate the number of divorces occurring in the cohort within an interval to the number of marriage-years experienced by the cohort during that interval. For this purpose we revert to the cohort of marriages exposed to the risks of both divorce and mortality.

The number of marriage-years experienced by the cohort during, for example, the (20, 24) interval is $L_{20,24}$, as defined above in equation (44). The number of divorces occurring during the interval is $D'_{20,24}$ and the duration-specific divorce rate during the interval is therefore $a_{20,24}$ divorces per marriage per annum, where

$$a_{i,j} = D'_{i,j}/L_{i,j} \tag{61}$$

Values of $L_{i,j}$, taken from *Table 5*, column 18, are repeated in *Table 6*, column 11. In column 12 we have $a_{i,j}$, found by dividing terms in column 3 by corresponding terms in column 11.

In *Table 9*, these Ngoni duration-specific divorce rates are compared with rates from some other societies.

TABLE 9 DIVORCES PER ANNUM PER 100 MARRIAGES EXISTING AT SPECIFIED DURATIONS: NGONI, U.S.A., AUSTRALIA, AND LONDON

	Divorces per annum per 100 existing marriages			
Nominal duration	*Fort Jameson Ngoni*	*U.S.A. 1955*	*Australia 1954*	*London 1939*
0		1·81		0·01
0–1	4·33			
1		2·51		0·01
2		2·54		
2–3	5·94			
3		2·21		
0–4			0·16	
2–4				0·06
4		1·88		
4–5	13·59			
5		1·59		
6		1·39		
6–7	5·68			
5–9			0·56	0·14
7		1·25		
8		1·13		
8–9	3·62			
9		1·09		
10		0·96		
11		0·82		
12		0·75		
13		0·70		
10–14	5·53		0·47	
14		0·66		
15		0·64		
16		0·62		
10–19				0·11
15–19	2·35		0·37	
17		0·60		
18		0·58		
19		0·56		
20		0·55		
21		0·53		
20–24	0·37		0·33	
22		0·51		
23		0·48		
24		0·45		
25		0·41		
26		0·38		
20–29				0·06

TABLE 9 (*contd.*)

	Divorces per annum per 100 existing marriages			
Nominal duration	*Fort Jameson Ngoni*	*U.S.A. 1955*	*Australia 1954*	*London 1939*
25–29	3·25		0·22	
27		0·35		
28		0·32		
29		0·30		
30		0·27		
31		0·25		
30–34	0·97			
32		0·23		
33		0·21		
34		0·19		
30–39			0·11	

Sources: Ngoni: 100 $a_{i,j}$ from *Table 6*, column 12.
U.S.A.: Jacobson (1959, p. 145, *Table 71*, column 2). These figures are with reference to 100 marriages extant at the beginning of the interval.
Australia: Day (1963a, p. 61, *Table 2*).
London: Hajnal (1950a, p. 187, *Table B*, column 6).

Despite substantial quantitative differences there is a broad similarity in the shape of the curves for the three modern societies, with a relatively quick rise to a maximum and a slow decline thereafter. The divorce rate is greatest for durations of from five to nine years in Australia and London, and in America it is greatest at two years' duration. The Ngoni curve has a maximum at from four to five years after marriage, but the first interval, centring at nine months after marriage, has a higher value than has the second interval. This reflects a real difference in divorce procedures in the two kinds of society. In modern societies divorce is typically sought only after considerable deliberation; the legal process lasts for months or even years, and it involves considerable expense. Most people enter marriage hoping that it will last for a lifetime and abandon this hope only slowly. The divorce rate during the first year of marriage is therefore relatively low. Among the Fort Jameson Ngoni a bride, even though marriage payments may have been made for her, may run away from her husband after only a few days and within a week or so she may be divorced. Despite its short duration this may be a proper marriage and not temporary concubinage. Hence the divorce rate during the first years of marriage is relatively high.

12. COLLECTING INFORMATION

This is as far as we need take these calculations. We have already taken them much further than the empirical data warrant. An elaborate analysis calls for a larger and more carefully collected body of observations than I have been able to employ, and the sophistication of the analysis has amply demonstrated the shortcomings of my field material. The small number of divorces occurring at long durations not only provides a very shaky basis for generalizations about divorce rates beyond the first decade and a half after marriage; it also entails a discontinuous distribution in the higher duration cells which makes an analysis based on intervals by single years quite inappropriate. The irregularities in the 6th-, 7th-, 8th-, and 9th-year intervals, as shown in *Table 4*, are also certainly due to biased estimation of the dates of marriage and divorce, and this must be regarded as poor field-work. My only defence is that in this paper I have been concerned primarily with demonstrating a technique of analysis and I have used as illustration the only body of field data available to me. I have argued in favour of certain methods of computation while conscious of the inadequacy of the data to which I have applied them. Indeed, these methods serve to make the inadequacy manifest.

For convenience I have brought together in *Table 10* the various definitions I have used. *En masse* they may seem formidable, but I hope that I have shown that only slight mathematical aptitude is needed to handle them and that their use leads to a greater degree of sociological understanding than would be possible through words alone.

The field procedures necessary for this analysis are remarkably simple. We begin by delimiting a sample, by selecting a segment of the society being studied, such as a village or clan or political sector, and we then examine the life histories of all the relevant individuals belonging to the chosen segment. We should indicate how the segment was chosen, how it was delimited, and its size, both absolutely and in relation to the whole society. It is desirable that the kind of segment selected should be such that each individual in the society belongs to one, and only to one, segment; but this is not always possible. It is also desirable that the segments should not vary widely in size; if they do, two (or more) samples should be made, one from a large segment and one from a small one.

Often we lack information on individuals who, in these terms, should form part of the sample. Even if we can find out nothing else about them, we should endeavour to estimate how many there are of these. In tabulations showing the distribution of individuals into different categories, as in a marital-status table, we can then include these individuals in an 'unknown' category. Where our units of tabulation are not individuals but events they have experienced, such as marriage and divorce, we cannot do this. We can however indicate the completeness of our sample by showing how many informants we used out of the total number possible, as well as providing an 'unknown' category for those events known to have been experienced by our informants but for which further information is lacking.

The minimum amount of information needed from each individual, man or woman, adult or child, in the sample to enable us to make the computations discussed here is as follows:

1. Name or other identification
2. Sex
3. Date of birth
4. Marital history, showing for each marriage:

   (*a*) date of commencement;

   (*b*) whether extant or terminated by death or divorce;

   (*c*) date of termination, if not still extant;

   (*d*) name or identification of spouse.

In some situations we may be able to determine the dates accurately, while in others we may have to estimate in decades. The more precise our observed data the greater the precision of our measures, but the method of computation remains essentially the same whether we are working to the nearest year or to the nearest five years.

It will be seen that the information required is not great and it can easily be collected as part of a systematic inquiry into topics such as marriage and fertility, kinship affiliation, or labour migration.

13. CONCLUSION

We are not here concerned with the full demographic analysis of marriage termination by death, but it should be noted that *Table 5* can be used in this connexion as well. We can show, for example, that, for most durations greater than three years, termination is more likely to have taken place by death of the man than of the woman. Among the Fort Jameson Ngoni, as in most societies, men are usually older than their wives and this may be part of the explanation. There are nearly twice as many women as men

TABLE 10 QUANTITIES USED IN COMPUTATIONS

	Columns where shown in Tables					
Symbol	*4*	*5*	*6*	*Relevant equations*	*Definition*	*Description*
$a_{i,j}$			12	61	$D'_{i,j}/L_{i,j}$	Duration-specific divorce rate
b'		f.n.		45	$L_{0,\infty}/N$	Mean duration of all marriages
b		f.n.		30	$E_{0,\infty}/G_{0,\infty}$	
c			f.n.	50	$Z_{0,\infty}/D'_{0,\infty}$	Mean duration, marriages ending in divorce
$D_{i,j}$	3	7	3			Sample marriages ending in divorce
$D'_{i,j}$		12		36	$D_{i,j}(1 + t_{i,j})$	Adjusted sample marriages ending in divorce
$D''_{i,j}$				34	$D_{i,j}\, t_{i,j}$	Hypothetical marriages ending in divorce
$E_{i,j}$	2	3				Sample marriages still extant
$e_{i,j}$		4		25, 26	$E_{i-2,j+2} - E_{i+2,j+2}$ or $E_{i-5,j-5} - E_{i+5,j+5}$	
$F_{i,j}$		10		33	$D_{i,j} + H_{i,j} + W_{i,j}$	Completed marriages in sample
$F'_{i,j}$		15		39	$F_{i,j}(1 + t_{i,j})$	Marriages in adjusted sample
$G_{i,j}$		5		2, 8–13, 15–18, 20, 21, 23, 24, 27, 28, 32	Various	Hypothetical completed marriages per annum
$H_{i,j}$	4	8				Sample marriages ending in death of husband
$H'_{i,j}$		13		37	$H_{i,j}(1 + t_{i,j})$	Adjusted sample marriages ending in death of husband
i					0, 1, 2, 3, …	
j					0, 1, 2, 3, …	
$K_{i,j}$				59	$T_i - T_{j+1}$	Marriages ending in divorce in mortality-free cohort
$L_{i,j}$		18	11	42, 43, 44	$(j - i + 1)(R_i + R_{j+1})/2$ for $i = 2, 4, 6, \ldots$ 10, 15, 20 …	Marriage-years experienced by cohort
$M_{i,j}$		6		29	$b\, G_{i,j}$	Hypothetical marriages in adjusted sample
$m_{i,j}$				52	$(H'_{i,j} + W'_{i,j})/R_i$	Observed probability of termination by death

TABLE 10 (*contd.*)

Symbol	Columns where shown in Tables 4	5	6	Relevant equations	Definition	Description
$m'_{i,j}$				54		Theoretical probability of termination by death
N		f.n.		40	$F'_{0,\infty}$	Number of marriages in sample
n				7, 14, 19, 22, 31	$G_{0,\infty}$	New hypothetical marriages per annum
$p_{i,j}$			9	56	$1 - q_{i,j}$	Probability of not ending in divorce
Q_j			5	46	$D'_{0,j}/N$	Cumulative chance of divorce
$q_{i,j}$			8	51	$D'_{i,j}/R_i$	Observed probability of divorce
$q'_{i,j}$				55		Theoretical probability of divorce
R_i		16	7	41	$N - F'_{0,i-1}$	Surviving marriages in cohort
$S(x)$				1		Chance of survival
T_i			10	57, 58	$100p_{0,i-1}$	Marriages surviving, mortality absent
$t_{i,j}$		11		35	$M_{i,j}/F_{i,j}$	Ratio of hypothetical to real completed marriages in adjusted sample
u						Any positive number
v						Any positive number
$w_{i,j}$	5	9				Sample marriages ending in death of wife
$w'_{i,j}$		14		38	$w_{i,j}(1 + t_{i,j})$	Adjusted sample marriages ending in death of wife
x						Any positive number
y				13, 18		Some positive integer
$Z_{i,j}$			6	47, 48, 49	$(i + j)D'_{i,j}/2$ for $i = 2, 4, 6, \ldots,$ 10, 15, 20 …	Marriage-years lived by marriages ending in divorce

f.n. = value shown at foot of table

in the sample and, whereas some of the men who used to live in the sample villages and whose wives have died are now labour migrants in the towns, comparatively few widows have become migrants. The figures as they stand appear to show that the additional hazards of child-bearing do not make termination by death of the woman as likely as might be expected. Any investigation of this point would have to allow for the unusual sex ratio and for differential rates of migration for men and women.

By calling upon further raw data, such as age of spouses at marriage, whether they were related to one another, whether they were married as Christians or pagans, how many children they had, what relatives they lived with, and the like, it is possible to analyse divorce frequency further. In our own society we often emphasize, and probably overemphasize (see Jacobson, 1950, p. 242 ff.), how divorce is more likely in a barren than in a fertile marriage. It would be well to know to what extent this is true of other societies where the rearing of children, and their social importance, is regarded in quite a different way (see Hsu, 1949, p. 105). Frequencies and rates can be calculated specific not only for duration but also for man's age, or for religion, or for social status. The particular line of inquiry followed will depend on the problem in hand.

Divorce is not one 'thing' and cannot be described by a single index or a single adjective. It is a social process that has many aspects; we can measure some but cannot measure others. Divorce in two societies may be similar in one respect and different in another, as we have seen by contrasting the Fort Jameson Ngoni and other societies. Some aspects are related to each other logically and we can define in advance the logical connexion between their various measures, as for example the equation connecting the three divorce ratios. We may assume *a priori* that there are other connexions in reality between aspects of divorce which may now appear independent. These connexions are properties not of our analytical tools but rather of the human societies we examine, and we may hope to discover them by further inquiry in the field. For example, is it true that as divorce becomes more frequent the time of greatest risk shifts from the second to the first quinquennium of marriage, as is suggested by the data in *Table 9*? In other words, if divorce is more likely does it come sooner? This kind of question can best be answered for simple societies with the help of tools such as those described in this paper. We may then go on to consider whether or not we are justified in treating as similar phenomena the comparatively rare terminations of marriage in, say, Zulu and Nuer societies, arising from conditions of extreme marital stress, and the comparatively frequent terminations in, say, Yao and Lozi societies, which appear to rise often from trivial precipitating causes and may have quite different social functions.

I am well aware I have constructed a pretentious superstructure on raw data that are quite unsuited to uphold it. My plea must be that, if we draw attention to the uses to which information of this kind can be put, workers in the field may be encouraged to collect more and better data.

from trivial precipitating causes and may have quite different social functions.

I am well aware I have constructed a pretentious superstructure on raw data that are quite inadequate to uphold it. My plea must be that, if we draw attention to the uses to which information of this kind can be put, workers in the field may be encouraged to collect more and better data.

J. A. BARNES

Genealogies

From the first the work of the genealogist in England had that taint of inaccuracy tempered with forgery from which it has not yet been cleansed.

O. BARRON, 'Genealogy'

IN many senses the most distinctive and fundamental human institution is the nuclear family, founded on the two concepts of marriage and parentage and consisting of man, wife, and children. It is not surprising that the family has provided us with a matrix for many other social institutions. The language of intrafamilial relations is used to define and describe relations between persons in different families and between groups of persons; the values conventionally associated with the family are transferred and transformed to refer to the affairs of the kindred, the community, and even the State; family membership and family position are used as criteria for membership and position in larger social units. The pedigree or genealogy, the 'account of one's descent from an ancestor or ancestors by enumeration of the intermediate persons', is used chiefly in connexion with the last of these processes. It is a statement of the way in which individuals are, or assert that they are, connected with one another through marriage and common parentage. The connexions stated in the genealogy are the grounds for assigning specific rights and duties, membership and status, to specific persons.

Relationships between ruler and ruled, between buyer and seller, between enemies and between friends, may all be defined and acted out in a bewildering variety of ways. But relations between kinsfolk are limited in a way that has no analogue in the domains of politics and economics. These limitations give to kinship systems those qualities of formal regularity and precision which have proved so tempting and perhaps so disastrous to generations of anthropologists. One salient characteristic of kinship systems is their concern with relationship rather than with status, or, in Service's terminology (1960, pp. 752–754), with egocentric familistic status and not with sociocentric status. In kinship there are, as it were, always two parties to be considered, for a man is never a son or an uncle merely on his own; he is always some specific person's son and some other specific person's uncle. It is true that a chief has his own subjects and that a priest serves a particular god and a particular congregation, but it is possible to visualize and to discuss the role and status of a chief or of a priest without constant reference to the identity of those whom he rules or serves. In the domain of kinship, however, the same individual, X, is the son of A and the uncle of B, and when we describe the entailments of being a son or being an uncle we have to discuss the actions of A and B as well as those of X. Furthermore, in kinship there are no logically privileged positions. Every man is someone's grandson and is potentially a grandfather of someone else. Each person may see himself spiderlike at the centre of his own web of kinship, but it is a web occupied by spiders like himself, each looking outwards at the others. A chief may dominate his subjects without the roles ever being reversed; but if in a kinship system a man exercises authority over his sister's son he does so only inasmuch as he is someone else's sister's son, and subject to that person's authority.

The characteristics of all kinship systems derive logically from the simple premises on which these systems are built. In general, each human is either male or female, has two and only two parents (one of each sex), may have siblings who share with him one or both parents, may marry, and may have children. In this context, whether social parentage is or is not identical with genetic parentage does not matter, for both follow the same logical model. These premises entail relationships between any individual and his (or her) mother, father, brother, sister, husband (or wife), son, and daughter, and by compounding these relationships we can specify as long and complicated a link through the kinship web as we wish. It would be possible to build a system of relationships using bricks other than those we have just listed, and in practice we find that criteria such as residence, political allegiance, age, and place of conception or birth are used along with parentage and marriage to define relationships that may still usefully be put under the broad rubric of kinship. In particular, many systems make use of order of birth as a distinguishing criterion, so that a man may have significantly different relationships with his older and his younger brother.

GENEALOGIES AND PEDIGREES

These, then, are the general properties of the system of kinship relations within which we find the specific statements of genealogies. The genealogy conforms to the logic of the system, and in analysis we use genealogies collected in the field along with other evidence to infer the properties of the kinship system generating them. In this sense the genealogy is an analytical tool used by those who study kinship. But in another sense it is a tool used by the actors who operate, and not merely observe, kinship systems. For many centuries written genealogies have been prepared in Europe as evidence of descent from a noble or landed ancestor and hence of the legal right to possessions and office. Analogous documents are found in many other cultures, as for example the printed genealogies of China and the genealogies written on barkcloth found among the Redjang of south Sumatra (Jaspan, 1964). In north India, the compilation of genealogies is the occupational prerogative of a special caste (Shah and Shroff, 1958). In Samoa, genealogies formerly committed to memory are now recorded in notebooks (Freeman, 1964, p. 555). The Old Testament includes many lists of descent from father to son and in numerous non-literate cultures there is formalized oral recitation of descent lines. These oral or written records are similar to the genealogies built up by the field ethnographer and, indeed, may form a substantial part of the evidence he uses to construct them, but they are not identical and it is useful to distinguish between them. Two terms, 'genealogy' and 'pedigree', are often used interchangeably for statements of genealogical connexion, and 'genealogy' is also used as an abstract noun for the study of these statements. I propose to extend the practice of many genealogists (e.g. Wagner, 1960) by using the word 'pedigree' for a genealogical statement made orally, diagrammatically, or in writing by an actor or informant. This usage is in conformity with Fortes's definition of pedigree as 'the charter by which any particular person presents himself as the descendant of a specified ancestor' (1959). Yalman (1963, p. 27), writing of the Kandyan Sinhalese, draws a distinction between 'pedigrees' which link living people with their dead ancestors, and 'genealogies' which link living people to others around them. In the terminology used here, these are all pedigrees, though of two distinct types. By 'genealogy', in the concrete sense, I mean a genealogical statement made by an ethnographer as part of his field record or of its analysis. In this essay I am concerned with both genealogies and pedigrees. In ethnographic inquiry it is often necessary to collect genealogical information about a much wider range of connexions than the people concerned normally include in their pedigrees. A pedigree is normally a contemporary statement, making assertions about connexions between people, many of whom died long ago, whereas in a genealogy the ethnographer seeks to establish how these people, during their lifetime, were thought to be connected to one another, as well as how these connexions are viewed now. The cultural milieu of the actors marks the method of construction of the pedigree, whereas the demands of science determine how the genealogy is recorded.

The collection of genealogies has long been regarded as part of the stock-in-trade of the ethnographer. Presumably knowledge of Western pedigrees must have prompted many a traveller in foreign parts to elicit and record genealogical information about the people he encountered. One of the first genealogies of tribal peoples to be published was collected by Sir George Grey (1841, II, pp. 391–394) in Western Australia. In the 1860s L. H. Morgan began his major work of investigating systems of kinship terminology throughout the world. His efforts fostered scientific interest in genealogical connexions but did not lead to an interest in genealogies themselves. It was not until W. H. R. Rivers published the results of his inquiries in the Torres Strait that the utility of genealogies for ethnographic inquiry began to be recognized (Rivers, 1900, 1904, 1910). Rivers was interested in genetic as well as socially recognized kinship and paid much attention to kinship terminology, but his method laid the foundation for later developments in social demography and the construction of statistical models, developments he was one of the first to advocate.

Kinship terms may be set out in either tabular or diagrammatic form, and in much ethnographic writing the diagram has the form of a genealogy. It is therefore important to distinguish between a genealogical chart and a terminological diagram. The pattern of a traditional diagram of kinship terms using conventional genealogical signs is determined by the logical structure of the terminological system, whereas the shape of a genealogy, shown diagrammatically, is determined by the fertility and nuptuality of the individuals it contains. For example, if there is a specific term for MBW (mother's brother's wife), this can be shown on a diagram by writing the term against the symbol for the only wife of the only brother of the mother of Ego. But if Alpha, a MB of Beta, has been married three times, and his numerous brothers have done likewise, a genealogy of Beta's relatives must show all his MBWs. On the other hand, Beta may perhaps have no sisters, and none would appear on his genealogical chart even though he knows the correct kinship term for sister. Hence a genealogy of Beta's relatives will take quite a different form from a diagram setting out the system of kinship terminology used by Beta and his fellows, though an incomplete description of the system may be given by writing against the name of each relative the kinship term for that person used by Beta.

The genealogy is also to be distinguished from what we may term the prescriptive diagram. This sets out how moieties, sections, sub-sections, lineages, and the like are related to one another, or how these relations are sustained by the marriage of persons in specified genealogical categories. Prescriptive diagrams show the logical interconnexions and entailments of a set of rules of marriage and recruitment to groups, but they do not necessarily conform to the genealogy of any set of related real individuals. Terminological and prescriptive diagrams are discussed later.

GENEALOGICAL NARRATIVES

Pedigrees have to be accepted for cultural and sociological analysis in whatever form they happen to arise in the field, but the ethnographer has a choice when organizing his genealogical information. A genealogy may be simply a transliteration of a pedigree, using universally recognized rather than local symbols; or it may be a record of the genealogical knowledge and assertions of a single informant; or it may be a construct made by the ethnographer from information supplied by several informants who may disagree with one another in a number of particulars. It may include a record of all the known connexions of a set of individuals or it may be limited to certain connexions regarded as important in a given context. It may mention only the name or sex of individuals or it may give dates of birth, marriage, divorce, and death, residence and changes in residence, type of marriage contract, occupation, or other personal characteristics. Deciding what social characteristics and what genealogical connexions are relevant at any stage in the analysis may be difficult, but for sound deductions there must first be a full systematic record of characteristics and connexions from which the appropriate extract can be made. I am not here concerned with how to plan and conduct a census of social characteristics and confine my discussion to the ways in which to elicit and record an account, as complete as possible, of real and alleged genealogical connexions.

For most purposes, the pattern of relationships of cognation and affinity in a community can be perceived more readily from a diagram or chart than from a narrative account. But, in the field, it is better to record fresh genealogical information in a notebook in narrative form rather than attempt to draw a genealogical chart at the dictation of an informant. A chart can be set out neatly only after it is known how many generations the genealogy covers and how many individuals have to be fitted into each part of the chart. Furthermore, for orderly presentation, each of the constituent cognatic stocks in the informant's kindred should first be entered on a separate chart. Later, information about kinsfolk belonging to several stocks can be extracted and combined in an illustrative genealogical diagram.

The large part played in the social life of any individual by the links he has or evokes with his several relatives has been conclusively demonstrated for a wide range of societies. Different lines of filiation are given different emphasis in the formation of social groups but everywhere cognatic and affinal connexions have some significance in social organization. Hence, even when studying the most strongly unilineal societies, it is good practice to record all that can be remembered of each informant's kindred, i.e. all the descendants of his ancestors, and as many of his affinal kin as seems appropriate. Adoption of this procedure dóes not in any way depend on whether or not the kindred, thus defined, exists either as a concept or as a *de facto* grouping in the thought and life of the society being studied. It is merely a way of making sure that the ethnographer leaves no possibly significant genealogical pathway unexplored. Indeed, this method of inquiry may well extend to individuals to whom a genealogical path may be traced, step by step, but whom the informant regards as not his kin. The boundary between kin and non-kin, if it exists, can then be determined accurately by exploring on both sides of it. Each of the partly overlapping cognatic stocks which together constitute an informant's kindred should be explored in turn. Information about clusters of affinal kin, other than his wife's cognates, can conveniently be recorded immediately after reaching the cognatic relative who links them to the informant.

Rivers describes how he collected systematically the names and relationship of each of his informant's kin, and his method can scarcely be improved, except for one alteration. I suggest that it is often useful, before beginning on a sequence of inquiries structured by the ethnographer, to record first whatever information about his kinsfolk the informant thinks important, in the form in which he presents it. In societies where pedigrees are significant, the volunteered information is likely to be the names of a single line of ancestors, listed in either ascending or descending order, or several lines may be given in succession. For the remoter generations, it may be that no information is available other than that embodied in these pedigrees. Alternatively, there may be no organized pedigrees at all, and the informant may offer only unorganized information which the ethnographer collates as he constructs his genealogies. The informant will almost certainly wish to talk about his kinsfolk in some order other than that to be described. The information he volunteers may be no more accurate or complete than the data collected by systematic inquiry later on, but it provides the best indication of how the informant perceives his kinsfolk and what version of their names, status, numbers, and relationships he wishes to present to the ethnographer.

After recording volunteered information, ask systematically about all the informant's relatives, skipping over relatives who have already been fully described unless it is found that in a new context fresh information about them may come to light. First, note the names, sex, occupation, and dwelling-place of the informant. Ascertain as accurately as possible when and where he (or she) was born and where he has lived. Note the names of each of his wives (or her husbands), whether or not he is still married to them, and record in each instance where the marriage began, when and how it ended if it is not still extant, the wife's date and place of birth and where she lives now, or her date and place of death.

Information on births, marriages, and deaths is more precise and more self-checking if these events can be dated. If there are no contemporary dated records, a local chronology can be constructed (Mitchell, 1949, p. 295). If ages are estimated from physical appearance, the estimates must be examined carefully to determine their likely accuracy, as discussed by Rose (1960, pp. 42–51) for an Aboriginal population. The ethnographer must make clear to his informants what kinds of parentage he is interested in, for social and genetic paternity are likely to differ in some instances in any society, and in some societies may often differ (see Stanner, 1960, pp. 253–254; Barnes, 1961a). Social filiation acquired at birth should be distinguished from filiation acquired by adoption, capture, or fosterage. Residence modifies or validates the rights, obligations, and actions of kinship in very many contexts and hence information on moves from one locality to another, for whatever purpose, should be recorded as fully as possible. It is also important to obtain as complete as possible a record of children born out of wedlock or in adultery; yet an ethnographer who asked persistently if the informant and each of his relatives had had extra-marital children would in many cultures encounter annoyance and hostility. Early in the interview the ethnographer can tell his informant that he is interested in these matters and that he will respect the informant's confidence; this may encourage the informant to volunteer information. In the procedure set out below, each set of full siblings is recorded separately; this is probably the clearest procedure for accurately determining social parentage when the informant is a man or when inquiring about a male relative, particularly in polygynous societies. After all a man's children by each of his wives have been noted, it may be possible to ask if he has had any other children. With a woman informant, and when inquiring about a female relative, it may be more effective to depart from the procedure as set out and to ask first for a list of all the woman's children in order of birth. Next inquire about her husbands and then go on to ask in turn about the identity of the father of each child. In this way, extra-marital and adulterine children may come to light.

Move to the first descending generation from the informant. Take the first wife and record the names of her children during her marriage to the informant, in order of birth. Ask if any children have been acquired by adoption or other means and distinguish them from the others. Begin with the eldest child and ask where he (or she) is living; record the names of his wives (or her husbands). Then ask for all his characteristics – date and place of birth (and of death), occupation, affiliation, modes of reference and address by the informant, and the like – as required (Elkin, 1933, pp. 263–264). Collect similar information about each of his spouses.

Move on to the second descending generation. Record the names of the children of the informant's first child by his first wife. Take the eldest child of this sibling set, grandchild of the informant, and note his characteristics, the names of his spouses, if any, and their characteristics. If this grandchild has had children, note the particulars of his spouses and children, and continue in this fashion until a generation of infants is reached. Only then do we start partly to retrace our steps. Exhaust each line of direct descent before beginning on the next. At each point, record the names of the whole set of full siblings before inquiring about the characteristics, spouses, and descendants of the members of the set. As soon as all the descendants and their spouses of the eldest member of a sibling set have been dealt with, move to the next member of the set and inquire about his characteristics, spouses, and descendants. Then move to the next younger member of the set and so on until the youngest member has been dealt with. In every instance all the descendants, with their spouses, of each of the informant's relatives are recorded before beginning on the descendants of that relative's next younger full sibling. Each time the youngest member of a sibling set, and his descendants, have been recorded, attention shifts to the next set of siblings, half-siblings of the previous set, or, if there are no more, to the next junior member of the sibling set under consideration in the adjacent higher generation.

When all the descendants, and all their spouses, of the informant and his first wife have been recorded, inquire about the names of the children of the informant and his second wife, and repeat the process. Move to the children by the third wife and so on until all his children by all his wives have been recorded along with their descendants. We then have recorded all the members, and spouses of members, of the cognatic stock of which the informant is the apex.

In the next stage, we complete the genealogy of the informant's kindred, and the spouses of his kindred, by taking his ancestors, one by one, and recording for each of them the membership of the cognatic stock which has that ancestor at its apex. To do this, ask the informant the names of his father and mother. Ascertain if these are his parents by birth or by adoption; if he is an adopted child, record both his natal and adoptive parents and kinsfolk. Inquire about other spouses, past and present, of his parents. Then take the informant's father as the point of reference and record all his descendants, and their spouses, in the same way as with the informant himself. The procedure will be exactly the same, except that one of the informant's father's sons by one of his wives will be the informant himself, whose descendants have already been recorded. After finishing with the informant's father, move to the informant's father's father and begin again. The process can be repeated for successively higher agnatic ancestors, so far as the informant's memory or the ethnographer's interest permits.

After all the descendants, and their spouses, of each member of the ascending agnatic line of the informant's ancestors have been recorded, begin exploring systematically all the other lines. If, for example, after finishing with the informant's father's father's father, it is found that the informant's father's father's father's father is unknown or of no interest in this context, come back to the father's father's father. His wives will have already been recorded: one of them is the informant's father's father's mother. Ask if she had other husbands and note the names of her children by each of her husbands. Proceed as before with the informant's father's father's mother as point of reference and record all her descendants and their respective spouses. Then inquire about her father and his wives, and take him as the next point of reference. After him, shift to his father, and so on as far as necessary. The same process of probing each line of ascent, first the patrilateral branch and then the matrilateral branch, continues until all lines have been exhausted. After all the descendants of all the known ancestors of any ancestor Gamma have been recorded, then and only then move to Gamma's wife, and record all her other descendants, her ancestor's descendants, and their spouses. When Gamma and his wife have been dealt with, move down a generation to their child Delta who is an ancestor of the informant. If Delta is a man, move to his wife Lambda, an ancestor of the informant, and move up through her ancestors. If Delta is a woman, then her husband's ancestors will have already been explored; therefore move down again to her child; and so on.

In this way, all the informant's cognates and all his cognates' spouses are included in the genealogical narrative. If this plan is followed, with an informant who knows the names of all his ancestors for four generations back but no farther, he and his thirty ancestors are used as apical points for reference in the following order (see also *Figure 1*):

Ego, F, FF, FFF, FFFF, FFFM, FFM, FFMF, FFMM, FM, FMF, FMFF, FMFM, FMM, FMMF, FMMM, M, MF, MFF, MFFF, MFFM, MFM, MFMF, MFMM, MM, MMF, MMFF, MMFM, MMM, MMMF, MMMM.

It needs a clear head not to lose the way through this genealogical maze. Even if the ethnographer knows the drill confidently, his informant may well lose his place, particularly if several of his relatives have the same name. Hence the ethnographer must be ready to vary his procedure to suit the way in which the informant thinks about his relatives. In some cultures, people think of the members of sibling sets with males in order followed by females in order, and not in the combined order of birth. It may then be difficult to obtain information on the relative birth order of a distant relative and his sister. The method suggested for taking ancestors as apical points of reference is appropriate for a patrilineal or cognatic society, but in a matrilineal society it may prove advantageous to take the matrilateral before the patrilateral branch at every point, so that the informant is asked first about the dominant line of ascent before his attention wanders and his interest flags. The appropriate order with matrilateral preference is shown in parenthesis in *Figure 1*. In a society with double unilineal descent, some other order may prove to be best.

FIGURE I EGO AND HIS ANCESTORS TO FOUR GENERATIONS DEPTH

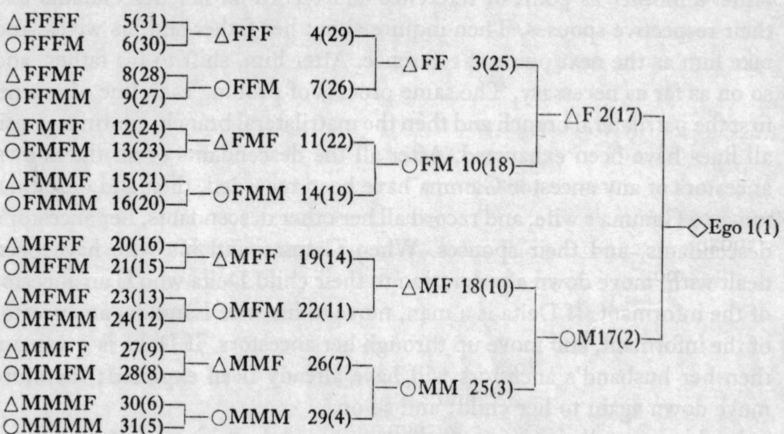

The numbers indicate the order in which ancestors are taken as apical points of reference with patrilateral (or matrilateral) preference.

In this method, ignorance takes care of itself, for the ethnographer moves on every time he reaches the limit of the informant's knowledge in any particular line, ascending or descending. In some societies, however, an informant may be able to recollect the names of some of the siblings of an ancestor without knowing the names of their parents. These siblings can be included if, every time he reaches the limit of knowledge in an ascending line, the ethnographer inquires about the names of siblings of the highest known ancestor, and then takes each sibling in turn as his apical point of reference. However, it is reasonable to assume that persons said to be full siblings but whose parents are unknown are less likely to have been full siblings in fact than are those whose common parentage is known.

Thus the method consists essentially in recording the names of members of the cognatic stocks descended from the informant and from each of his ancestors, along with the spouses of members. The narrative should therefore include all the informant's known cognates and their spouses. For many purposes this may be sufficient, but sometimes it is necessary to collect information about more affinal relatives. For example, the ethnographer may be interested in finding out how well acquainted the informant is with his affines; or the informant's spouse may not be available to speak about her (or his) own cognates; or certain affinal links, e.g. between brothers-in-law, may be known to be socially important. Among the Hanunóo, for example, a man regards all his wife's 'consanguineal' relatives as members of the widest category of his kin equally with his own (Conklin, 1964, p. 49).

The same procedure may be applied taking the informant's spouse as starting-point and recording her (or his) kindred and their spouses exactly as with the informant's own kindred. It will scarcely be necessary or feasible to explore the whole kindred of each of the informant's cognate's spouses, but it may be worth while noting, in respect of each spouse encountered in the course of the narrative, the names of his or her parents and full siblings. Explore the origins of all adoptive children, and note the new filiation of children who have been adopted by others.

The procedure described here is built on the assumed reliability of the steps from child to parent, from parent to children, and from one spouse to the other. This assumption is probably justified for most societies but the ethnographer should not merely take this for granted. He should verify that in the society being studied individuals are associated unambiguously with others as parents and as spouses.

Kinship systems may be found universally, but nevertheless we have to remember that marriage and parentage, as social and not biological concepts, are sometimes defined ambiguously and applied equivocally. In particular, the ethnographer should not read into his charts greater clarity and consensus about the relationships prevailing between distant ancestors than actually exist among his informants. Some peoples are quite uninterested in their ancestry but will answer questions to please the inquirer. The ethnographer should be ready to modify his method of inquiry if there is persistent vagueness, uncertainty, and inconsistency about who was married to whom and who their children were. For example, if a culture stresses age-set placement rather than filiation, it may be necessary to develop a technique of inquiry in which individuals are first located by age-set and then linked up as far as possible with their parents and children (see Goldenweiser, 1937, pp. 316–317). If names are regularly inherited, it may be difficult to know which holder of a name is being discussed at any time; nicknames may then serve to identify successive holders. It may be necessary to deal in sequence with all those who held the same name, irrespective of their relative position genealogically. Likewise, if every individual takes many names in succession, as in some systems of teknonymy, nicknames may be useful to determine identity (Holmberg, 1950, p. 51). Prohibitions on mentioning the names of relatives, or of the dead, or on saying one's own name, present special difficulties, and it may be necessary to adopt special procedures to overcome them. Informants may be readier to speak about the relatives of others than they are to discuss their own, so that the ethnographer never makes his informant the point of reference of the genealogy he records. Some names may have to be whispered, or revealed through an intermediary or when no one else is is present. For some purposes, photographs can be used. Stanner (1936, p. 208) reports how some Australian Aborigines, when teaching each other a new sub-section system, used twigs and marks on the ground as signs for individuals who were being discussed. This device may help an informant to concentrate his attention while his genealogy is recorded.

GENEALOGICAL CHARTS

As soon as the genealogical narrative is completed, it can be summarized in diagrams or charts. Indeed, it is good practice in the field to summarize every portion of genealogical narrative diagrammatically as soon as it has been recorded. In a community where many or all are related to one another, the testimony of each informant will overlap in part with the information supplied by others. Genealogical charts reveal quickly whether these testimonies conflict and where they confirm one another. Even illiterate informants, who cannot read a genealogical narrative, can quickly learn to understand a chart and can see how their testimony is being put to use, particularly if the charts are drawn in several colours. Composite charts may be built up from data contained in the narratives of several informants, if these do not conflict. Charts summarize and rearrange the information contained in narratives, but some details have to be omitted. A chart that included all the information of a narrative might well be too crowded to read quickly. With care it should be possible to show clearly on a chart dates of birth, marriage, and death; clan, moiety, or section affiliation; place of birth; and present residence. Lengthy life histories and similar information that may rightly form part of a genealogical narrative are usually out of place on a chart, though special symbols may be employed to indicate in very summary fashion histories of migration and the possession of other selected characteristics (see Barnes, 1947, p. 51). Likewise, it is quite impracticable, in most instances, to attempt to include all the kinsfolk mentioned in one informant's narrative on a single connected chart. Attempts to show on one chart all the kinsfolk of all the members of an interrelated community are even more likely to end in confusion. The connecting lines become so long and criss-cross one another so much that the chart cannot serve its prime purpose, to clarify for the ethnographer the pattern of interrelationship in the community.

It is much better to treat each section of an informant's kindred separately, each with its own chart, with some system of cross-referencing from one chart to another. There are two obvious ways of dividing up a kindred, into cognatic stocks or into unilineal segments, a unilineal segment being in fact merely a special kind of partial stock. If a kindred is divided for diagrammatic purposes into cognatic stocks, many individuals will each be eligible to appear on several charts, while the informant himself can appear on them all. A unilineal arrangement eliminates repetition, but used in a cognatic society it may mislead the ethnographer into attributing social existence to a unilineal group or a distant kinship link that in fact is nothing more than his own analytical construct. For example, Peters reports that although he recorded ostensibly agnatic links, based on common patronyms, between the ancestors of groups of Lebanese peasants, he doubts very much whether the peasants conceive of their relations in this patrilineal form. Peters says that when they were asked to volunteer accounts of their kin, they gave complex bilateral connexions within a range of some two generations only (1963, p. 184). If each chart shows all or part of a stock, repetition of information can be avoided by cross-referencing, but it is often useful to accept some repetition in order to bring together on the same chart the kinsfolk and sets of cousins who habitually interact. Even in a society with strong unilineal descent, it may be worth while showing how individuals would belong together in notional cognatic stocks, so that the possible significance of ties of complementary filiation may be assessed.

There are several ways of setting out a genealogical chart. Some written pedigrees employ what has been called a 'multiple balloon form' (e.g. Peters, 1963, p. 182; Jaspan, 1964) in which individuals closely related to each other are enclosed in a line. In medieval Europe pedigrees were drawn with curved radiating lines resembling the foot of a crane (*pied de gru*, *petigrewe*) and indicating the links between siblings and parent (Round, 1895; Sweet, 1895). In the sixteenth century this style was replaced in England by the rectilineal tabular form known today (Wagner, 1960, p. 323). Chinese genealogies are set out in similar form, with a circle as the sign for a male, and with brothers arranged across the page in order of birth, the eldest on the right. In one modification of the rectilineal method, the highest generation is located not at the top of the page or on the left, but in the centre, and successive generations are shown in concentric circles (e.g. Holleman, 1949, p. 51). The popular notion that a pedigree is a genealogical 'tree' appears to be derived from the Roman civil and canon law concepts of *arbor civilis* and *arbor consanguinitatis* (Hale, 1820, p. 335; Pollock and Maitland, 1898, I, 297). The individual who is the point of reference is seen as located on the trunk of the tree, with his descendants lower on the trunk, his ancestors higher up, and his collateral relatives in the branches (e.g. Domat, 1777, I, 405, reproduced as *Plate 1*).

To illustrate an argument or to support an analysis a variation of this form is sometimes appropriate, but for charts of cognatic stocks that are essentially summary records rather than illustrations, a different layout is recommended. In these charts of record it is often better, particularly if personal names are long and sibling sets numerous but memory of early generations poor, to take a horizontal rather than a vertical temporal axis. Write the names of those in the highest generation not at the top of the page but at the left-hand side (e.g. Quain, 1948, p. 87). Allow two adjacent columns, not one, for each generation, the left hand for members of the stock and the right hand for their spouses. Use large sheets of paper ruled with lines or squares; double foolscap sheets are large enough to take five or six generations, the span of much ethnographic information. If the stock is too numerous to be written on one sheet, use several, marked so that they can be aligned with one another. On the diagram indicate sex by a symbol. The traditional symbols, ♂ for male and ♀ for female (also used to indicate the planets Mars and Venus respectively), are best avoided. Follow the convention, advocated also by the International Federation of Eugenic Organizations, of a circle as the symbol for female and a diamond for an individual of unknown or unspecified sex (Gates, 1946, p. 3). In ethnographic work the use of an equilateral triangle for a male is now well established (Royal Anthropological Institute, 1951, p. 52), despite an earlier proposal that this symbol should stand for an individual of unknown sex (Royal Anthropological Institute, 1932, p. 120). Some writers use a square for unspecified sex, but this usage should be avoided, because in genetics a square normally indicates a male. Many writers indicate whether an individual is alive or dead by the use of an outline or a solid symbol;

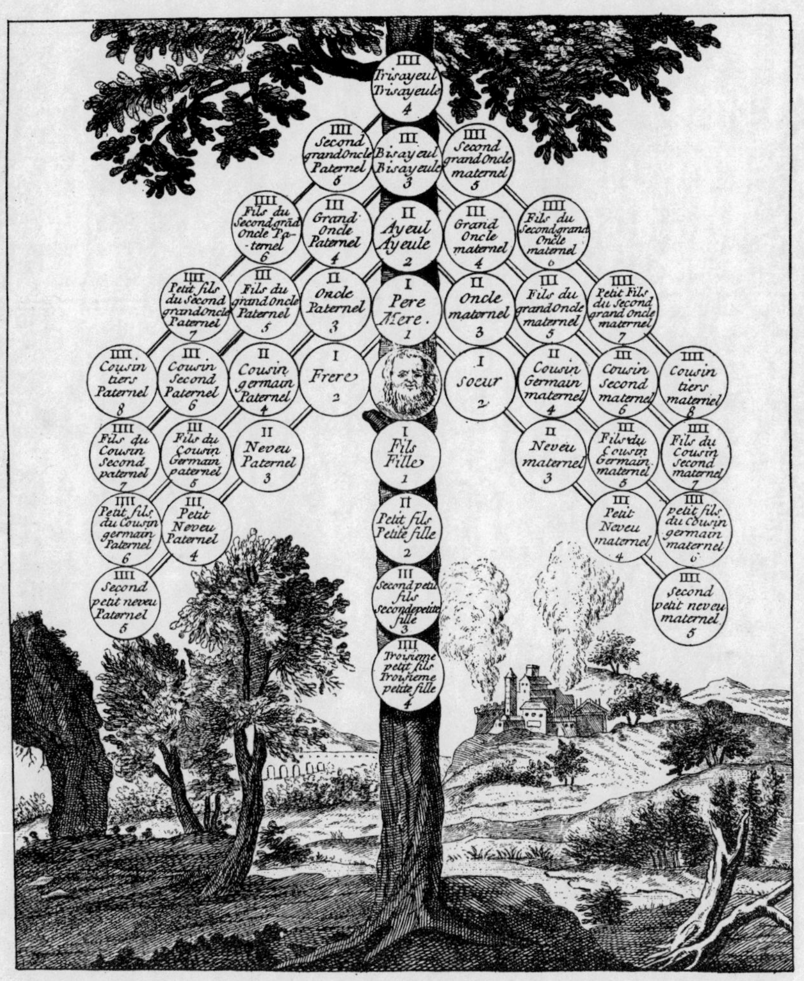

PLATE 1 An eighteenth-century French *arbor consanguinitatis*. The Arabic and Roman numerals indicate degrees of consanguinity according to Roman civil law and Christian canon law respectively. *After Domat* (*1777, I, p. 405*)

if this convention is followed, the date of the information must be shown. Rivers indicated living individuals by underlining their names, and some writers still follow him, as with the convention of writing the names of males in capital letters (1900, p. 74). The link between spouses may be shown by one of the conventional signs for marriage, but on a stock chart the abbreviations H and W for husband and wife may be preferred, preceded by a numeral showing the chronological order in which spouses were married, or alternatively their rank among co-spouses (see Culwick, 1932). Show the extent of full sibling sets with a vertical line. Indicate multiple births by joining the sex signs for the siblings concerned to the same point on this line, or by linking them with an additional vertical line.

To construct a series of record charts, begin with the highest ascending ancestor or ancestral married pair in each line of ascent from the informant. Set out for each of these ancestors or pairs their descendants and spouses of descendants, generation by generation, down to babes in arms. Identify each cognatic stock by a code letter or number. Whenever a set of full siblings is reached that has already been entered as part of some other stock, decide whether anything is to be gained by repeating the information in a new context of cousins. If not, merely refer to the earlier stock where the information can be found, and on the chart of that stock refer forward to the later stock to which it is linked. Thus suppose that a man Alpha, is married to Beta and they have children, Gamma and Delta. Then on the chart of stock *a*, consisting of the descendants of some ancestor of Alpha, we have Alpha as a cognatic member and Beta as his wife. Their children are included as members in the next generation. Similarly on the chart of stock *b*, the descendants of some ancestor of Beta, we have Beta as a member and Alpha as her husband. Note on chart *b* that Alpha belongs to stock *a* and that his children by Beta are shown on chart *a*; note on chart *a* that Beta belongs to stock *b*.

Record charts provide checks on the internal consistency of separate genealogical narratives and on the compatibility of each informant's narrative with all the others. The range of genealogical knowledge and interest among informants is made manifest. The genealogical and other information contained in the narratives and summarized on the charts should be checked further against other sources, for example, the results of a census of dwellings and of face-to-face encounters in the community. A census may reveal the existence of members of the community, particularly children, who have been omitted from the genealogies but who may be related genealogically to their neighbours. The omission may be due to forgetfulness or concealment by an informant, or to the ethnographer's failure to probe along an unexpected genealogical track. Questions asked about unidentified persons seen at ceremonies and other gatherings may bring to light distant genealogical connexions that have been overlooked and may stimulate informants to remember details they have forgotten (see Murdock, 1951, pp. 7–8).

Rivers regarded the collection of genealogies as a method of 'collecting social and vital statistics' and he was primarily interested in the information contained in genealogies about members of recent and present generations. Long lists of distant ancestors he regarded as 'of little value for the investigation of social organization' (Rivers, 1906, p. 461). Pedigrees stretching back through many generations may have greater value than Rivers thought, but the division of interest is valid. With present and immediate past generations, the ethnographer is usually mainly concerned to establish as well as he can what happened in fact, whereas with earlier generations he is more interested in discovering how the living perceive their ancestors; establishing what actually happened in the past, who married whom and what were the names of all their children, is often quite beyond his grasp.

Rivers first collected genealogies in connexion with psychological testing, but after completing his first field expedition came to realize their value for other inquiries (1900, p. 74). Genealogical information can be used for a study of the demography of a community, of its patterns of marriage, fertility, migration, and the like. Conditions in one generation may be contrasted with those in another, and some indication gained of the direction and extent of change. Genealogies must not however be treated as if they contained random samples of a wider population, for the probability that an individual will occur in a genealogy collected by the ethnographer varies with the individual's fertility, the longevity of his relatives and descendants and similar factors (see above, pp. 54–55). Apart from this statistical application, genealogies bring what Rivers called 'a concrete element into anthropological work which greatly facilitates inquiry' (1906, p. 465. See also Rivers 1914, I, 55–60). Questions about past or possible behaviour can be linked to named actors, and the information received is likely to be more precise and more revealing. Actors observed at a ceremony, quarrelling, working, discussing, become not mere adults, or co-villagers, or litigants, but are seen by the ethnographer as identifiable and unique individuals enmeshed in a network of genealogical ties which influence their actions in varying degrees (see Goodenough, 1951, p. 9). The sociological value of genealogical inquiry in any community is determined by the extent to which in that community genealogical ties influence social action. But in any kind of society genealogical knowledge, just because it is specific and private rather than public, is likely to help the

(▲Robert tembo
W ●Jane
[Monga])

▲Harry tembo
? – 1916
Wv2 ●Polly
mvula
[? Makwakwa]

▲William tembo ⊙
1898–1921 [50]

○Nelly Makwakwa
1901–
1919H △George nsefu 1896– Makwakwa

○Jenny nsefu 1920–1922 Makwakwa
△David Ndola 1923–
Wo unk Ndola
△Jacob unk 1927–

▲ Alan 1903–1920 [50] ⊙

○Maria 49
1905–
1920Hd2 △Paul mwale 1895– 49

△Thomas mwale 50
1920–
1941Wa4 ○Emily lungu 50 ex Malengo 1923–

△Claude mwale 63
1942–
1963Wk2 ○Ann zulu 63 1948– ex Monga

○nny 63 1964–

○Peggy 52 1947–
○Molly 49 1949–
△Edward 55 1953–
○Sally 55 1953–
△Robert 50 1958–

△John 73 1910–
1916We3 ○Ellen nyoni 73 — see e3 →

○Matilda 13 1878–
1892–1900 1Ħ △Jan mwale Kabulu 1873–

○Sophie mwale Wanga
1893–
1913H △Otto nkosi 1882– Wanga

△Japhet nkosi 1927– Wanga

△Paul 49 1895–
1920Wd2 ○Maria tembo q.v.

1915 2H △Daniel banda 13 1885–

△Moffat banda 15, 16
1916–
1938W ○Kate pili 15 1921– ex Mponda

○Jill banda 1940– Makwakwa
1959H △Emrys daka Makwakwa

○Selina daka 1961– Makwakwa

△Charles 55 1943–

1941 2Wk3 ○Joy culu 16 1918–

△Martin Katete 1943–
○Clara 57 1944–

β↓ γ↓

LEGEND

5d2	Sheet identification: village 5, stock d, sheet 2
( )	Information within brackets repeated from previous sheet 5d1
Wv2	Wife a member of stock v of this village and shown on sheet 2 of that stock
Makwakwa	Underlining indicates place name, showing present domicile
13	Resident in house 13 in this village
[Monga] [7]	Square brackets indicate former place of residence
nsefu	Absence of initial capital indicates descent name
2W	Second wife
Ħ	Former husband, marriage ended in divorce
ex	Comes from
unk	Name unknown
unk	Whereabouts unknown
nny	Not named yet
see e3 →	Descendants of this married couple shown on sheet e3 of this village
q.v.	*quem* (*quam*) *vide*, whom see elsewhere on this sheet
⊙	Died unmarried without issue
▲1898–1921	Dates of birth and death
1919H	Date of marriage
1892–1900Ħ	Dates of marriage and divorce
α β γ	Marks for aligning this sheet with adjacent sheets 5d1 and 5d3

ethnographer to demonstrate that he is interested in the members of the community he is studying, that he does not treat them as if they were all alike but knows something about each of them. In this way, the ethnographer shows that he is not an ignorant stranger but a would-be friend.

The procedure described for human populations can be applied with little modification to obtain genealogies of domestic animals, and with rather more modification narratives and charts may be obtained for villages, clans, and other social units that proliferate, fuse, and die out. In some instances there is a close but varying connexion between the proliferation of social groups and of the human families that belong to them, and this connexion may be shown on a genealogical chart (e.g. Barnes 1954, *Diagram 1*).

PEDIGREES

Many people cannot remember and are not interested in the names of ancestors they have never seen. In literate societies, records of ancestry may exist in archives yet be rarely consulted, while in non-literate societies knowledge of ancestors and past events may pass into oblivion because nothing is done to preserve it. In at least one society, Bali, a system of teknonymy positively ensures that the names and relationships of ancestors are systematically forgotten (Geertz and Geertz, 1964). Genealogies collected from these societies will necessarily be short, spreading over six generations at most. On the other hand, in other societies, people can remember, or say they can remember, the names of quite remote ancestors and they may be able to produce written records or ostensibly standardized oral accounts of ancestry through many generations. Regarded as historical records, these pedigrees are often manifestly untrue. As long ago as the sixteenth century, Calvin ridiculed the Emperor Maximilian who 'was induced by a silly trifler to believe that he had traced his lineage to Noah's ark' (*Commentary* on Isaiah xix. 11). Elizabeth I of England deduced her pedigree from Adam (Round, 1930, p. 5). In the nineteenth century, McLennan assembled many examples of fraudulent pedigrees 'to show the readiness of men in all times to fabricate genealogies' (1896, p. 117). Critical study of the Old Testament revealed the mutual inconsistency of the several lines of ascent and descent it contains and, in view of the link between Biblical studies and anthropology in W. Robertson Smith (1903), it is surprising that extensive pedigrees from tribal peoples, where textual criticism was not available as a check on validity, were accepted at their face value for so long (Cunnison, 1959, p. 111; Piddington, 1956; see Pei te Hurinui, 1958). Krämer, in his work on Samoa (1902), was one of the first ethnographers to give detailed attention to pedigrees, while modern interest in how peoples perceive their ancestry owes much to Evans-Pritchard's work on the Nuer (1940).

The maximum number of possible lines of ascent that could possibly be recalled by an informant doubles with each successive generation. If cognates have married each other in the past, some or even all of these lines may be identical and the number of different lines is reduced (see Christian, in Blackstone, 1800, p. 205, cited in Freeman, 1961, pp. 206–207). If there are written records from the past, it may be possible, though often laborious, to construct partial or complete 'descents' (Burke, 1864), showing all the ancestors of a selected individual for several generations back. This is sometimes done for monarchs who are well documented, but even in literate societies there is usually only selective interest in tracing ascent. One line or sometimes two out of many possible lines are remembered and the others are forgotten completely or traced only a little way. Commonly the remembered line is either patrilineal or matrilineal, and we then find that the same unilineal emphasis is present in what is remembered of the cognatic stock stemming from these ancestors. Thus if an informant can remember in the fourth ascending generation only one of his ancestors, his FFFF, then he is likely to be able to remember only that man's sons, not his daughters. All that is remembered more than a few generations back is, in fact, a pedigree and no amount of persistence by the ethnographer will bring to light genealogical connexions, distant in ascent or collaterality, that have no contemporary significance for the informant and for his group. We are then dealing with a different category of ethnographic fact, and have to handle it differently. There is no sharp dividing line between genealogical links embodied in a pedigree and recent links that would eventually have been forgotten but which have been elicited by the ethnographer, but the transition is real. In both parts of the genealogy, the limits of knowledge provide clues to the patterns of interaction and affiliation of the informant.

Pedigrees may be invoked in many different contexts, and within one society pedigrees may be associated with several kinds of social groups and statuses. Each group may have its own pedigree memorializing its founders and acting as a charter for its present activities, but the pedigrees pertaining to several groups are not necessarily genealogically or chronologically compatible with one another. Genealogical myths may follow a standard pattern but the ethnographer should not be surprised if, misinterpreted as historical accounts, they are plainly inconsistent. For example, Cunnison (1957) has shown how, for the Luapula peoples, royal pedigrees take one form and lineage pedigrees another, the latter containing only two significant generations. This reduction to two generations is facilitated by a system of kinship terminology in which members of alternate generations are equated. Peters (1960) has described some of the processes at work among the Bedouin of Cyrenaica whereby the pedigree of a group comes to be an agreed statement about its relationship to its environment and to neighbouring groups, and these and similar processes probably operate among other peoples (e.g. Bohannan, L., 1952; Bohannan, P. J., 1954; Cunnison, 1959; Freedman, 1958, pp. 70–72; Ṣalisbury, 1956, p. 4). It seems likely that in most instances the number of generations covered by the pedigree, from the oldest remembered ancestor to the living, remains approximately constant, and that the names of the older ancestors, and their relation to one another, remain fixed. A named ancestor Alpha is said to be, say, ten generations back from an adult informant today; then it is probable that thirty years ago the informant's father was likewise thought to be ten generations away from Alpha and, unless conditions change, the informant's son will also be separated from Alpha by ten generations. This is achieved by continual modification of the pedigree. Peters distinguishes several processes: the pedigree is foreshortened by telescoping, i.e. by the omission and elision of ancestors in intervening generations; ancestors with similar or identical names are fused; persons whose names are inherited are fused with their successors; a person with comparatively few surviving descendants is shifted to become the child of one of his or her more prolific siblings; cousins who live together or whose descendants live together become siblings. For the Bedouin, these processes occur, says Peters, because 'the genealogy must always represent an ordered grouping, and these people live on strips of territory . . . The main landmarks of the Cyrenaican ecology are fixed points which cannot be manipulated to fit in with the genealogy; it is the genealogy which must be altered to comprehend the distribution of people in their ecological setting' (1960, p. 38).

Bedouin pedigrees fall into three parts, and Peters (1963) has analysed the pedigrees of 'Learned Families' among Lebanese Muslims in much the same terms. The higher generations constitute the 'cultural past' and the composition of this section of the pedigree is, as a first approximation, constant through time. Recent generations appear in the pedigrees more or less as they lived; this section of the pedigree demonstrates demographic experience fairly accurately. In between is an 'area of ambiguity' and it is here that the pedigree is continually under revision; this is the area about which living informants are likely to disagree with one another. This tripartite model may well hold for pedigrees found in other cultures, with major ecological changes reflected in a revision of the 'cultural past';

changes in social organization, in particular in the alignment and relative size of unilineal groups, shown in the 'area of ambiguity'; and demographic facts preserved for a few generations in the lower reaches of the pedigree (see Shah and Shroff, 1958). For the Bedouin, the 'area of ambiguity' lies at and around the fifth ascending generation (Peters, 1960, p. 40), which suggests that demographic accuracy disappears at the point when we reach those individuals who died before the oldest people now living were born. Gulliver, writing about the Jie, for whom 'history only begins two generations ago, or even more recently', gives instances of the fusion of brothers in the first and second ascending generations (1955, pp. 104–117). Likewise Salisbury's material from the Siane of New Guinea (1956) shows that, among a people with very little interest in ancestry, pedigrees may be demographically inaccurate even in the first ascending generation.

ILLUSTRATIVE GENEALOGICAL DIAGRAMS

When the record charts have been completed, covering information elicited in genealogical narratives as well as that drawn from written and oral pedigrees, the ethnographer is well equipped to carry out his analysis. Even if the analysis is delayed, the charts are of value, for they make his field notes easier to understand. I regard the preparation of these diagrammatic records as part of the 'minimum obligation' every fieldworker has to organize his data into a form that is intelligible to others (American Anthropological Association, 1964).

In general, the text of an analytical exposition will stand by itself, but it will often help the reader if he is given genealogical information in diagrammatic form. An illustrative diagram will usually contain only an extract of a record chart, or it may draw on information contained on several charts. Names may be unnecessary, or may be replaced by coded information. The layout will depend on how much information is needed, and what point the writer is trying to drive home. If an illustrative diagram contains only a few individuals, these can be identified merely by letters, but with more than a dozen individuals to be identified, it is convenient to use letters to distinguish the generations, and to number serially all the individuals shown on the diagram in each generation (e.g. Mitchell, 1956, Appendices). Use a vertical or horizontal temporal axis, as convenient. It may not be necessary to allow separate columns or rows for spouses, and the marriage link can then be shown by a symbol. The clasped hands and bow knots used by Blackstone (1800, p. 240) to denote marriage and the joining of two descent lines are scarcely appropriate today. Avoid the × sign; the 'equals' sign (=) is adequate if there is monogamy and if husband and wife can be drawn adjacently on the diagram, but in general the ⊐ or ⊔ sign, depending on whether the temporal axis is horizontal or vertical, is best. The link between siblings is shown likewise ⊏ or ⊓, and the existence of other siblings not specified on the diagram may be indicated by extending the ligature, as ⊏ or ⊓. If there are many long parallel lines on the diagram, so that sibling and spouse ligatures cannot readily be separated, the spouse link may be drawn with a thicker line or double lines, though possible confusion with the International Federation of Eugenic Organization's sign for consanguineous marriage must then be guarded against (Gates, 1946). Turner (1957, Appendix) uses a line of dashes and dots for marriage between relatives, and dotted lines are customarily used for non-marital unions. Classificatory sibling links may be shown by dashed lines, preferably with the letter K written on the line. If two unconnected lines have to cross one another, make a loop, } or ⌒, in the line running perpendicular to the temporal axis. Avoid the appearance of a cross by offsetting the connecting lines on opposite sides of marriage and sibling ligatures. Thus, for example, show a man, his wife, and their three children as

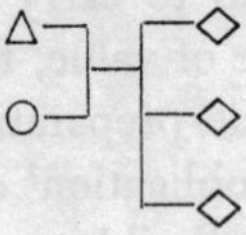

and not

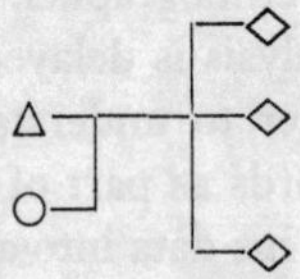

Show multiple births as stemming from the same point on the sibling ligature (Royal Anthropological Institute, 1951, p. 53). Some writers incline sibling sets at a slight angle to the vertical (or horizontal) to suggest the passage of time between successive births. Quasi-genealogical links to god-parents, foster-parents, and captors, or special links between siblings or co-wives, can be indicated by special symbols. Parts of several intermarrying stocks may be shown on the same diagram.

It is often necessary to refer to single genealogical relationships. These may be illustrated in a diagram, but a method is also needed to specify relationships succinctly in ordinary text. Radcliffe-Brown (1930) developed a system of notation that some ethnographers have used in their field notebooks but which seems not to have found favour in print. Writing out relationships in full, step by step, using a series of genitives, is cumbersome if there are many steps, and in a language such as French, lacking a genitive form, their expression is even longer. Murdock (1947, p. 56) introduced a set of two-letter abbreviations now in wide use. A single-letter set, used in this essay, was developed by the Rhodes–Livingstone Institute (Colson and

Gluckman, 1951, p. xx) and is gaining acceptance. It uses fourteen units to build up whatever relationship is required.

F father	P parent	M mother
B brother	G sibling	Z sister
H husband	E spouse	W wife
S son	C child	D daughter
+ elder		— younger
++ eldest		—— youngest

Thus for example MFBSS stands for mother's father's brother's son's son; HM ++ B stands for husband's mother's eldest brother. Half and step relationships are shown by the link through the common relative. Thus FS stands for paternal half-brother, MH stands for step-father, and HW for co-wife. Additional symbols can be added as required. If a distinction is needed between classificatory and narrowly-interpreted relationships; inverted commas may be used for classificatory relationships.

TERMINOLOGICAL AND PRESCRIPTIVE DIAGRAMS

The study of how people address and refer to their relatives is best carried on by observation of speech and writing in real situations of everyday life, but the analysis of these observations may be facilitated by systematic and formal inquiries about the way in which kinship terms are employed. Morgan prepared for use by his correspondents a series of more than two hundred questions (Smithsonian Institution, 1862; Eggan, 1960, p. 184) about the terms used for relatives, specified in fairly precise terms, e.g. father's brother's great-grand-daughter, mother's mother's brother's great-grandson (Morgan, 1870, pp. 4–7, 110), but there does not seem to be any attempt to link these questions with real relatives of an informant. Howitt, probably in 1874 (Mulvaney, private communication), suggested in a circular for similar purposes that his correspondents should use sticks or other objects to represent hypothetical individuals standing in specified genealogical relationships to one another, and that informants be asked to state how these individuals would call one another (Mulvaney, 1958, p. 310). Rivers collected information about the way in which his informants called those real relatives whose names he had recorded, and this he regarded as the 'first and most obvious value of the genealogies' (1900, p. 77). Rose has recently drawn attention to the uncertainty found among some Australian Aborigines about what term to apply to specified relatives who are dead, and has developed a method, using photographs, of asking each informant for the term used for each of his fellows (Rose, 1960, pp. 21–34).

The ethnographer should remember that a variety of criteria, some genealogical and some not, may influence an informant's choice of kinship term. If the informant is related to a relative by more than one genealogical path, there may be two or more terms he can use that are equally valid; alternatively one path alone may be significant. Relative and absolute age and relative and absolute sibling rank are often significant. Some egocentric kinship terms are used also as terms of reference or address for persons in sociocentric or non-kin statuses, as with the use in English of 'father' as the title for a priest, or 'auntie' by a boy for a female adult friend of his parents. Sometimes a term is applied thus in a sociocentric sense to an individual who happens to be a kinsman of the speaker, as when a parishioner addresses his great-uncle the priest as 'father'. The ethnographer has therefore to be on his guard against misinterpreting apparently anomalous uses of kinship terms due to the intrusion of other kinds of status (see Schneider and Roberts, 1957, pp. 17–18). Likewise, in studying modes of address, he should remember that the way in which A addresses his relative B in the presence of C may depend as much on the identity and status of C as on the genealogical link between A and B.

Information on the use of kinship terms, however collected, can be set out in tabular form (Royal Anthropological Institute, 1951, p. 81) or on a skeleton genealogical diagram (e.g. Morgan, 1870, p. 45), with the individual who is the point of reference designated as Ego. Some earlier writers designate him Hypotheticus, Propositus, or Titius (Blackstone, 1800, p. 203). Pollock and Maitland (1898, I, p. 297 ff) pointed out long ago how misleading were genealogical diagrams developed for the Roman system of inheritance when applied without modification in the exposition of the English system; in the former a kindred can be depicted as a single cognatic stock but in the latter system this cannot be done. Likewise many systems of kinship nomenclature do not easily fit a standard genealogical skeleton, and linked relationship terms, as Firth (1936, p. 254) calls them, cannot be shown at all without introducing a special notation. Even an elaborate genealogical diagram may prove to be a cumbrous form of record and a complete break with the genealogical method of presentation is then called for. Componential diagrams (e.g. Wallace and Atkins, 1960; see Burling, 1964) lie outside the scope of this paper, but reference may be made to the admirably rigorous procedure for the analysis and exposition of kinship terminology set out by Conklin (1964) which would seem to be applicable to any society where terms are used systematically.

If the traditional genealogical form is retained, the diagram can ramify outward from Ego in every possible direction as far as required, and this may seem an easy way of summarizing a first field record of terminological usage. But if taken farther, this procedure has several hazards. In analysis, it will be found with many systems of terminology that not only can several adjacent positions on the diagram be fused because they carry the same term (e.g. FB and FZ when known by the same term fuse to FG, provided their spouses, descendants, and affines are also not distinguished from one another), but other non-adjacent positions can be fused by postulating the appropriate kind of cognatic marriage. For example, if W and MBD carry the same term, then the structure of the terminological system may be made manifest by drawing a diagram in which Ego is married to his MBD. Many, though probably not all, terminological systems which are conformal in this sense with some variety of cognatic marriage are found in societies where there is a prescription or preference for that kind of marriage, and the exposition of these prescriptions and preferences is directly facilitated by the existence of the appropriate terminological system. The same diagram may then serve to illustrate both the terminological system and the marriage rules (e.g. Warner, 1958, p. 59). Analytically, these two features are quite distinct, and it is important not to confound them, as well as to avoid the even more serious error of thinking that the diagram is a genealogy. Another hazard arises because it is often convenient to illustrate a rule by showing marriage between persons who are as closely related genealogically as the rule permits, although the rule may be equally well satisfied by marriage between persons whose genealogical connexion is more distant but is classified with the closer relationship. This convention permits the simple though very summary diagrammatic representation of rules of considerable complexity. It can also mislead. Thus, suppose the rule states, as among the Kumbaingeri (Radcliffe-Brown, 1930–1931, p. 263), that a man should marry a woman who is classified terminologically as his 'MBD' but who is not his actual MBD. It would then be misleading to illustrate either the rule or its associated system of kinship terminology by a diagram showing Ego married to his actual MBD.

The same caution applies, though with less force, to diagrams showing the rules of recruitment to moieties, sections, and sub-sections. These differ more in appearance from genealogical diagrams, and illustrate rules that, in some societies at least, are followed with fewer infractions than are marriage prescriptions. The rules of a section system may be shown merely by writing against each individual shown on a skeleton genealogical chart his or her section affiliation, but two other methods are also employed. Radcliffe-Brown (1910) introduced diagrams in which recruitment to sections (or sub-sections) is shown by arrows placed on either side of a table of intermarrying sections. This method has been widely used, but unfortunately the order of intermarrying pairs is arbitrary and it is possible

FIGURE 3 ARANDA AND MURNGIN SUB-SECTION SYSTEMS

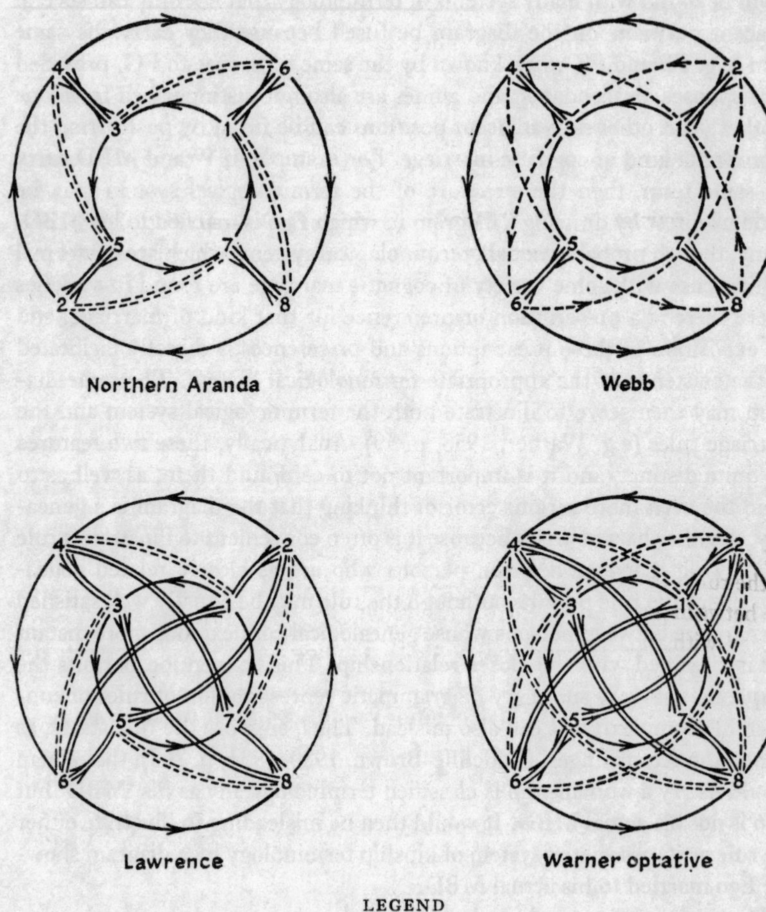

LEGEND

Matrilineal cycle | Patrilineal cycle
Woman-to-husband link | Patrilineal couple

Common Characteristics

Matrimoieties	(1357) (2468)	Patrimoieties	(1458) (2367)
Matrilineal cycles	1 → 3 → 5 → 7 → 1 2 → 4 → 6 → 8 → 2	Sets of alternating generations	(1256) (3478)

Differentiating Characteristics

	Northern Aranda	*Webb*	*Lawrence*	*Warner optative*
Intermarrying pairs	(1, 6) (2, 5) (3, 4) (7, 8)	(1, 2) (3, 4) (5, 6) (7, 8)	—	(15, 26) (37, 48)
Marriage cycles	—	—	1≻6≻5≻2≻1 3≻8≻7≻4≻3	—
Patrilineal couples	(1, 8) (2, 7) (3, 6) (4, 5)	—	(1, 4) (2, 7) (3, 6) (5, 8)	(15, 48) (26, 37)
Patrilineal cycles	—	1≻4≻5≻8≻1 2≻3≻6≻7≻2	—	—
Compatible marriage rule	MMBDD	MBD	MBD	MBD

Note: In the notation used in Barnes, *Inquest on the Murngin*, the Webb system shown here is the normal version, and the Lawrence system shown is that version proposed by Lawrence and Murdock.

to give two apparently different presentations of a single system by altering the tabular order (Stanner, 1936, p. 201 f.n. 4). This drawback is avoided in a less used but clearer and more flexible method, based on an indigenous system of representation recorded by Deacon at Balap in the New Hebrides (1927, pp. 329–332). In this method, the closed property of the system is brought out by drawing the symbols standing for units of the system at regular intervals on a circle or series of concentric circles. Many variations in detail can be introduced, depending on the argument the diagram has to support (e.g. Lane, 1960, 1962; Lawrence, 1937, pp. 342–343; Lévi-Strauss, 1962, p. 109). As an example, the formal distinctions between the Aranda and Murngin systems of eight sub-sections are shown in *Figure 3*.

J. VAN VELSEN

The Extended-case Method and Situational Analysis

ETHNOGRAPHIC fieldwork is guided, but not necessarily determined, by the anthropologist's theoretical approach. The reader of ethnographic monographs as a rule can never be certain what kind of material the anthropologist has recorded in his notebooks, but there is evidence to suggest that anthropologists with contrasting theoretical frameworks collect different kinds of material and use different methods to gather it. This is particularly true of three successive schools of British anthropology, with which alone I am concerned here, which I have labelled 'pre-structuralist', 'structuralist', and 'post-structuralist'. In this essay I shall be concerned with what Gluckman (1961a) has called the 'extended-case method', but which I prefer to call, for reasons stated elsewhere (van Velsen, 1964, p. xxv), 'situational analysis'. This refers to the collection by the ethnographer of detailed data of a particular kind. But it also implies the particular use to which such data are put in analysis, above all the attempt to incorporate conflict as a 'normal' rather than 'abnormal' part of social progress.

THE STRUCTURALIST SCHOOL

Pre-structuralist anthropologists were concerned with custom *per se*. Customs from different areas and different periods were juxtaposed and compared with little regard for the total social context of each particular institution. In their search for material, these students meandered all over the globe and through the ages with little concern about questions of spatial or chronological delimitation. In this search they often called in the help of travellers, missionaries, administrators, *et al.*; the collection of material did not require personal observation by the anthropologist. Sir James Frazer is an obvious example of this school: he carried on a voluminous correspondence with administrators and others in many parts of the world in search of material for his books; but there are plenty of more recent instances of such anthropological *Wanderlust*.

A radical departure from this method came when fieldwork began to be carried out by professional anthropologists for whom the theoretical approach to the collection of ethnographic material went hand in hand with the observation of human behaviour in groups. Without belittling the impact, at the time, of men like Rivers, Haddon, and Seligman, one may date the development of modern British anthropology from Malinowski and Radcliffe-Brown, both of whom published their first major works in 1922. While Malinowski was the practitioner of new fieldwork techniques and functional analysis, Radcliffe-Brown was the theoretician of what has often been referred to as the 'structuralist' school. In this kind of structural analysis the emphasis was on social morphology: individual variations were smoothed away in favour of structural regularities. Observed behaviour and interpersonal relationships were abstracted in the form of structural relationships between groups and these structural relationships were further abstracted in the form of separate systems: economic, political, kinship, etc. Though it was admitted that these systems were linked, the problem of dealing with the linkage in an analytical framework was not satisfactorily solved. For instance, Fortes, in *The Dynamics of Clanship among the Tallensi*, states that the membership of ritual congregations partly overlaps with that of unilineal descent groups. He concludes that this overlap contributes to social cohesion. He also states that the web of extra-lineage kinship ties created by marriage has the same effect. But he does not describe the social processes through which this cohesion is actually achieved. In fact, by analysing some of the cases that Fortes used to illustrate structural principles, and by putting these cases back into their situational context, Sommerfelt (1958) has demonstrated that overlapping membership need not in itself positively contribute to cohesion or form a basis for alliance: it may mean no more than neutrality in armed conflict.

As fieldwork became the accepted method by which anthropological material was gathered, the emphasis gradually shifted from a study of societies as wholes to particular communities or segments of societies. Anthropologists, particularly those working within a structuralist frame of reference, have thus become more conscious of the need for delimitation. The boundaries of their inquiries are generally those of a whole tribe at a particular moment in time. This moment is generally the present, i.e. the ethnographer's present, but in fact inquiries have often been pushed back into the past in order to discover a purer tradition (e.g. unadulterated by European contacts); hence the term 'ethnographic present'. Unfortunately, this mixing of material from the past and the present is not always as well controlled as it should be and frequently deteriorates into a haphazard mixture of data derived from different periods and, because conditions have changed, from different social, political, and economic conditions (see van Velsen, 1965).

The 'structural frame of reference', according to Fortes (1953, p. 39), 'gives us the procedures for investigation and analysis by which a social system can be apprehended as a unity made up of parts and processes that are linked to one another by a limited number of principles of wide validity in homogeneous and relatively stable societies.' This passage sums up the salient features of the structural approach. Structural analyses are primarily concerned with relations between social positions or statuses rather than with the 'actual relations of Tom, Dick, and Harry or the behaviour of Jack and Jill' (Radcliffe-Brown, 1952, p. 192). There is clearly a preference for abstractions as against the particulars on which these abstractions must necessarily be based. Indeed, Radcliffe-Brown emphatically rejects the particular (which he appears to equate with the unique) behaviour of Jack and Jill as unsuitable for an 'account of the form of the structure . . . even though it may go down in our field notebooks and may provide illustrations for a general description' (loc. cit.). I will discuss the other two features of homogeneity and stability below (p. 136). For the present the important point is that actions of individuals become submerged in general principles which may be the anthropologist's abstractions or informants' statements; these latter, of course, may be abstractions themselves. This type of analysis does not allow for the fact that individuals are often faced by a choice between alternative norms. Thus Evans-Pritchard writes: 'We would remark that the contradiction we have alluded to is on the abstract plane of structural relations . . . It is not to be supposed that behaviour is contradictory . . . There may sometimes be conflict of values in the consciousness of an individual, but it is structural tension to which we refer' (1940, pp. 265–266). Thus the structuralist view is that each individual has a clearly defined status in the kinship system with equally clearly defined rights and duties towards other kinsmen. But the chances are, particularly in small-scale tribal societies, that many, if not most, people can claim to be genealogically related in more than one way to any other person within the same relatively small area – e.g. a village, or neighbourhood, or chiefdom – where social intercourse is most intense. And one is likely to find that an individual has a choice as to which particular kin relationship he wishes to utilize, depending on his objectives in the particular situation. Moreover, in a classificatory kinship system behaviour is not determined solely by kinship, as is so frequently implied or explicitly stated. Individuals are often faced by a choice or even conflict not only within the kinship system (e.g. one set of kin relationships as against another set) but also between kin relationships and, say, relationships based on residential grouping.

In any society, then, the individual may at times have to make a choice between a variety of mutually contradictory norms. Thus the norms relating to a man's status as son, husband, father, prime minister, or chief are unlikely to be mutually compatible in all respects. Though ethnographic accounts with a structural frame of reference may mention or imply such inherent contradictions, they do not treat them as a datum that has to be analysed just as, and with reference to, other observed data. Instead, the emphasis is on consistency, possibly highlighted by exceptions. But inconsistency and contradictions between various sets of norms in different fields of action are a feature of all societies. To live with these inconsistencies by manipulating the norms in such a way that people can continue to stay together in social order is a problem that members of any society have to solve. It is, therefore, also a problem worth studying for the anthropologist. Thus Turner (1957) tells us how, among the Ndembu, the two dominant principles influencing residence in villages, viz. maternal descent and virilocal marriages, are irreconcilable. Consequently, marriages are unstable, fission within the village is frequent, and there is a high degree of mobility of villages and individuals. However, this instability of the secular social structure is counteracted by 'ritual performed by cult associations that cut across villages, vicinages, and even adjacent chiefdoms of Lunda origin . . . [and which thus keeps] the common values of Ndembu society constantly before the roving individualists of which it is composed' (p. xxi). And he found that people who, in the context of internal village relationships, 'appear to be exceptions to the rule that [when a village splits up] uterine siblings secede together', perform, in the wider system of inter-village relations, 'an essential function . . . [in] preventing the total estrangement of groups divided initially in anger'. 'Thus,' Turner concludes, 'apparent exceptions to statistical regularities obtained from genealogical data on village fission prove to be themselves regularities within a wider system of social relations' (p. 232).

What distinguishes this kind of analysis from classical structural models is the type of material collected in the field and, given the different theoretical approach, the different use made of it. The works of Evans-Pritchard, Fortes, Firth – to mention but a few exponents of the structural method – clearly are based on a great number and variety of observed and recorded actions and, presumably, informants' statements of ideal norms of behaviour. However, they appear to have viewed and recorded the actions and interpersonal relationships from the standpoint of the structural principles to be abstracted from them later. At any rate, their works do not contain correlated case material illustrating social processes; what records of people's actual behaviour do find their way into their analyses usually serve merely to illustrate certain aspects of the models abstracted from unpublished case material. I have already noted how Radcliffe-Brown considered that the actions of particular individuals should not appear on the pages of a monograph. However, it is clear from these ethnographic accounts that there were variations from the abstracted regularities which they presented *and* that the authors were aware of them. To quote Radcliffe-Brown again: 'the general or normal form of this [structural] relationship [between mother's brother and sister's son] is abstracted from the variations of particular instances, though taking into account those variations' (loc. cit.). But he does not make it clear how such variations can be and are incorporated into the general norm. Similarly, Evans-Pritchard writes: 'political actualities are confused and conflicting . . . they are not always . . . in accord with political values' (1940, p. 138). Unfortunately, the authors do not indicate what made them decide that their models represent the general rules and that the 'variations' or the 'confusing and conflicting actualities' are merely exceptions which do not come into the scheme of their analysis. The reader is inclined to ask: How 'ungeneral' are these variations, etc.? To take the Lakeside Tonga as an example, a structural model would present matrilocality and matrilineal descent as the pattern of village residence and mode of descent and would treat instances of persons who do not live matrilocally or who do not succeed to office matrilineally as exceptions. And certainly the Tonga themselves stress that the matrilineal principle and matrilocal residence are two dominant values in their society. However, I found that I could no longer meaningfully talk about the 'exceptions' when I found that some 40 per cent of my sample did not live matrilocally. I had to show why those who do not live matrilocally do not do so; I tried to find some regularity in the irregularities (see van Velsen, 1964).

Richards's work is written within a predominantly structural frame of reference, but we begin to get some of the case material on which her analysis is based. I am referring to her detailed description of Kasaka village (Richards, 1939, pp. 154–183). The members of this village emerge from the social structure as personalities. It should be noted that these individual Bemba receive attention not because they are law-breakers or 'deviants' in some other way. The following quotation gives Richards's own summing-up of – as she calls it – this 'sketch of an actual community': 'the individual characters, with all their temperamental and physical peculiarities and the dramatic incidents of everyday life, seem to stand out in bold relief, while the formal patterns of kinship, which we have just described, fade from view. We are watching a number of people who like or hate to share their food, or to prepare it in common, and not plotting a system of relationships on a kinship chart. But this is, of course, how the scene appears in the context of everyday life' (p. 160). She is also more explicit about her method of collecting field data: 'The abstractions of the anthropologist are based on two types of material: viz. statements of natives as to what they believe they do, ought to do, or would like to do, and his own observations of a number of human beings of widely different personalities, reacting to a set of tribal rules in different ways – conforming to them or rebelling against them. A concrete account of the distribution of food in three family groups will not only enable the reader to visualize the whole process, but *will give him an idea of the kind of observations upon which these generalizations have been based*' (p. 160; my emphasis).

Although I agree with her distinctions, I would prefer to make a further one. Informants' statements could be further categorized as: explanations or interpretations of particular actions or events, on the one hand, and informants' opinions as to ideal norms in response to the fieldworker's questions about hypothetical situations (e.g. 'If a man kills game, how should he divide it?'), on the other hand. Statements of either type are nothing but views held by particular members of the group the anthropologist is investigating. Such statements should be considered as an aspect of the behaviour of these persons and treated as such and they should therefore be related to the informants' position in the group and the informants' involvement in the actions in question. They should also be related, quantitatively and/or qualitatively, to behaviour in similar circumstances of other members of the group. Informants' statements, of either type, should be treated as the historian treats his sources: they are, that is to say, value judgements and should, therefore, be considered as falling within the category of data referred to earlier as observed behaviour. In other words, such statements should not be used as if they were objective, analytical observations by outsiders. The sociological evaluation of actions and other behaviour is the anthropologist's job, and the sociological evaluation of the same actions, etc., may well be very different from their social evaluation by local informants. After all, one cannot expect untrained informants, be they Bemba headmen or white-collar workers in London, to present the anthropologist with sociological analyses of behaviour observed in their respective communities. To do so would be to assume, as many laymen do, that to be a member of a community is to understand it sociologically.

Anthropologists frequently do not distinguish between these various types of data or, in other words, they do not treat informants' statements with the caution they deserve, being merely one type of observed behaviour. At any rate, the reader often does not know – because it is not indicated by the author – whether the author's generalizations or statements of norms and values are the result of his examination of all types of observed behaviour (including informants' statements of norms and values), or whether they are the people's own evaluations. Thus, with regard to cross-cousin marriages the reader is too often asked to accept without much evidence that this type of marriage, where it is allowed, is a preferred type of marriage because it strengthens the bonds within a particular group. Thus Richards (1950, p. 228) states that among the Bemba cross-cousin marriage in general – i.e. a man marrying his father's sister's daughter (FZD) or his mother's brother's daughter (MBD) – increases the stability of the extended family unit. The reason she gives is that the son-in-law moving into his wife's village is not a stranger and is 'closely identified by descent with the leading men of the group'. This is not very convincing, as I have pointed out elsewhere (van Velsen, 1965, pp. 183–184). Considering that the Bemba marry uxorilocally, one would have thought that this applies only to the man marrying his MBD; the man marrying his FZD is not matrilineally related to his father-in-law. Indeed, Richards mentions that cross-cousin marriage of the MBD type is the more common. This would seem to indicate that the whole question of the stabilizing influence of cross-cousin marriage is more complicated than would appear from her statement. In any case, it may be true that a cross-cousin husband is not a 'stranger' in, and is already 'closely identified' with, his wife's village, but this does not exclude the possibility that he may be even more closely identified with another village whose pull may eventually prevail. One wonders whether Richards's generalization is based on an analysis of observed behaviour or whether it is largely a reflection of Bemba views. My own experience among the Lakeside Tonga was that whenever I asked general questions about cross-cousin marriage, I was invariably given views very similar to those recorded by Richards. However, these views did not tally with other data that I collected. And I was forced to the conclusion that, contrary to the Tonga view, in fact only cross-cousin marriage of the MBD type could possibly have the greatly desired effect of preventing a man's children from moving to their mother's village. But even in this type of marriage the desired effect was likely to be counteracted by a potentially disruptive effect, inherent in this type of marriage, in the political field (see van Velsen, 1964, pp. 128 seq.).

Structural analysis has provided us with outlines where previously there were none; it has opened up new fields of interest. To mention but one example: the work of Fortes and Evans-Pritchard on the Tallensi and the Nuer respectively presented morphologies of viable political systems that operated despite the absence of specialized institutions of government.

Before the publication of their work, political systems were invariably assumed to be based on some form of a hierarchy of bearers of state authority. Thus Malinowski, writing before these developments, superimposes upon his Trobriand material a hierarchy of chiefs. Uberoi (1962), re-evaluating Malinowski's ethnographic data in the light of more recent theories, has demonstrated that Malinowski's hierarchical political structure for the Trobriands does not tally with Malinowski's own ethnographic data (cf. Powell, 1960). On the other hand, the development of anthropological theory, as well as the striking changes that have overtaken many societies of the kind anthropologists have conventionally studied, have led to an increasing questioning of some of the basic assumptions of the structuralist position.

VARIATION, CHANGE, AND THE CONFLICT OF NORMS

As we have seen, structural analysis aims at presenting an outline of the social morphology; consequently there is a marked emphasis on consistency so that variations are ignored in its abstractions. This outline is reduced – in Fortes's words – to 'a limited number of principles of wide validity' from which the rough edges and loose ends have been removed. On the other hand, as Schapera (1938, p. 29) has pointed out: 'culture is not merely a system of formal practices and beliefs. It is made up essentially of individual reactions to and variations from a traditionally standardized pattern; and indeed no culture can ever be understood unless special attention is paid to this range of individual manifestations.' In other words, norms, general rules of conduct, are translated into practice; they are ultimately manipulated by individuals in particular situations to serve particular ends. This gives rise to variations for which the structuralist writer does not account in his abstract model. He may not even consider these variations particularly relevant and he will therefore ignore them or fail to explain how they fit into his frame of general principles of wide validity. Alternatively, he may mention that there are variations, but dismiss them as accidental or exceptional. In this way, too, variations are not fitted into the structuralist framework. Moreover, labelling this category of observed data 'exceptional' or 'accidental' does not solve the problem for, after all, they do occur within, and are part of, the same social order that the ethnographer has set out to investigate and describe.

I am now able to return to a point mentioned above (p. 131). The statements of Fortes and Evans-Pritchard quoted earlier indicate that a structural analysis assumes homogeneity and relative stability in the society or community studied. And there has been a tendency to look for these conditions of homogeneity and relative stability in an era preceding the ethnographer's personal observations of the people studied, e.g. before the influence of European or any other foreign culture was supposed to have made itself felt. This was not merely the result of a Rousseauish romanticism, a nostalgic hankering for 'unspoilt cultures'. The structural frame of reference is unsuitable for the analysis of conflicts of norms and of the resultant choice of action open to individuals. Such mutually conflicting norms are particularly apparent in societies that are experiencing the pervasive influence of other cultures, e.g. the introduction of a new religion, new trade goods, or a governmental bureaucracy. The older – and even some rather more recent – structural analyses have tended to ignore problems of change and to consider, instead, individual choices of action arising from new situations as exceptions to, or distortions of the 'proper', that is traditional, norms. This approach leads to conjectural 'history' or a 'reconstruction' of the traditional system of norms (see, e.g. Hammond–Tooke, 1962, and also van Velsen, 1965).

Such considerations have prompted a reaction among some anthropologists against the structuralist's over-emphasis on consistency and on the formal and ideal norm. There has been an increasing interest in the problem of conflicting norms, including norm conflicts resulting from foreign cultural influences. Moreover, they have begun to move into urban communities, studying trade unions and other aspects of urban, industrial living, both in countries with a long-established industrial economy and in countries whose economies were, until comparatively recently, based largely on subsistence production. Consequently, they are becoming more aware of the contradiction between the observable realities of wage employment, labour migration, cash-crop production, etc., and the older assumptions of consistency, homogeneity, and relative stability. Moreover, the isolation, for analytical purposes, of the units of study is becoming increasingly complicated (see Gluckman, ed., 1964, especially Chapters 2–6). And even in the study of relatively isolated and small communities of the Highlands of Australian New Guinea – to quote one instance – Barnes (1962) found one could not usefully apply the structural models of kinship and political systems that were first formulated in the African field.

One way in which this reaction has expressed itself is in an over-emphasis on actual behaviour: particular events and relationships are treated as unique and there is a reluctance to relate them to a general frame of reference. For instance, Bohannan (1957) describes the legal system of the Tiv as if it were unique and thus incapable of comparison with the legal systems of other peoples including the English and American systems. Indeed, his description would seem to deny, by implication, that the Tiv possess a legal *system* because he treats each dispute as if it were unique, that is, it is not settled with reference to a general body of norms. Bohannan writes: 'The decision [of the court] seldom overtly involves a point of law, in the sense that we think of a rule or a law. . . . The purpose of most *jir* [viz. judicial hearing] is, thus, to determine a *modus vivendi*; not to apply laws, but to decide what is right in a particular case. They usually do so without overt reference to rules of law' (p. 19). (Note that Bohannan uses the general term 'decision' and does not make it clear whether he refers to the court's *verdict* or to the sanctions it imposes as a *result* of its verdict.) One wonders how a court – any court – can 'determine a *modus vivendi*' (or 'settlement' as Bohannan calls it elsewhere) which is considered *right* by all parties without reference to a commonly accepted body of norms; whether this reference is overt or implicit is of little significance. In any case, the cases quoted by Bohannan do not support his statement. For example, Case No. 8 is concerned with the legal custody of a girl who had been reared by her maternal grandmother. The girl's father wanted his daughter returned to him. Very early on in the case one of the members of the court 'hearing this much of the matter, observed that there seemed no problem . . . [the grandmother should receive a reward for rearing the girl, but the girl's] filiation was not in doubt'. In my view this statement would seem to indicate that courts in their *verdicts* are guided by – and apply – certain norms. Moreover, it is clear from the rest of this case (and, indeed, from several other cases quoted by Bohannan) that Tiv courts do abide by certain norms and are not prepared to compromise on them for the sake of an amicable settlement between the parties. The cases also appear to indicate that Bohannan's statement about the courts' aiming at a *modus vivendi* or settlement may apply to the courts' sanctions rather than to their verdicts.

Bohannan, when discussing the underlying methodology of his book, distinguishes between the '"folk system" of interpretation' of the Tiv and the 'analytical system' of the anthropologist (p. 4). Nevertheless, his account of the Tiv legal system would seem to be based predominantly on one type of data only, viz. observed actions, excluding the ideal norms to which the Tiv adhere or say they adhere. But this ignores the fact that the social anthropologist is concerned with people who live and act within a certain social order and whose actions must therefore have some reference to established and accepted norms of conduct. Ideal norms of conduct and actual behaviour are necessarily closely interconnected. Thus Devons (1956) has argued that although a formal rule of conduct, whether in a business concern, in a voluntary organization, or in the political field, may be ignored in practice and have become a myth, theoretically the rule is still valid and part of reality. Devons's article was in response to one by Finer (1956), who dealt with the role of interest groups in politics. Devons opposed the view that political behaviour can be 'explained and understood exclusively in terms of the interaction between . . . [interest] groups' and he denies that 'the notion of government as the pursuit of a wider public interest [is] just a sham, a myth'. Instead, Devons posits that 'The ideal of the public interest and the practice of interest groups are both part of political life, and any satisfactory view of politics must comprehend both, contradictory though they are. We get a misleading view if we attempt to explain the reality of political behaviour exclusively in terms of one or the other. The reality is a complex interaction, admittedly not easy to disentangle or to explain.' Devons further notes that 'The tendency to construct theoretical explanations exclusively in terms of either principles or practice' is common with regard to discussions not only of political behaviour but also of business and other organizations.

One aspect, then, of the reaction to structuralism as formulated by Radcliffe-Brown and developed by some of his students, has been a growing desire among anthropologists to understand how people actually live with their – often conflicting – norms; how they operate these norms and manipulate the choices open to them. I quoted earlier Evans-Pritchard's footnote regarding the 'political actualities [which] are confused and conflicting'. Now, Gluckman has suggested (1955a, pp. 1–26), using Evans-Pritchard's own extensive data, that in the latter's analysis of Nuer society a vital part is missing, namely how the Nuer reconcile or utilize the conflicting demands of patrilineal descent and the affective bonds of matrilateral kinship. And he has hypothesized that a deeper understanding might be gained of the Nuer feud by considering the political importance of matrilateral kinship. Indeed, all of Gluckman's work is pervaded by the notion that conflicting norms, i.e. individuals' conflicting loyalties to different groups, based on different principles of organization, may ultimately contribute to social and political cohesion. Similarly, Colson (1953) describes in some detail a situation in which individuals' conflicting lineage, marital, and residential loyalties help, in the end, to solve a dispute arising from a case of homicide.

This approach calls not only for the recording and presentation of 'the imponderabilia of actual life' (Malinowski, 1922, p. 18) but also for co-ordinated accounts of the actions of specified individuals. Barnes (1958) has noted the 'shift away from the collection of statements about the customs and the details of ceremonial behaviour to the study of complex social relationships . . . [with the consequent] emphasis on actors rather than informants'. Thus records of actual situations and particular behaviour have found their way from the fieldworker's notebooks into his analytical descriptions, not as 'apt illustrations' (Gluckman, 1961a, p. 7) of the authors' abstract formulations but as a constituent part of the analysis.

I have called this way of presenting and handling ethnographic data 'situational analysis'. By this method the ethnographer not only presents the reader with abstractions and inferences from his field material but also provides some of the material itself. This puts the reader in a better position to evaluate the ethnographer's analysis not only on the basis of the internal consistency of the argument, but also by comparing the ethnographic data with the inferences drawn from them. Particularly when several or most of the actors in the author's case material appear again and again in different situations, the inclusion of such data should reduce the chance of cases becoming merely apt illustrations. I am not implying that ethnographers working with a structural frame of reference do not have any accounts of actual situations in their notebooks or do not publish any. Rather, as I have already indicated, the difference would appear to lie in the fact that structural descriptions do not give us a series of connected events to show how individuals in a particular structure handle the choices with which they are faced. In fact, Radcliffe-Brown's statement quoted above indicates that he was not concerned with this problem.

Regarding the relationship between actual behaviour and generalized description, I have argued that situational analysis offers better opportunities for integrating the accidental and exceptional with the general than does a structural analysis. If this can throw more light on, and give greater depth to, the total process of social life in societies that appear to have clear-cut formal structures, I would maintain that this approach is *a fortiori* applicable, if one has the same ends in view, in the case of those societies such as, say, the Tonga of Malawi, or of Zambia, or some of the tribes of the Highlands of New Guinea, which lack this characteristic. When the agents in the system are not clearly structured, enduring corporate groups but rather individuals interlinked through continually changing alignments in small and often ephemeral groups, one cannot talk meaningfully about exceptions.

I have contrasted the aims and methods of anthropologists writing in the structuralist tradition with the types of problem in which many anthropologists of a younger, post-structuralist, 'generation' have become interested. In doing so I wished to indicate that our criticism of the structuralist tradition is a matter of amplification and difference of emphasis rather than a radical departure from this tradition in the way that the new fieldwork techniques and analytical methods of the structuralists differed fundamentally from those of the pre-structuralists. The structural frame of reference is still a prerequisite for anthropological analysis. But we now want something in addition: the statics of the structure, 'the permanent edifice in which social relations and activities are congealed' as Fortes put it (1945, p. 232), should be supplemented and enlivened by an account of the actions – both 'normal' and 'exceptional' – of the individuals who operate the structure, i.e. the processes going on within the structure. We seek to relate the deviations from structural regularities to regularities of a different order, namely the interpretation of a social system in terms of conflicting norms. This new emphasis not only demands a different type of field material but also raises the question whether and in what form this material should be presented to the reader. While a structural analysis aims at integrating the generalizations and abstractions into a coherent account, no effort is made to integrate the various pieces of case material either with one another or into the analysis, and, indeed, if this is done, as Sommerfelt (1958) has shown, the result may be that a case that was meant to illustrate a particular generalization may in fact invalidate it. By contrast, a situational analysis pays more attention to the integration of case material in order to facilitate the description of social processes.

SITUATIONAL ANALYSIS AND FIELDWORK

I suggested at the outset that the ethnographer's fieldwork methods are guided by his theoretical approach; they are not necessarily determined by it. For instance, Firth's theoretical views are in some respects very similar to those I have discussed here with reference to situational analysis. Surprisingly, however, there are few signs that Firth has applied these theories to the analysis of his own ethnographic material, even in his most recent work. Firth has written (1964, p. 43): 'If social structures *are* models, then we can call social organization the "reality". But even if they are not merely models, then as the set of primary forms of the society, they need supplementing by studies of process.' And again: 'One may describe social organization, then, as the working arrangements of society. It is the process of ordering of action and of relations in reference to given social ends, in terms of adjustments resulting from the exercise of choices by members of the society' (1964, p. 45). However, these and other interesting, dynamic theories appear to have been ineffective as guides – let alone as determinants – in Firth's ethnographic work. In his replication study of the Tikopia (1959), he mentions the increased influence of Christian mission teachers and also of the British administration. The book provides ample evidence that these conditions have widened the choice for Tikopia individuals between alternative norms of behaviour. But Firth does not describe 'the exercise of choices by members of the society'. Rather, the book is mainly concerned with the exercise of choices by the society. Indeed, we seem to be dealing with two different meanings of the term 'choice'. In his theoretical statements, which I have quoted above, Firth would appear to use the term in the sense of the selection by individuals of alternative norms of behaviour within a persisting social structure. That is also the sense in which I have used the term in this essay. In his replication study, however, Firth uses the term in the sense of a collective, cultural 'decision'. This sense of the term choice has an historical connotation: it is only afterwards that the investigator can state that 'things have changed'. It refers to the end-result of a process of change wherein, over a period of time, individual members of the society make individual choices in particular situations: some selecting the traditional norm and some selecting the novel, rival norm, or, again, the same people now selecting the one and now the other, with an overall trend in favour of the novel norm. It is only when the latter has become universally accepted that the investigator can state that 'a village has chosen progress'. It is this kind of 'before and after' treatment which dominates Firth's replication study: he constantly juxtaposes what he found in 1929 with what he found in 1952. The intervening *processes* of change (not to be confused with the *stages* of change) are barely revealed. This approach also tends to emphasize changes of customs. Hence the reader is constantly confronted by statements such as: 'There seems, however, to have been a progressive modification in the Tikopia marriage ceremony, by cutting down the number of formal acts. Some traditional food exchanges had been abbreviated [viz. in 1952 as compared with 1929] . . . These reductions were done not only in Christian marriages; pagans had followed suit . . . the practice of ritual capture of the bride . . . seemed by 1952 to have been finally abandoned . . .' (1959, p. 204). Thus Firth in his ethnographic studies deals largely with the change from (or the 'choice' between) one 'set of primary forms' and another but neglects the problem of individuals choosing between one set of structural norms and another.

Nevertheless, Firth's emphasis on choice in his concept of social organization is an important mark of the trend in recent anthropology away from a preoccupation with social structure as such. Related to this trend is the growing interest in social processes, including the study of regularities in the variety of actual individual behaviour within the social structure. My own view is that situational analysis may prove very useful in dealing with this process of optation, that is, selection by the individual in any one situation from a variety of possible relationships – which may themselves be governed by different norms – those relationships which they consider will serve their aims better. The particular relationships and norms selected are likely to vary in regard to the same individuals from one situation to another and in regard to similar situations from one individual to another.

A related problem of sociological significance where situational analysis would appear to be relevant concerns the discrepancy between people's beliefs and professed acceptance of certain norms on the one hand and their actual behaviour on the other. Such discrepancies, I have argued, cannot be explained away by relegating them to the category of data called 'exceptions'. They are after all part of the field of study and may on closer analysis disclose their own regularities. Moreover, actions that to other members of the society and to the ethnographer may appear to be in conflict may be explained by the actors themselves in terms of that norm or a different one. I have also laid stress on the structuralist's perhaps necessary assumption of consistency, and have observed that a characteristic feature of both unstable and non-homogeneous societies is variation: variations over time in the case of the former, and in the case of the latter synchronic variations as between constituent parts of the society. As a method of integrating variations, exceptions, and accidents into descriptions of regularities, situational analysis, with its emphasis on process, might therefore be particularly suitable for the study of unstable and non-homogeneous societies. Mitchell (1960, p. 19) has argued this with regard to the study of social relationships in plural societies where we are clearly 'not dealing with an integrated cultural system but with one in which quite disparate systems of belief may co-exist and be called into action in different social situations'.

This stress on the study of norms and actual behaviour in a variety of different social situations for the handling of certain analytical problems also calls for different techniques of fieldwork and presentation of the data. In the first place, it requires a greater emphasis in fieldwork on the recording of the actions of individuals as individuals, as personalities, and not just as occupants of particular statuses. Thus in order to perceive – and later to describe – the process of optation – it is necessary to record, in meticulous detail, the actions of certain specified individuals over a period of time. When such a series of related case material is later presented in the analysis, the As, Bs, and Cs of so many of the situationally isolated 'apt illustrations' will lose their anonymity and, instead, will regain their identity as Tom, Dick, and Harry, or Jack and Jill: they are now actors in a series of different circumstances who make greater or less use of (i.e. manipulate) an element of choice of norms to suit the requirements of the particular situation. To give his case material this historical perspective the fieldworker will face certain problems. He may decide to limit the time depth to his period of observation. But this limit may be too restrictive and he may be forced to take into account events that occurred before he commenced his inquiries. The ethnographer who wants to record case *histories* will therefore have to supplement his own, observed, data from other sources such as informants' memories, court records, and other documentary and non-documentary sources. However, the ethnographer should be aware that there is a difference of type between these two categories of data. In contrast to the observed data, the other sources of information may contain an element of bias which is not always easy to evaluate. (This observation is not quite as obvious as it might appear. Anthropologists working in tribal societies have frequently displayed a remarkably uncritical attitude towards informants' statements about past events or conditions. For instance, informants' comparisons of present moral laxity with 'the old days', when those guilty of extra-marital sexual relations would have been burnt, have often been reported and apparently accepted at face value without any attempt at critical evaluation.)

An example of the diachronic treatment of the actions of specified actors in on-going structural relationships is a series of cases related by Middleton (1960, pp. 129–229). These cases are set in one local community, among the Lugbara. They cover a period of about one year and are based on Middleton's own observations, although he had to rely for the necessary background information on informants' memories; but he is careful to indicate who tells what. Ostensibly these cases are mainly concerned with sacrifices to ancestral ghosts as a result of personal misfortune. But they do more than illustrate the norms, values, and practices of Lugbara ancestor worship and religion. This series of cases shows the growing rift between two lineage sections in one local community, leading to their separation. Middleton interprets this series of cases as a struggle for power carried on in ritual terms.

In contrast to this integrating treatment I now quote the following isolated items of information from Firth (1959). On p. 246 he records an interview with two Tikopia chiefs, Fangarere and Taumako. He 'discussed with them the lineage structure of their clans in 1952. Each of them was concerned to give a separate identity to quite small units which previously I had regarded as simply component parts of larger ones'. It was chief Fangarere in particular who 'insisted on characterizing most units which lived separately as individual units, . . . [saying] "It is appropriate for them to stand separately".' Firth does not attempt to explain this attitude by relating it to other events or the chief's (or chiefs') particular position, or by putting it in some other way in a wider social context. Then, on p. 280, we read that the old chief Fangarere died in 1940 and was succeeded not by his eldest son, as would have been 'normal', but by his eldest son as a Christian chief Fangarere *and* by a younger son as the pagan chief Fangarere. The reader, not unnaturally, wonders whether there might possibly be any connexion between these two pieces of information, particularly since there are one or two other isolated references to the Fangarere chief which make him seem somewhat 'exceptional'. To heighten speculation, Firth insists on referring to the Fangarere chief without specifying whether it is the pagan or the Christian one.

The use of extended-case material of the kind that Middleton employs is aimed then at illuminating certain regularities of social process, not at highlighting personal idiosyncracies. Therefore in collecting and presenting data on the actual behaviour of individuals reference must always be made to the norms which govern or are said to govern that behaviour. Thus one will be able to assess whether deviation from certain norms is general or exceptional, why such deviation occurs, and how it is justified. The ethnographer should seek in each instance the opinions and interpretations of the actors and also those of other people, not in order to find out which is the 'right' view of the situation but rather to discover some correlation between the various attitudes and, say, the status and role of those who have those attitudes.

Such detailed investigation requires the ethnographer's close acquaintance with individuals over a lengthy period of time and a knowledge of their personal histories and their networks of relationships. In view of the fact that the ethnographer's period of research is generally limited to two or three years or even less, this means that he has to limit his area of research: to 'do' a whole tribe, or the trade union organization, or an urban area may not always be possible. This leads us to the question of the typicality of the anthropologist's analysis. This question may be of particular relevance if the anthropologist's main concern is to present the culture (the customs) or the structural principles of his unit of research. I am arguing, however, for the analysis of social processes. This means a different kind of fieldwork, viz. more intensive research within a smaller unit.

The definition of the geographical, cultural, economic, and political boundaries of one's unit of study and its excision from larger – and perhaps hitherto more conventional – entities, poses a difficult problem. And the question arises to what extent the smaller units can still be considered 'units'. In reply I would point out, in the first place, that isolation for analytical purposes should not be confused with *de facto* isolation. In tribal studies the tribe has too often been treated as if it were factually isolated from external cultural, economic, and political influences. Certainly in

Africa, tribal societies have been much less isolated, particularly since European colonization, than has far too often been assumed by anthropologists, historians, and others. In the second place – and following from the preceding point – the question of isolation is not one that suddenly arises when one studies, say, a village instead of the whole tribe, or one trade union, or even just a branch of a trade union, instead of the entire national trade union organization, or one urban area, or even only a part of it, instead of the whole country. It would be truer to say that it is only comparatively recently that we have become aware of the problem of the definition of the unit of study in relation to the larger entity of which it is a part. Therefore, the analytical isolation of, say, a village, as a unit of study instead of the whole tribe, is a relative problem. For instance, few have ever questioned the appropriateness of a study of the Trobriands which, as Malinowski so successfully demonstrated, were very much part of a large archipelago. Certainly, Malinowski himself did not show any concern with the problem of the delimitation of the Trobriands as a unit of study. Clearly I am not arguing that the Trobriands are not a proper analytical unit. On the contrary, I am merely arguing that to excise, for analytical purposes, a small area from the Trobriand Islands would not create a new methodological problem compared with the excision of the Trobriand Islands from the rest of the '*kula* ring'; both involve the problem of analytical isolation (see Gluckman ed., 1964).

One final observation on this point: it should be noted that there has been a tendency for the units of study to shrink: from the limitlessness of the *Wanderlust* school to just a few villages (or even only one) in a tribal society, or a branch of a trade union, and so forth. This is not necessarily the expression of a passion for rarefied detail. On the contrary, this trend might well yield the kind of material that will enable us to lay a better foundation for large-scale cross-cultural comparison: it is a matter of *reculer pour mieux sauter*.

I now sum up briefly my main points on the recording of cases within a situational frame of reference. One of the assumptions on which situational analysis rests is that the norms of society do not constitute a consistent and coherent whole. On the contrary, they are often vaguely formulated and discrepant. It is this fact which allows for their manipulation by members of a society in furthering their own aims, without necessarily impairing its apparently enduring structure of social relationships. Situational analysis therefore lays stress on the study of norms in conflict. The most fruitful source of data on conflicts of norms is, not unexpectedly, disputes, whether aired inside or outside courts. Descriptions of 'primitive law' frequently imply that all disputes are simple cases of 'breaking the law' and that argument therefore is concerned with the 'facts' of the case while there is tacit or express agreement among all parties concerned as to the applicable norm or norms. This ignores the point that in any society one is likely to find a large category of disputes where argument is mainly concerned with the question of which of a number of mutually conflicting norms should be applied to the undisputed 'facts' of the case. Given this point of view, it becomes important to obtain different accounts and interpretations of disputes or other particular events from a variety of people rather than to search for the *right* account or interpretation of these events. The latter approach is more that of the 'look for the wise old men of the village' school and of the lawyer. For the sociologist interested in social processes there are no right or wrong views; there are only differing views representing different interest groups, status, personality, and so forth. It follows from this, secondly, that as much as possible of the total context of the cases should be recorded – the cases should be presented situationally – and the actors should be specified. For instance, bridewealth disputes may well involve more than merely a demand for an unpaid bridewealth. It may be the vehicle for a dispute in another field (e.g. political) which for one reason or another cannot be discussed *as* a political dispute (see, for instance, van Velsen, 1964, p. 125 *et passim*). Finally, in the field one seeks interconnected cases within a small area involving a limited number of *dramatis personae*. Such cases should later be presented in the analysis in their social context as part of a social process and not as isolated instances illustrating, more or less aptly, a particular generalization.

The following two examples show the practical application of the situational approach. Mitchell (1956), one of the first anthropologists to use connected cases in this way as a basis for – and integrated with – his analysis of the composition of the Yao village, gives a series of cases of witchcraft accusations and divinations (pp. 165–175). These cases cover a period of eight years going back several years to a date before the author's arrival on the scene. They are ostensibly concerned with personal misfortunes such as death and difficult childbirth. Treated as isolated instances, these cases might have been used to illustrate more or less appropriately Yao notions of sorcery. But Mitchell presents his cases in the total context of a particular village and thus describes the process of the widening cleavage between the lineage sections in the village and its ultimate split into two separate villages. The book contains similar data from other villages and they are presented by the author together with an account of the structural principles of Yao residential and kinship groups. Presented in this way the many instances of quarrels, bitter accusations, and other symptoms of disunity do not lead to the conclusion that we are confronted by a 'disintegrating society' (e.g. as the result of British occupation). Instead, the author shows that such periods of bitter and frequent quarrelling are not symptoms of 'social pathology' but inherent in the life-cycle of the Yao villages from foundation through growth to dispersal.

Turner (1957) has elaborated this type of analysis. His book is also mainly concerned with the developmental cycle of the village, in this case among the Ndembu. Running right through his structural analysis of the Ndembu village, and integrated with it, is a series of 'social dramas': a series of cases which are all set in one village and centre upon a man called Sandombu who struggled against many odds for political office but failed. Turner describes ritual as a mechanism of redress which tends 'to come into play in situations of crisis where conflicts have risen in and between villages as the result of structural contradictions, rather than of the law-breaking activities of malicious or ambitious individuals' (p. 330). This author's aim, too, has been 'to show how the unique, the haphazard and the arbitrary are subordinated to the customary within a single, if changing, spatio-temporal system of social relations. . . . [and] to show how the general and the particular, the cyclical and the exceptional, the regular and the irregular, the normal and the deviant, are interrelated in a single social process.' He therefore considered it 'necessary to take a single village as my universe' (p. 328). Turner, like Mitchell, pushes the starting-point of his cases back to a date well before he began his investigations. Both authors, however, indicate where necessary who the informants are for particular stories or other pieces of information. This helps the reader to place the cases in their social context. Both Mitchell's and Turner's studies are structural analyses, but I suggest that they have been able to approximate more closely to the observed reality by adding another dimension, namely an analysis of social process, that is, the way in which individuals actually handle their structural relationships and exploit the element of choice between alternative norms according to the requirements of any particular situation.

CONCLUSION

In this essay I have outlined methods of analysis and fieldwork from the comparison of haphazardly collected customs, through the more modest but sociologically more fruitful structural method with its emphasis on social morphology, to a method that aims at analysing the interrelation of structural ('universal') regularities, on the one hand, and the actual ('unique') behaviour of individuals, on the other.

Although I am of the opinion that the fieldworker's theoretical approach is of primary importance with regard to the type of material he seeks, and although I think that fieldwork methods can be prescribed only in general terms, I have made some suggestions regarding the collection of the type of material that is most likely to satisfy the demands of some of the present theories. These demands are for a synchronic analysis of general structural principles that is closely interwoven with a diachronic analysis of the operation of these principles by specific actors in specified situations.

is of primary importance with regard to the type of material he seeks, and although I think that fieldwork methods can be presented only in general terms, I have made some suggestions regarding the collection of the type of material that is most likely to satisfy the demands of some of the present theories. These demands are for a synchronic analysis of general structural principles that is closely interwoven with a diachronic analysis of the operation of these principles by specific actors in specified situations.

PART TWO

Selected Problems: Data and Methods

T. S. EPSTEIN

The Data of Economics in Anthropological Analysis

DESPITE the existence of a number of classic studies in the field, 'primitive' economics has remained one of the most neglected branches of anthropological inquiry. Today, however, there are signs that this situation is changing. An increasing number of anthropologists are showing awareness of the importance of economic data to the analysis of social systems. Interest has been further stimulated by the problems posed as once isolated subsistence societies are drawn more and more closely into the world cash economy. These are matters of concern to the administrator and the economic planner, but they also involve the social anthropologist interested in studying the processes of social change. Many fieldworkers today therefore collect quantitative data on such topics as exchange, consumption, and production. But since few anthropologists have had any serious training in economic theory, they often have no clear idea what data to collect when they are in the field or how later to compile and present the material they do gather. Consequently much of the data so patiently collected remains unprocessed or, if published, at once exposes the writer to severe criticism.

The methodology of economics differs greatly from that of social anthropology. Much of modern economics tends to be concerned mainly with macrocosmic studies carried out with carefully prepared sampling techniques based on available statistics. By contrast, the social anthropologist often focuses attention on a small unit, which he examines for its internal systematic interconnexions. In these studies he has usually to collect his own quantitative data, a procedure which may make it impossible for him to generalize about the society at large (see above, p. 15). Collecting the kind of statistics with which economists work is made possible only by the existence of a complex social system, dominated by the institution of the market, whereby all values can be expressed in terms of a common denominator – money. Comparable institutions are of course frequently absent in primitive societies. There is therefore the problem of collecting the kind of information in these societies which the economist regards as the *sine qua non* of economic analysis. This in turn points to the more fundamental question whether the tools of analysis, which have been developed within the context of industrial, market economies are indeed applicable to societies organized on very different principles. Only after some consideration of this issue can we go on to discuss the character of 'economic' data in primitive and peasant societies, the methods by which they may best be collected, and the way in which such data also serve to illuminate the organization of social relationships.

On the basic question itself there are some differences of opinion. Among economists, Goodfellow (1939, p. 3) has remarked: 'When it is asked, indeed, whether modern economic theory can be taken as applying to primitive life, we can only answer that if it does not apply to the whole of humanity then it is meaningless.' Among anthropologists, Herskovits, too, has affirmed his belief in the universal applicability of economic theories, a conclusion that derives from his view (1952, p. 294) that 'the basic problem is universal: not only to have enough to eat to keep alive, but also to satisfy the demands of personal tastes, religious rules and a multitude of social obligations, all as important to the life of the group as mere subsistence is to the life of the organism'. But such views have not gone unchallenged, and they have indeed been repudiated by a number of scholars. Thus Dalton (1961), for example, has asserted categorically that 'economic theory cannot be fruitfully applied to the study of primitive communities'. Adopting a similar line of argument, Sahlins (1960) has made the point that anthropologists are wont to identify the economic sub-system of a culture, 'an economy', with 'economizing' – that is, applying scarce means against alternative ends. This distinction has been elaborated in Dalton's paper where he defines an economic system as relating to 'the provision of material goods which satisfy biological and social wants' whereas 'economizing' refers to 'a special set of rules designed to maximize the achievement of some end or to minimize the expenditure of some means' (1961, p. 6). From this point of view each and every society may be seen as having an economic system. Thus, as Dalton comments, 'with unambiguous meaning one can talk about the economic system of Imperial Rome, of the Kwakiutl Indians, of the Benedictine Order of Monks, of 19th century England, or of Soviet Russia – meaning nothing more than the organizational structures and processes through which material goods are provided'. 'Economizing', on the other hand, is not a trait universally characteristic of social life, and not all societies are amenable therefore to the methods of economic analysis. 'Economizing' in this context appears to imply the need for a common measure of value. In a modern industrial society such as our own this function is served by the price mechanism which acts as a general measuring-rod. But in primitive and peasant societies such a yardstick is not available, and even where they have come within the orbit of the wider cash economy there are still likely to be large sectors of economic organization which remain outside the monetary exchange system. This is the basis of Sahlins's argument that the absence of a generally accepted medium of exchange among primitive peoples implies that they do not have to make economic choices: they do not have to 'economize'. He states (1960, p. 391): 'The question is whether economic choices are specifically determined by the relative values of the *goods* involved. If so, as can be true only in a price setting market system, then the entire economy is organized by the process of maximization of economic value. If not, as in primitive societies where price fixing markets are absent and social relations channel the movement of goods, then the economy is organized by these relations.'

Sahlins seems here to be viewing economic theory as somewhat rigidly committed to the assumption of a rational *homo economicus*, an assumption which stresses material as against non-material incentives. From such a standpoint the time and effort the Kwakiutl Indian invests in the preparation for his potlatch might well strike the economist at first glance as 'irrational' behaviour. For as Goldman observes (1937, p. 91), 'the economic motives are only incidental to potlatching, as indicated by the fact that one gains even greater prestige by destroying property'. The Kwakiutl gives to shame his rivals and to gain prestige for himself and his descendants. Prestige gained in this way thus rates higher than achieving maximum material gain for oneself and one's family. But are the Kwakiutl thus motivated by non-material incentives so different from those who live in a price-setting system? Factory workers may prefer the congenial company of their mates to a better-paid job in a strange environment or entrepreneurs to establish their business in a pleasant but more remote location rather than in the heart of an industrial area where production costs would be lower. Economists have thus had to introduce the concept of non-monetary advantages into their analyses. Robbins (1935, p. 16) has defined economics as the science that studies human behaviour as a relationship between ends and scarce means that have alternative uses. He defined the field, that is to say, in terms of choice; and the task of the economist is thus concerned with all aspects of human behaviour that involve choice. Clearly it is easier to study those forms of behaviour which are readily measured in terms of money, but this is a matter of convenience and expediency rather than principle. The problem of choice is not limited to exchange economies. All human activities involve the expenditure of time, for example, and time is a scarce resource in all societies. From this point of view society may be regarded, to quote Burling (1962, p. 811), 'as a collection of choice-making individuals whose every action involves conscious or unconscious selection among alternative means to alternative ends. The ends are the goals of the individual coloured by the values of his society towards which he tries to make his way. They may include prestige, love, leisure, or even money.' In making their selections individuals are in fact 'economizing' their use of time.

In handling the problem of choice, one of the concepts that economists work with is that of opportunity cost. By this is meant that the 'cost' of something, in the final analysis, is that thing which was most nearly chosen instead, the alternative which was forgone (Benham, 1948, p. 6). Thus among ourselves a man may decide to take a Continental holiday with his family rather than to buy a new car. The 'cost' of the holiday in this sense is the car he would otherwise have bought. But the concept also applies where it is time that provides the measure of value. As Benham points out, a man may decide to work overtime: the 'cost' of the things he buys is the leisure he has forgone. Similarly, in pre-industrial societies, if men prefer to sit around and smoke and chat rather than go off and clear more bush for cultivation, the 'cost' of their leisure is the additional food they forgo. Or again, if a man decides to plant a field with rice rather than millet, the 'cost' of the rice is the millet crop he has forgone. If the time involved in cultivating rice and millet is alike, whereas the yields differ, the real cost of rice in terms of millet can be easily calculated. Assuming that the same area under rice yields only half the quantity of rice as compared with millet, the cost relationship between rice and millet is obviously two to one. In this way it is possible to calculate real costs even in subsistence economies provided that input and output of crops can also be measured.

Firth (1956, p. 72) has remarked how in modern industrial societies economists have worked out an elaborate technique for the study of economic organization, and have produced a body of generalizations upon it, but he adds that it is still a matter of argument how far this technique and these generalizations can be applied to the study of primitive communities. There are aspects of modern economic theory, for example certain concepts developed by Keynes to examine the flow of money incomes, where it would clearly be absurd to expect applicability to the circumstances of primitive life. On the other hand, once it is recognized that there are criteria of value other than money, and that time may serve as such, it becomes apparent that many of the basic concepts of modern economic analysis may have immediate relevance for the study of tribal and peasant societies.

The point of view I am expressing here has been developed most systematically and applied most consistently by Salisbury (1962) in his study of the Siane. The New Guinea Highlands is one of the most remote parts of the world, and it was not until 1933 that the Siane were first contacted by Europeans. Salisbury visited them in 1952. He thus had the rare experience of being able to study the workings of a primitive economy many of the traditional features of which were still functioning effectively. One of the most fascinating aspects of Salisbury's study is that he was in a position to hold all other factors constant and concentrate upon one variable, namely the consequences of the introduction of steel axes not merely for the Siane economy, but for their social and political life in general.

The Siane traditionally distinguished between three types of economic activity: subsistence food-getting, concerned mainly with the strengthening of intra-clan links; luxury trading, which meant establishing 'diffuse personal relations between individuals in situations where no clan obligations exist' (p. 106); and *gima* ritual exchanges, which regulated the relationships between corporate groups. 'The one resource used in all activities is the *time* of the participants. At all moments an individual has to choose whether or not he will enter a situation where a specific activity would be appropriate. At all moments the cost of doing one activity is the activities of other kinds which must be forgone' (p. 106). In such circumstances, therefore, the careful collection of time budgets becomes one of the fieldworker's most important tasks. In fact, the fieldworker cannot possibly hope to observe the daily activities of more than three or four individuals at any one time. Hence it is advisable to compile a stratified random sample of the total population being studied. Through census and other material the general characteristics of the population at large should already have been established. Now, therefore, it can be stratified by such criteria as age, occupation, social and/or economic status, and educational qualifications. Age and social status probably provide the easiest basis for stratification. Salisbury stratified his sample of 12 men, randomly selected, in terms of social status. The unit of measurement he employed was the day or half-day of work. He followed each of his 12 informants for three different weeks in the year and recorded the way they spent their days. He classified their activities into 10 different categories calculating the percentage of time spent on each by each stratum of his sample, as well as by the average Siane (p. 219). By observing the same tasks performed with stone tools and with steel axes, he was also able to calculate the time saved by the use of the latter. Thus he could show the change in the allocation of men's time brought about by introduction of the new tool. Similarly he was able to calculate the labour cost of the various capital goods owned by one small group of Siane. By noting carefully how many individuals were required for how many days to complete a certain task, for instance, the building of a man's house, he could calculate the labour required for the production of different capital items. In this way, through the use of time budgets, it is possible not only to show the allocation of time as between different tasks, which reflects the values of a society, but also to compile input data for productive as well as non-productive property.

An important aspect of production in horticultural societies is of course the direct assessment of yields per unit of cultivable land. Among peoples like the Siane, however, harvesting methods may make such estimates difficult since they only collect small amounts of produce at a time. However, Salisbury has shown how an indirect estimate can be made on the basis of consumption figures. Each month one day, or week, may be randomly chosen during which the total food consumption of the sample households, or of one settlement, is weighed and checked. This information can then provide the basis for a calculation of the average annual food consumption per individual. Then the garden lands of the sample have to be surveyed and, keeping in mind the bearing period of garden land and the consumption needs of the population, the yield per acre of land in real terms can be estimated. By keeping a careful account of quantities of consumption and property as well as of time allocation, Salisbury was able to give a full and fascinating account of Siane economic activities, as well as some of their implications for other aspects of Siane social life. For example, the introduction of steel axes resulted in reduced labour input in the subsistence sector. The Siane spent the freed time on increased trading, *gima* exchanges, and on new activities such as work for the administration and on football.

But groups so remote and isolated as the Siane are becoming increasingly rare. Many anthropologists, at any rate, find themselves working in societies where the economy is already partially monetized. Yet even in these cases it may be necessary to handle economic data in other than monetary units. Thus Bailey (1957), in his study of Bisipara, found it necessary to employ units of paddy, and worked out annual income per head in terms of paddy units. 'Rice is the main crop. Rich landholders differ from poor in their stock of rice and not in growing other crops. . . crops other than rice are not important . . . the word for "food" is the same as the word for "cooked rice" . . . Rich landowners can be distinguished from poor by measuring their income of rice and ignoring secondary crops' (p. 279). Though Bailey shows income totals in real terms, i.e. units of paddy, he does indicate the average annual price per unit of rice, and in other contexts presents statistics, for example the expense account of a funeral, in monetary terms. Such a step, of course, can only be taken where it is possible to establish prices for food and other commodities produced and consumed in the subsistence sector of an economy, because there are links with the wider market economy.

The size of the total universe studied determines how far it is possible to collect economic data for the whole of the society or whether a sample has to be taken. I have found by experience that a fieldworker and one or two research assistants are unable to collect detailed statistics for more than 50 or 60 households in one year of study. If the total universe is composed of more than about 300 individuals, i.e. about 60 households, it is necessary to work by sampling. It is not always reliable, however, to use census information collected for individuals as a basis for sampling. It is true that in some societies the individual may figure as an independent economic entity. Thus the Turners (1955) report that the Ndembu regarded the earnings of each individual man, woman, or child as his or her own possession to be used as he or she thought fit. But this kind of economic independence is unusual in primitive society and in the case of the Ndembu operated only in certain contexts. More often individuals participate in economic activities as members of families or households. Where common residence and membership of a household coincide, that is where men, women, and children living under one roof share in the production and consumption of goods, it is easy to sort census material into households. On the other hand, there are many societies where it may be difficult to decide who belongs to any particular household (Deane, 1949, p. 46); for example, the Siane have men's houses where all initiated men stay, while each married Siane male builds a separate hut for his wife, children, and pigs. In this case, common residence cannot provide a criterion of household composition. Again, the individuals who share in consumption may differ from those who participate in productive activities: an unmarried Tolai youth usually cultivates his own gardens but takes most of his meals with kinsfolk (Epstein, T. S., 1965). In these difficult cases where household membership is not clearly definable in terms of common residence it is advisable to take the housewife as the centre of the household: whoever helps her regularly to produce the food she cooks should be counted as belonging to her household. In polygynous societies this will mean that the husband is included as a member of each of his wives' households. If more people share in the consumption than in the production of goods, this can be recorded as presents given on the part of the donor household and gifts received by the recipient household.

Once the composition of the individual households has been decided, the task of sampling itself has to be tackled. One can take either a fully random or a stratified random sample. Since the total universe being studied will usually be no larger than 250 households, it is advisable to stratify the sample in order to include all categories of the population. If we wish to weight the sample for economic status, we need to have information on the economic status of each of the households in the population. The type of basic economic data needed will depend on a knowledge of the major sources of wealth in the society under study. For example, in India lands have been surveyed, precise records exist, and farmers know the area of their holding. It is thus possible to collect details of land-holding under different types of tenure, and different types of crop in rural settlements where land is the major source of wealth. By contrast, in New Guinea, where land has not yet been surveyed, the number of coconut and cocoa trees as well as the number of food gardens may have to be taken as indices of economic status. In some circumstances, it may be necessary for the fieldworker to survey the land himself, a very tedious but most informative activity. If cattle or pigs are a major source of wealth, then the number of these animals owned by each household has to be ascertained. In order to devise economic categories on the basis of which the sample is to be stratified, it may be useful to allocate point values to the economic resources of the households. For example, in my study of Wangala, an irrigated village in South India, I gave each household a point value according to the size of wet and dry land-holding. As I found the price relationship between wet and dry land to be three to one, I allocated twelve points for one acre of wet land and four points for one acre of dry (1962, p. 42).

Since the size and age composition of households vary considerably, it will be necessary to introduce the concept of the 'consumption unit'. This involves the weighting of the various household members according to their sex and age. Different coefficients may be employed for this purpose. In my own Indian study I accepted Lusk's coefficient, which accords weights as follows:

Household members	*Consumption unit*
Males above 14 years	1·00
Females above 14 years	0·83
Males and Females of 10 years but below 14 years	0·83
Males and Females of 6 years but below 10 years	0·70
Males and Females of 1 year but below 6 years	0·50
Males and Females of below 1 year	Nil

Bailey used a less complex coefficient. He 'considered all persons of fifteen years and over as full consumers, those from ten to fourteen as half-consumers, those from two to nine as quarter-consumers' (1957, p. 277). He ignored children under two years old since he found that the amount of rice they ate was negligible. Salisbury employed an even simpler index. He assumed that children eat half what an adult eats (1962, p. 79). But whatever the coefficient employed it should aim at evening out the differences in the sex and age composition of different households. For example, one household may be composed of three adult men, two adult women, and two adolescent children with a points allocation of 100, while another may just be made up of a young married couple with their five small children and a points allocation of 90. On this basis both households might well be put into the same economic category, whereas the latter is clearly richer than the former. It is therefore essential to weight the households' points allocation according to the consumption units they contain. If we divide the number of allocated points per household by the number of consumption units each contains we arrive at a points allocation per consumption unit per household. The range and frequency distribution of points per consumption unit will then determine the economic categories. For instance, if the range is one to thirty-five and there are only one or two households with a points allocation per consumption unit of more than thirty, then the economic units may conveniently be sorted into three categories, i.e. one to 10 points, 11 to 20 points, and 21 and over.

When the households have been sorted into the various economic strata, the size of the sample has to be decided upon. If the universe is composed of, say, 250 households, a sample of 50 involves the random selection of 20 per cent of the units in each of the economic categories. The larger the proportion of the households in the sample to the total number of households, the smaller will be the probable difference between the results of the sample and the results to be expected from the total universe (Yule & Kendall, 1958, p. 433). Once the stratified random sample has been compiled, the selected households must be subjected to intensive and, if possible, exhaustive inquiry. However, should it prove impossible to compile a statistically valid sample, a small number of households may be selected and treated as individual cases, subjected to the same exhaustive inquiry, in order to illustrate the social life of the people studied. But since the selection is not random, results will not allow for generalization over the whole society under review.

PREPARATION OF SCHEDULES

The ideal way to collect all information is by personal participation or observation. However, this is rarely possible. When the sample householders go off in different directions to their various tasks in the morning, it is clearly impossible to follow all of them in order to observe their activities.

SCHEDULE A

TIME SCHEDULE

Se. No.......................................
Code No.....................................
Date ....

Name	Se. No.	Monday		Tuesday		Wednesday		Thursday		Friday		Saturday		Sunday	
		M	A	M	A	M	A	M	A	M	A	M	A	M	A

SCHEDULE B

BUDGET SCHEDULE (TOLAI)

Village.......................................
Hamlet ....
Name of HH...............................

Se. No.......................................
Code No.....................................
C.U. No.....................................

Date	Expenditure					Income				
	Item	No.	Source	Price	Value	Item	No.	Source	Price	Value

The systematic collection of economic data requires, therefore, a number of different schedules dealing with the various aspects of production, consumption, and exchange. Though these schedules will have to be completed on the basis of interviews, it is important to carry out periodic checks on the reliability of informants' data. Another safeguard as to the reliability of data is the thorough examination of each sample household. If the same aspect of economic life is approached several times from different angles, inconsistencies in the data will soon be revealed: for example, if a farmer tries to exaggerate his crop yield while wanting to underestimate his income, this will soon show up and act as a pointer to the fieldworker to check the matter or pursue it further.

The nature of some of the material to be collected and recorded is set out in a number of schedules that I devised in the course of my fieldwork, which are appended here. The form that the schedules take will vary of course with local conditions, but in preparing them the following points seem worth bearing in mind:

1. Each completed form should be easily identifiable and cross-referenced with other records referring to the same household. For example, my input and output schedule for paddy (Schedule C) bears a serial number derived from the census cards, as well as a *kathe* number – *kathe* being the Mysore village land survey record. Each completed schedule could thus be easily identified in terms of other information relating to the same household. Moreover, the information could readily be cross-checked with the village land records, which had been copied out previously.

2. It is worth trying to incorporate as many pertinent questions as possible. It is far better to leave some questions on the form unanswered than to discover later on, possibly when the fieldwork has been completed, that certain vital information that could have been obtained is missing. For example, I included in the input and output schedule for paddy questions relating to the annual paddy payments given to village functionaries with whom Peasant households have a hereditary relationship. Although this information was not strictly relevant to the input and output of paddy as such, it helped to throw light on the economic interdependence of Peasant and Functionary castes in the Indian village.

3. It is always advisable to have spare columns on each schedule for additional information that may emerge in the course of an interview. Provision must also be made for totals to be entered when the schedules have otherwise been completed.

Schedule C

INPUT–OUTPUT OF PADDY PER ACRE (LAST CROP)

H.H.		Caste		No. of H.H. members	Kathe No.	Se. No.
Total Acreage: Paddy Acreage Last Crop: Paddy Acreage Previous Year: Paddy Acreage Next Crop: Reason for Change:	Wet:		Dry:	How Many Paddy Fields? Why Not Adjacent? How Many Crops per Year? Which Crops? How Big is Nursery?		Tax: Water rate: Contribution:

	Output			Consumption				Sale			Paddy Payments							
	Quantity	*Price*	*Value*	*Quantity*	*Price*	*Value*	*Period*	*Quantity*	*Price*	*Value*		*Quantity*	*Price*	*Value*		*Quantity*	*Price*	*Value*
Paddy Hay Sesame											Pujari Aradya Dhobi Barber Smith				A.K. Labour			

	Bullock	Iron Plough	Wood Plough	Rope	Yoke	Cart	Sickle	Crowbar	Pickaxe	Harrow	Basket	Mortar Pan	Spade	THR in Yard
Own, Loan, Hire Price Maintenance Duration														

SCHEDULE C—*Continued*

Operation		*Labour*				*Bullocks*			*Ploughs*						*Carts*			*Seeds and fertilizer*	*Nur-sery*	*Own acre*
		Unpaid		*Paid*					*Iron*			*Wood*								
		Male	*Female*	*Male*	*Female*	*Own*	*Loan*	*Hire*	*Own*	*Loan*	*Hire*	*Own*	*Loan*	*Hire*	*Own*	*Loan*	*Hire*			
	No.*	No. D	No. D	No. DR	No. DR	No. D	No. D	No. DR	No. D	No. D	No. DR	No. D	No. D	No. DR	No. D	No. D	No. DR		Q V	Q V
1st Ploughing																		Horsegram		
Sowing and manuring of pulses																		Sesame		
Nursery:																		Jola		
Ploughing																		Greengram		
Manure																		Bengalgram		
Sowing																		Tagani		
Fertilizer																		Appsanabu		
1st Harvest																		Paddy		
2nd Ploughing																		Salt		
Levelling																		Ash		
Plant removal																		Oilcake		
Transplanting																		Cowdung		
Weeding																		Total		
Fertilizer																				
Cutting																				
Bundling																				
Thrashing																				
Treading																				
Transport																				
Milling																				
Irrigation																				
Cutting and rebuilding bunds																				

D = day; Q = quality; R = rate; V = value

No.* = number of times individual operation performed

Schedule D

BUDGET SCHEDULE (S. INDIA)—EXPENDITURE

Informant: Caste: CU. No. Se. No.

	Quantity	*Period*	*Source*	*Price*	*Value*	*Remarks*
Rice						
Ragi						
Jola						
Pulses: Cowgram						
Peadhal						
Horsegram						
Blackgram						
Bengalgram						
Greengram						
Tagani						
Chilly						
Salt						
Tamarind						
Coriander						
Lemon						
Onions						
Garlic						
Potatoes						
Beans						
Pumpkin						
Cucumber						
Radish						
Greenleaves						
Herekaye						
Surekaye						
Badanekaye						
Karebe						
Spices: Asafoetida						
Mustard						
Pepper						
Fenugreek						
Cinnamon						
Cumminseeds						
Poppyseeds						
Cloves						
Oil: Castor (seed)						
Coconut						
Groundnut						
Coconut						
Copra						
Wheatflour						
Soji						
Jaggery						
Sugar						
Milk						
Buttermilk						
Butter						
Coffee						
Tea						

SCHEDULE D—*Continued*

	Quantity	*Period*	*Source*	*Price*	*Value*	*Remarks*
Meat						
Fish						
Fruit: Plantains						
Oranges						
Guava						
Groundnuts						
Eggs						
Pansupari: Betel leaves						
Arecanuts						
Kadepudi						
Calcium						
Tobacco						
Cigarettes						
Beedi						
Matches						
Snuff						
Intoxicant						
Hotel						
Cinema and Drama						
Transport						
Fuel						
Kerosine						
Soap						
Soap powder						
Clothes: Men						
Women						
Children						
Services: Guru						
Priest						
Education						
Medical						
Barber						
Laundry						
A.K.						
Puja Articles:						
Sandalwood sticks						
Camphor						
Vermilion						
Turmeric						
Flowers						
Rent						
Interest						
Gifts						
Feast						

Schedule D—*Continued*

INCOME

Informant: Caste: CU. No. Se. No.

	Quantity	*Period*	*Source*	*Price*	*Value*	*Remarks*
Sales: Sugarcane						
Jaggery						
Paddy						
Ragi						
Bullock						
Cow						
Calf						
Buffalo						
Goat						
Sheep						
Poultry						
Wool						
Hide						
Butter						
Milk						
Eggs						
Pots						
Bricks						
Tiles						
Services: Guru						
Laundry						
Repairs						
A.K.						
Ornaments						
Hire: Cart						
Bullocks						
Implements						
Gifts						
Rent: House						
Land						
Interest						
Wages						

INDEBTEDNESS

	Amount	*Lender*	*Date incurred*	*Reason*	*Interest*
Debt:					

Schedule D—*Continued*

INDEBTEDNESS

	Amount	*Borrower*	*Date incurred*	*Reason*	*Interest*
Loans:					

SAVINGS

Amount	*Period*	*Institution*	*Source*	*Interest*

Schedule E

PROPERTY SCHEDULE (TOLAI)

Se. No.....................................
Code No.................................
Name of HH.......................... C.U. No..................................

Item	*No.*	*When acquired*	*Source*	*Price*	*Value*	*Remarks*
1. Clothes:						
Laplap						
Shirt						
Blouse						
Singlet						
Brassiere						
Trousers						
Belt						
Tie						
Towel						
Handkerchief						
Raincoat						
Umbrella						
2. Ornaments:						
Earrings						
Noserings						
Necklace						
Belt						
Armband						
Elbowband						
Headband						
Watch						
Ring						

Item	No.	When acquired	Source	Price	Value	Remarks
3. Luxury articles:						
Gramophone						
Pictures						
Toys						
Books						
Pen						
Pencil						
Pipe						
Bicycle						
Sewing machine						
Razor						
Guitar						
4. Agric. tools:						
Knife						
Axe						
Hoe						
Spade						
Shovel						
Digging stick						
Grass-knife						
Scraping-knife						
Half-knife						
Cocoa-hook						
Hammer						
Saw						
Nails						
5. Livestock:						
Fowl						
Pig						
Goat						
6. Vehicles						
Truck						
Jeep and Land Rover						
7. Car Accessories:						
Wheel						
Tyre						
Jack						
Wheel spanner						
Spanners						
Pliers						
Screwdriver						
Petrol tank						
Springs						
Hoist						
8. Household articles:						
Bed						
Bed mat						
Blanket						
Pillow						
Mosquito net						
Table						

Item	*No.*	*When acquired*	*Source*	*Price*	*Value*	*Remarks*
8. Household articles—*Continued:*						
Chair						
Lamp						
Torch						
Tin trunk						
Wooden box						
Stone						
Pot						
Pot stand						
Frying pan						
Kettle						
Dish						
Cup						
Knife						
Fork						
Spoon						
Basket						
Water bottle						
Water drum						
Water tank						
Broom						
Iron						
Mirror						
Comb						
Bag (Men's)						
Bag (Women's)						
Lock and key						
Scissors						
Needle						
Thread						
Mat						
Plate						
Store						
9. House:						
Copra drier						

	Bank	*When started*	*Amount*	*Remarks*
10. Savings				
11. Tambu				

Se. No.	*Code No.*	*C.U. No.*	1	2	3	4	5	6	7	8	9	10	11

PRODUCTION STATISTICS

In many underdeveloped societies cultivation of crops provides the major source of livelihood. What follows here, therefore, is a discussion of the way crop input and output details may be collected. However, data on other productive activities, such as animal herding or crafts, may be gathered in the same way.

When compiling production schedules it is important to bear in mind what kinds of question the schedule is being designed to answer. One such question of immediate importance is what is the degree of self-sufficiency of the household and how far it is necessary to call in outside labour. Thus my own inquiry in Wangala clearly indicated that the richer the household the less the participation of wives or daughters in productive activities. It had become a matter of prestige for a farmer to be able to hire female labour rather than have his own womenfolk help in cultivation. This was in striking contrast to Dalena, where other prestige criteria operated (1962, p. 237).

Again, one needs to examine the extent to which agricultural labour is hired and the system of payment in operation. Where cash wages are paid, it is important to establish the additional non-monetary rewards, such as meals, quantities of crop or hay, etc. In my Wangala study I discovered five different types of labour relationship, each defined by the nature of the reward (1962, p. 72). It also emerged that the relationship between a farmer and his agricultural labour was of a much more personal nature when labour was rewarded in kind. Other social, political, and economic obligations reinforced the labour relationship. By contrast, whenever wages were paid in cash, the relationship between employer and worker had more of an impersonal, contractual nature. Provision has thus to be made in the schedules for recording the different types of reward.

Another important matter requiring attention is what tools and other aids to production are employed, their value, and whether they are owned, loaned, or hired. This information is important not only for calculating the overhead or indirect cost of cultivation, but also because it throws light on the network of economic relations – for example, whether ploughs are bought from a village carpenter or blacksmith or whether they are imported from the nearest town. It may also illuminate the prestige structure: for instance, in Wangala, ownership of a pair of bullocks and a cart was a matter of prestige, even though such productive aids were often underemployed because of the small size of the farmer's land-holding. By contrast, Dalena farmers looked upon bullocks as commercial commodities: they tried to buy them cheaply and re-sell to the highest bidder.

Frequently it will be found that the size of the area under the particular crop investigated differs between various farmers: one may cultivate paddy on a plot of two acres, while another may plant the same crop on a plot of no more than half an acre. In such cases each sample farmer should be asked to supply the information relating to the area that he has actually been cultivating for the last crop. The problem of having to reduce to a common denominator all the different areas under cultivation in order to calculate input and output per acre will have to be faced when the statistics are computed. Though most farmers seem to have a pretty good idea of the number of labour days each operation requires, they are much vaguer on the yield of crops. This is particularly so with subsistence crops, such as paddy or millet, of which only a small proportion may be offered for sale. It may therefore be necessary to establish the average weight per sack of crop, if it is to be stored in sacks, or the average weight carried away on a cart, if the crop is carried by cart to its storage place. It will then be quite easy to find out how many sacks or cart-loads were harvested from a particular field, and to calculate the total weight harvested. The same technique may, of course, also be employed to find out the quantity of hay or subsidiary crops harvested. However, when gardens are highly interplanted and crops cannot be stored, or are never harvested at one time but collected as and when required, it may prove impossible to collect input and output data. The Tolai, for example, interplant young coconuts with taro, yam, sweet potatoes, and other vegetables. Women collect the vegetables from their garden as they are required for cooking. Where, as in this instance, it is impossible to collect production statistics, then, as we saw earlier, details of how the sample householders spend their time have to be carefully collected. These time schedules will indicate the labour performed, and budget data can then be used to show the output of crops.

Before the data derived from the completed schedules can be computed into meaningful statistics, several points may have to be settled. First of all, there is the problem of establishing a common denominator for the different acreages for which information has been collected. Unless there is evidence to the contrary, it is quite justifiable to assume constant cost of production, that is, that the cost of cultivating one acre is double that of half an acre. Thus the first task in computing production statistics is to convert all the data supplied by informants into figures applying to one acre. Then the problem arises of evaluating subsistence labour, as well as rewards paid in kind. If there is an accepted daily wage rate operating in the society then it is possible to evaluate subsistence labour at this rate. Similarly, if there is a market price for the quantities of crop, hay, or food, given in kind, their cost can be easily established. However, it is important to remember that from the farmer's point of view the cost of his family's labour is unimportant; his chief interest is the difference between his outlay and income, that is, the farmer's total wages and profits.

The calculation of overhead expenditure for the different crops is another major problem in the preparation of crop statistics. Unless land is frequently bought and sold it will be very difficult to estimate the price of any particular piece of land. This makes it impossible to include landed property as part of agricultural capital or to include an interest charge on investment in land among items of overhead expenditure. However, depreciation of implements and draught animals can be calculated according to their span of life. For example, if bullocks have an expected working-life of about 15 years then their annual depreciation can be taken to be 7 per cent. As soon as depreciation, maintenance, and interest charges for agricultural capital have been calculated on the basis of the information extracted from the completed schedules, there is the further difficult task of deciding the allocation of subsistence and cash overhead expenditure among the acres under the various crops cultivated by each sample farmer. If, for instance, a farmer cultivates three or four different crops and employs his agricultural capital on all of them, how can we decide how much of the overhead expenditure should be allocated to each crop? From the information collected, however, it may be possible to calculate the average relationship between the utilization of the major items of agricultural equipment, such as draught animals, carts, and ploughs, on the different crops cultivated. Thus in my study of South Indian villages I found this relationship to be 60 per cent for cane, 20 per cent for paddy, and 10 per cent each for the two types of millet cultivated. If a farmer cultivated one acre each of the four major crops and his total cash or subsistence overhead expenditure was Rs.100, Rs.60 would be allocated to his acre of cane, Rs.20 to his acre of paddy, and Rs.10 to each of his two acres under millet crops. Weights may, therefore, be calculated on the basis of which overhead expenditure can be fairly distributed over the various crops.

CONSUMPTION STATISTICS

The collection of household budgets is coming to be recognized as an essential part of anthropological fieldwork. This is so because budgets can throw light on a number of problems with which the social anthropologist is concerned. Consumption statistics must be collected from the same households, or economic entities, from which the production data were collected. Altogether it is important to use the same sample households for all quantitative inquiries in order to be able to check the consistency and reliability of data.

Budgets can be collected in different ways. The two most obvious are: first, daily inquiry of expenditure and income for certain periods in a year (see Schedule B); second, the completion of carefully prepared questionnaires in the course of two or three lengthy interviews (see Schedule D). The first method is preferable if time in the field permits it. The ideal method would, of course, be to have income and expenditure personally recorded by the fieldworker or his assistant for every day of at least one year. However, this is usually quite impracticable. It may therefore be necessary to limit the inquiry to relate to one week of each month or even to only two or three months per year, depending on the seasonal variations. The second method is less time-consuming, since two or three visits twice or three times a year suffice to complete the questionnaire. But it is much less reliable and also requires a much more lengthy and detailed preparation: all possible items of income and expenditure have to be listed before the questionnaire can be drawn up. In each case, whether budget data are collected daily or at a few interviews, the schedules should provide for the gathering of information on the quantity of each item earned or spent, its source – that is, where it was purchased or whether it was a gift from relatives or friends – and its price, if it is known to the informant.

Budget data may be limited to purely cash transactions. In this connexion Mitchell (1949b, p. 50) writes: 'There can be no doubt that the recall of the various moneys spent and gained over the period of a year can at the most be approximate', yet 'the relative infrequency of the possession of money by the semi-subsistence cultivators allowed them to immediately answer that the money was spent on this or that' (p. 51). However, in order to get an adequate picture of the economic and social life of a people it is essential to study not only the cash income and expenditure of households, but also the extent of subsistence production, barter, and gifts. Informants will probably be unable to indicate the prices of self-produced consumption items. However, provided there are established links with the wider cash economy, it is usually possible to convert the quantities of subsistence production into money values. This simply involves checking prices at the nearest market; allowance has to be made here for seasonal variations.

One of the major difficulties in collecting budget data lies in the fact that in pre-literate societies people rarely employ standardized units of measurement. Therefore in order to assess the food intake of households the research worker should seek to weigh each item before it is cooked or eaten. However, the time consumed in this type of survey is enormous. Yet with the co-operation of informants it is often possible to get a fairly accurate picture of consumption even without this extremely time-consuming research method. All the fieldworker has to do is to prepare a vessel small enough to hold the least quantity of items consumed, then fill the container with the different commodities used by households and weigh each lot. If the housewife is prepared to measure every item in this container before it is cooked or consumed in her household, this should provide reasonably reliable details of consumption.

If the society has not yet developed any links with the wider cash economy, then calorific values may be used as a common denominator for the different items consumed (Platt, 1962). However, if prices can be established for subsistence consumption, then the value of each item can be calculated: the value of each item simply represents the product of the quantity multiplied by the unit price. Of course it must be remembered that the total of subsistence consumption entered on the expenditure side of the budget must also be entered under household income. If the budgets have been collected on a daily basis, then the values of the different categories of income and expenditure have simply to be added up in order to arrive at totals for the period for which the inquiry was carried out, i.e. usually one month at a time.

On the other hand, if the income and expenditure questionnaires have been completed during a few long interviews, it will frequently be the case that the informants have given details of their income and expenditure in units of different periods for different items, for example, consumption of rice per day, expenditure on spices per month, and income from milk per week. If this is the case, quantities of items have to be computed on the basis of a common denominator, e.g. one month, before values can be calculated. Thus while the method of daily budget collection involves more time-consuming observation and interviewing, the second method of completing questionnaires requires much more preparation before the inquiry and also more intricate calculations afterwards. A further drawback of the second method is the liability to error of budget data drawn from informants' memories: informants may quite genuinely not remember details of their income and expenditure correctly, or they may be tempted to exaggerate or understate their consumption or earnings. For instance, when I collected budgets in Wangala I encountered one sample householder who persistently overstated his expenditure, presumably in order to impress me, while he understated his income so as to arouse my pity and secure my help. In some societies informants may be reluctant to divulge their earnings and savings in order to protect themselves from demands for help from their kinfolk. As the Turners remark (1955, p. 29), in all peasant societies 'behind the facade of publicly vouchsafed information there exists a background of social intrigue and conflict within and between groups and this background conditions the type and amount of information given'.

The construction of household income and expenditure accounts will frequently involve the separate interviewing of different members of the household. This may be so even in small households composed only of a young married couple and their small children. In societies where the cultural pattern is such that husband and wife have extremely segregated conjugal roles, it will usually be found that the wife knows little about her husband's income and the way he spends it, while he in turn may know nothing about her consumption and expenditure. Furthermore, it has to be remembered that children, too, often have a small income of their own, which is frequently overlooked by the adult members of the household. The culture pattern of the society will determine whether budget item interviews have to be conducted separately with each member of the household or whether they can be held in the presence of all or most household members.

If certain kinds of expenditure are concentrated in certain periods every year, details should be collected separately, and then averaged out on the basis of yearly or monthly average expenditure. For example, if new clothes are regularly bought only once a year during July for the harvest feast then, if budgets were collected during July, the expenditure on clothes would be exaggerated, whereas if budgets were collected in any other month no expenditure on clothing would be included in the data. Similarly, income which all households may get at the same time each year, e.g. payment for sugarcane sold to a sugar factory, must be averaged out over the period of a whole year. If occasional expenditure, as on weddings or funerals, happens to occur during the period for which a budget is collected, details of these expenses should be carefully recorded, but not included in the calculation of average household budgets. Thus income and expenditure for which there is no chance distribution among householders throughout the year must be given special treatment in the compilation of average income and expenditure accounts.

In order to compare household budgets and to calculate meaningful averages it is important to use the concept of the consumption unit as common denominator. Therefore all household totals have to be divided by the number of consumption units each contains. Another point to remember when preparing budget statistics is to present not only averages, but also frequency distributions for each item of income and expenditure. This helps to show much more clearly the extent of economic differentiation. The more ambitious social anthropologist may also employ standard deviations, coefficients of correlation, and other statistical techniques as the occasion demands.

I have already remarked that occasional expenditure on weddings, ceremonies and feasts, mortuary rites, and so on must be collected separately from household budgets. Since there are likely to be only a small number of these occasional expenses in a small community in the course of a year, it will be advisable to collect full details of expenditure for each event. The statistics can then be presented as case studies to illuminate certain aspects of social life. Thus Bailey (1957, p. 64) gives one expense account of a funeral to show how social pressures operate to force next of kin to indulge in excessive expenditure on mortuary rites. This in turn explains the sales of land to realize assets in order to cover funerary expenses. I myself have used wedding expenses for selected households to illustrate the different degrees of economic differentiation emerging in Wangala and Dalena (1962, pp. 103, 264). Of course, it is not sufficient simply to record the expenditure incurred on these occasions; information must also be collected on how the expenses were covered, i.e. how much was met out of savings, realization of assets, or loans.

Budgets and occasional expenditure indicate the flow of income and expenditure in a society. But no account of the economy can be complete without information on accumulated assets, i.e. productive and non-productive property. This can be obtained only after the fieldworker has familiarized himself fully with the way of life of the people he studies. He must prepare a fully exhaustive list of all possible items of productive and non-productive property (Schedule E) a household might possess. Then he has to inquire from each of his sample households the number of each item owned, how long ago they were obtained, and, if purchased, at what price. If informants are price-conscious, they may even be able to indicate the present resale value of old items of property. All this information gathered together should give a fairly complete picture of property-holding in the community. A major difficulty in this context is in evaluating the different items of property and deciding the present economic value of old items of property. Where there is a ready market for second-hand goods it will be quite easy to verify the market prices indicated by informants. In my inquiries in India and among the Tolai of New Britain I found that informants were usually quite keen to establish the total value of their property and were therefore extremely co-operative in giving this information. Many an Indian villager enjoys going through the bazaars inquiring the market price of old items similar to those which he has in his possession. His estimate of his old property's market prices tends therefore to be fairly reliable. But among the Tolai where there was no ready second-hand goods market available, it was necessary to take the replacement value as the price of old commodities. Household totals of non-productive property, like budgets, have to be divided by the number of consumption units each contains, so as to allow for comparison between different households. Items of non-productive property may be sorted into different categories: for example, personal property, including clothes and ornaments, household chattels, and house property (Epstein T. S., 1962, p. 57).

Where productive property consists largely of purely agricultural assets, details will already have been collected in the course of input and output inquiries. However, where other than agricultural assets are in existence, or where it is impossible to collect production statistics, full details of all capital assets should be recorded on the same basis as for non-productive property.

The compilation of input and output statistics and the collection of family budgets and the details of productive and non-productive property might seem at first sight to yield information of a kind that is likely to be of interest only to economists. This is not so. For the use of detailed quantitative economic data may serve to raise questions about the nature of social relationships in the community that might not otherwise be posed, or at least posed in the same way. To take an example from my own field-work in India: the collection of input and output data in the villages of Wangala and Dalena showed up distinctly the existence of a traditional relationship between Peasant masters and their Untouchable servants in Wangala and the absence of such a relationship in Dalena. This led directly to the quest for other differences in social structure as between the two villages, and to the attempt to explain them. It is doubtful whether the differences would have emerged so clearly or whether I would have posed my problem in quite the same way had I used a purely qualitative approach. In the same way the examination of household budgets can throw light on many aspects of social life that might otherwise remain obscure. The distribution of the different items of income and expenditure per consumption unit, or average budgets per consumption unit calculated separately for each of the strata in the sample, will clearly indicate the type and degree of economic differentiation in the group. Such material also brings out the way in which economic differentiation expresses itself: whether the wealthy spend more on larger quantities of more expensive foods or on different and more costly items of clothing, whether their expenditure is purely personal or constitutes an investment in social relationships. This in turn at once raises questions about the coincidence of economic, social, and political status and may point to important sources of cleavage within the community (Epstein, A. L., 1963). Finally, it may be noted how even property inventories may be relevant for anthropological purposes. Thus the inquiry into non-productive property in Dalena showed the importance attached to possession of items such as fountain pens, gold watches, and bicycles even by those for whom they had no utilitarian value. In Dalena, too, there was a considerable range in the type and cost of new housing. In Wangala, by contrast, economic differentiation did not emerge so clearly in the holdings of non-productive property as in the examination of expenditure on weddings. Such differences between the two villages could be related to the different ways in which the villages were integrated into the wider society.

The discussion in this essay has mainly centred upon such economic activities as production and consumption in primitive and peasant societies. My principal aims here have been to demonstrate that many of the data with which modern economic analysis occupies itself are also available in less advanced economies, and to indicate the means by which they may be assembled in the field. Once the general principle is conceded by the fieldworker, and the art of devising and administering schedules has been mastered, the technique can readily be extended to the examination of the systems of distribution and exchange and other aspects of the economy I have not been able to treat in detail. Clearly, the quest for quantitative economic data makes heavy demands of the fieldworker – it requires time, energy, and an infinitude of patience. But it can also offer rich rewards in the form of a heightened understanding of the inner workings of a society, particularly one that is in the process of rapid social and cultural change.

V. W. TURNER

Aspects of Saora Ritual and Shamanism

An Approach to the Data of Ritual

SOME time ago I was asked to write a review of Verrier Elwin's book, *The Religion of an Indian Tribe*, a descriptive account of the religious beliefs and practices of the Hill Saora of Orissa. I jumped at the chance, for I had collected comparable field data in a Central African society, the Ndembu of Zambia. Elwin's book, I hoped, would shed light on some of my own problems, particularly on the relationship between ritual and social structure. But, in this respect, I was disappointed. For Elwin does not write as a social anthropologist, but as an eclectic ethnographer, and where he interprets, he uses the language of a theologian. He gives exhaustive lists of the names and kinds of mystical entities believed in by the Saora, describes in cultural detail many sorts of ritual to propitiate or exorcise them, and contributes a most valuable section on shamanism. From all this he concludes that 'the whole structure of Saora theology and mythology may be regarded as an attempt to make the mystery and horror of the unseen more bearable'. The burden of the 'wholly other' was too great for them to bear, and so they produced ghosts, who were related to them, deities who had the same desires and passions as themselves. Such ghosts and gods might still be alarming and dangerous, but they were not overwhelming; rationalization, of however simple a sort, had drawn their sting. This formulation may well meet with the approval of the theologian or the psychologist of religion, but the social anthropologist would, I think, examine the same sets of data in a different conceptual framework and require additionally a fuller treatment of the social background of Saora religion than Elwin has given us. For religion, particularly in tribal societies, bears the imprint of many features of the social structure. Crucial religious symbols, for example, may represent a society's articulating principles of social organization. The dominant symbol of the girl's puberty ritual among the Ndembu, for instance, is a tree which exudes a white latex when cut. As a religious symbol this tree ranges in meaning from 'mother's milk' (primary sense) to 'matriliny' (a much more abstract significance). Other symbols may represent social *groups*, *categories*, or social *positions* (in a perduring system).

Furthermore, performance of rituals may make visible specific structural aspects of the situation to which they refer, as, for example, the local or tribal hierarchy of authority or patterned opposition between the sexes. And to obtain an adequate understanding of a given performance, the investigator must take account of the idiosyncratic relations obtaining between particular groups at that time. Relations between village pressure groups may, for example, influence the allocation of roles in a particular performance of ritual. These considerations entail the collection of systematic data about the *social field* in which ritual is observed. (Although I write as an Africanist about Indian data, I would like to stress that we have many common problems and must find common methods of tackling them if social anthropology is to develop a genuinely scientific basis).

The methods I shall use to interpret certain features of Saora ritual have been fruitfully applied by anthropologists to the study of societies with widely differing ethnic and cultural backgrounds. I hope that this will serve as an adequate excuse for my presumption in analysing Indian data although I have never done fieldwork in India.

Let me try to show with the help of three examples how Elwin might have clarified certain features of Saora ritual if he had made a prior analysis of the social system. On p. 411, he cites the case of two brothers who lived together with their father, until his death, when each set up a separate establishment. Shortly after one of the brothers had built his new house, he became very ill. He summoned a diviner-shaman, who ascribed his illness to the affliction of three gods. These gods had been regularly worshipped by his father, and his brother had painted an ikon (i.e. a sacred drawing, on an inner house-wall, dedicated to gods and spirits) in their honour. The shaman, impersonating the three gods, declared to the sick man that 'this man's father used to worship us, and so did his brother. So long as he lived with them he joined in the worship, but now he has separated from them, he neglects us. If he wishes to recover he must honour us in his house also'. The patient begged the shaman to paint an ikon to the gods, sacrificed a goat before it, and we are told that he recovered from his illness.

In this case, reference is made to no less than five categories of social relationships: father–son, brother–brother, shaman–patient, shaman–god, moral offender–god. Indeed, the shaman performed two roles that in Saora society are often undertaken by different individuals, those of diviner and doctor. Does Elwin supply us with sufficient background material to enable us to put these relationships in their relevant structural context?

Unfortunately he does not, for his main interest in this case is in Saora iconography. We do learn, however, from the Introduction to the book, that the 'one essential unit of the Saoras is the extended family descended from a common male ancestor'. But it is impossible to discover whether 'the extended family', called *birinda*, is really a paternal extended *family* or a *patrilineage* with internal segmentation, or whether the same term covers both meanings. Again, Elwin says next to nothing about the modes of succession and inheritance, whether these are dominantly adelphic (along a line of brothers) or filial (from father to son). He does indeed mention that a man's 'paddy fields are divided among the sons', but on the other hand he cites a murder case (on p. 539) in which 'a youth named Turku killed his paternal uncle Mangra in a dispute over a field'. On the following page he mentions how quarrels over the inheritance of a palm tree from which wine is made 'often lead to tragedy, for these trees are the most cherished of a Saora's possessions'. An uncle killed his nephew in one such dispute and in another a nephew killed his uncle. I presume that the term 'uncle' in these cases refers to 'father's brother', although Elwin does not make this clear. From these cases, it would appear that there was no clear rule of inheritance, and that the death of any man with property was the prelude to sharp disputes between persons belonging to several categories of his close paternal kin. In the ritual case mentioned earlier, one may not be far off the mark in inferring that the brothers had quarrelled, since the shaman states that the patient had 'separated' both from his father and from the brother who had continued to worship his father's domestic gods. It may very well have been that the brothers had disputed over their share of the inheritance, and that the brother with the superior share had continued to worship his father's gods. But Elwin does not tell us this, nor does he tell us whether the patient was the elder or the younger brother.

In view of the widespread belief in tribal societies that spirits and gods frequently afflict the living with illness and misfortune to punish them, whether for quarrelling openly with their kin or for harbouring malignant wishes against them, it seems feasible in this instance that the shaman, using the idiom of mystical affliction, was in fact redressing a breach of the customary norms governing behaviour between seminal brothers. At the same time, the ritual he performed would seem to have had the effect of restating and reanimating the value set on patriliny. For the patient's recovery was made dependent on his consenting to worship his father's gods. After the ritual both brothers worshipped the same gods, and were presumably reconciled.

One learns further that it is believed that the gods actively intervene to punish breaches between living kin and to maintain the continuity through time of patrilineal ties. The shaman mediates between gods and men and makes the wishes of gods known to men. One is led immediately to inquire whether the shaman may not perform a structural role of great importance in the day-to-day adjustment or adaptation of Saora society, since it would appear that one of his tasks is to re-establish the social order after disputes have led to the breaking of certain of its relationships. For example, in the case cited, patriliny is asserted as an axiomatic value. Now, patriliny is a principle that apparently governs a number of quite distinct sets of relationships in Saora society. It appears to govern domestic relationships in the household. But it also seems to articulate households that are spatially distinct and may even belong to different quarters and villages. In ritual, *patriliny* is asserted as a unitary value that transcends the different kinds of relationships governed by patrilineal descent, and also transcends the conflicts of interests and purpose that in practice arise between paternal kin. This case also leads one to inquire whether the position of shaman may not be structurally *located* outside the local or kinship sub-divisions of the Saora social system. The shaman may well have no structural links to either of the parties in a dispute. It is also possible that he has the permanent status of an 'outsider' or 'stranger' who has little stake as an individual in any of the ordered arrangements of secular society. He appears to mediate *between* persons or groups as well as between gods and ancestors, on the one hand, and the living, on the other. And as he mediates he mends not only the idiosyncratic tie that has been broken, but also adjusts a far wider set of relationships that have been disturbed by the quarrel. Let me give another illustration of the redressive role of one of these functionaries, this time of a female shaman, or *shamanin*, to use Elwin's term. Incidentally, it is worth noting in connexion with this concept of the shaman as an 'outsider' that shamanins outnumber shamans, although in secular political and social life women rarely occupy positions of authority or prestige.

This second case is dominantly concerned with affinal relationships, although the patrilineal basis of Saora society is an important factor in the events described. A man's wife died and a year afterwards a girl came 'of her own accord' to live with the widower. She fell ill, and her illness was attributed by a diviner-shamanin to the first wife's spirit. It would seem, although Elwin does not mention this, that the husband had *married* the girl before she became ill. The shamanin, reputedly possessed by the spirit, declared to her, 'What are you doing in the house I made? I was there first, and you have entered it of your own accord, and have never given me a thing.'

On the shamanin's advice the husband instituted a ceremony of friendship (*gadding*) to bring his two wives, the living and the dead, together.

Another shamanin acted as officiant, and said to the husband speaking as the spirit, 'Why did you bring this woman into my house? I had a little sister; she was the girl you should have married. She would have looked after me properly.' The husband replied, 'But that was the very girl I wanted to marry. I went to her father's house for her. But the old man made such a fuss that we quarrelled. Then this girl came. She works well; you ought to be pleased with her.' The shamanin, acting in the character of the dead wife, agreed to make friends with the new wife, and gave the latter a cloth and bracelets (supplied by the husband) in token of ritual friendship. Two funerary priests, dressed up to represent the two wives and carrying bows and arrows, then mimed the antagonism of the two wives, while bystanders threw ashes over them. In Africa the throwing of ashes might have represented in some tribes a symbolic 'cooling' of the anger, but Elwin does not explain the significance of this act for the Saora. In the end the funerary priests drank together, embraced and fondled one another, thus dramatically portraying the end of the dispute.

From these events we may infer that the Saora practise the sororate. Indeed, Elwin states elsewhere that they do, and also that sororal polygyny is not uncommon. In this respect the Saora resemble many other patrilineal peoples. The data also shows that the bond between seminal sisters is highly valued. It would also appear that most marriages are arranged, for the second wife is blamed for coming to live with the widower *of her own accord*. Her action, it is implied, disregarded the values attached to the sororate (a form of marriage that maintains the structural relations between patrilineal groups), to the relationship between sisters, and to the custom of arranging marriages. The husband tries to defend the new wife by claiming that he had tried to fulfil Saora norms by marrying his deceased wife's sister. Her father was in the wrong, he suggested, for 'making such a fuss' that they quarrelled. If Elwin had been interested in sociological problems he would have inquired more closely into the content of this alleged quarrel, which might conceivably have thrown light on the nature and functions of bridewealth among the Saora. One would like to know, for example, whether a woman's father has to return her widower's bridewealth, if the widower does not marry her younger sister. In the case we are discussing the husband might have claimed the return of his bridewealth, rather than marry a little girl. Or the father might have wanted to marry his younger daughter to another, perhaps wealthier husband, and this may have occasioned the 'fuss' he made. It appears probable that neither the husband nor the father desired a radical breach in their relationship, for the symbolism of ritual friendship between dead and living wives seems to signify that the new marriage was accepted by the kin of the dead wife. In this connexion, it would have been interesting to know the social composition of the ritual gathering, whether representatives of the dead wife's paternal extended family (*birinda*) were present or not, and whether they partook of the sacrificial meal with the husband. Again, since each *birinda* has its hereditary funerary priest, one would like to know whether the two funerary priests who mimed conflict and reconciliation between the dead and living wives represented the *birindas* of the women. Elwin does not give us this kind of information.

What we can say, however, is that both the diviner-shamanin and the doctor-shamanin who performed the friendship ritual reaffirmed a number of Saora norms and values in a situation following their breach or neglect. The doctor-shamanin fulfilled the further task of reconciling the various parties to the quarrel. Through her mediation their relationships were realigned, so as to take into account the fact of the new marriage.

In the case just mentioned the agent of affliction was a spirit, not a god. It is possible that different kinds of mystical beings are invoked to explain misfortune in connexion with different kinds of social relations. It may be merely that gods and spirits are invoked haphazardly according to the caprice of diviners. At any rate, the difference in the afflicting agency does not seem to depend upon the severity of affliction, for both gods and spirits are believed to have power to *kill* the living. My own guess is that gods are regarded as agents of affliction where emphasis is laid on the general interests and values of Saora society, or when general disasters, like plagues, strike the people; while spirits are brought into account for misfortunes arising from open quarrels and concealed hostilities within its component sub-groups. The point I wish to make is that if the investigator had been concerned with the sociology of Saora religion, awareness of such problems would have influenced his selection of data.

My last example of the interdependence of aspects of ritual and social structure is a fragment of a genealogy. It is a very odd genealogy indeed, for it portrays marital and blood ties between human beings and spirits. The human beings are Saora shamans and shamanins. The spirits are not ancestor-spirits but a special class of mystical beings called tutelaries by Elwin, who are believed to marry diviner-shamans and shamanins, to possess them in trances, and to assist them in divining into the causes of misfortune and illness. The genealogy is extracted from an autobiographical text recorded by Elwin from a famous shaman, who was both diviner and doctor (p. 258). This shaman's father, who was also a shaman, was said by his son to have had four children by his tutelary spirit, two boys and two girls. One of the spirit-sons became the tutelary husband of a shamanin, in a village about three miles to the north, and one of the spirit-daughters became the tutelary wife of a shaman in another village. It would appear from this and similar texts that shamans and shamanins are in the habit of linking themselves to one another by collaborating in the manufacture of fictitious or, rather, fantasy genealogies of this sort. The Saora, in real life, attach a political significance to inter-village ties of affinity, perhaps because they have no indigenous centralized political authority, but live in autonomous villages, each largely self-supporting and self-contained. Shaman-diviners express their professional unity in the idiom of affinity and kinship, and fabricate genealogies in which the significant links are unseen, fictitious beings.

There is another curious feature about these fictitious genealogies. Many of the marriages between diviners and their tutelary spouses would be reckoned incestuous if they were between living Saora. Thus, on p. 435, Elwin describes how a shaman married the tutelary daughter of his father's father, in other words his father's spirit-sister. On p. 149, a shamanin is recorded as having married her deceased mother's tutelary, i.e. her spirit step-father. Another shaman married his spirit-cross-cousin, and cross-cousin marriage is forbidden in real life. Moreover, irregular forms of marriage are practised between humans and tutelaries. One shaman and a male spirit lived in polyandrous marriage with a female tutelary in the Under World, where ancestor spirits and tutelaries live, and whither the shaman believed he went in dream and trance (p. 436). Another shamanin was married to two tutelaries simultaneously (p. 138).

These examples suggest that at least some of the fictitious genealogical interconnexions between living shamans and shamanins arise from fantasies of incestuous matings and irregular forms of marriage. Once again, in another aspect of his social personality, the shaman is placed outside the rules that govern ordinary secular life. The genealogies also express his privileged position as well as his estrangement, for he enjoys considerable prestige and may become a wealthy practitioner. For he is privileged to transgress rules that others must obey. When we come to consider what sorts of person become shamans and shamanins we may also feel justified in saying that the strong elements of fantasy in these genealogies may arise from the fact that many shamans feel dissatisfied with their real kinship connexions and with their positions on real genealogies. In other words the complicated syndrome of the fantasy genealogy may contain an aspect of *psychological compensation*. Such compensation may be related to a number of characteristics of the typical shaman, some of which we will consider later, such as physical inadequacy or low secular status. The shaman or shamanin seems to be a person who is in some way extruded from the structured sub-groupings of his society, or who voluntarily disaffiliates himself from them, and who compensates by becoming a representative of the total system, regarded as a simple homogeneous unit. He is at once within and outside his society. Another aspect of compensation for personal inadequacy or structural inferiority may be expressed in the fact that tutelary spirits are often supposed to be Hindu or Christian Doms, not Pagan Saora. These groups, who oppress the Saora in secular life, are wealthier, and more powerful than they are. And like shamans themselves, Dom and Paik tutelaries have the further attribute of *externality* to the structural order of Saora society. But I shall return to this topic when I have made an attempt from Elwin's somewhat sketchy material on Saora social organization to determine just what are the major sub-units of Saora society and how they are interconnected and sub-divided.

The Hill Saora inhabit the Agency Tracts of the Ganjam and Koraput Districts of the modern state of Orissa. Saora are mainly distinguished from other peoples by linguistic and cultural criteria, and by the occupation of a given territory. The most typical of these Saora live in the Gumma and Serango *Muttas* or sub-divisions of the Ganjam District, and in the villages within ten miles of Pottasingi in Koraput. Not all Saora living in this area are Hill Saora though most of them are. Hill Saora live in long streets, in which they build little shrines; they erect menhirs (stone memorials) to the dead, whom they cremate; they sacrifice buffaloes to the dead; shamanism is the most conspicuous feature of their religion; they engage in both terraced and shifting cultivation; they have a peculiar form of dress. Other Saora are becoming assimilated into the surrounding populations, and are losing their language; and they have begun to worship Hindu gods, to adopt Hindu food taboos, and to wear different clothes and ornaments from the Hill Saora. The Hill Saora have no overall centralized political organization of their own. The Koraput Saora have no overlords or landlords, and pay taxes direct to the State. But the Ganjam Hill Saora territory is divided into tracts of land under the rule of feudal overlords called Patros or Bissoyis. Each of these overlords has a small army of 'home guards' called Paiks. The 'environment' of the Hill Saora includes, therefore, Hindu Bissoyis and their Paik retainers, who live in their own villages. It also includes Christian Doms, who inhabit separate hamlets, sell cloth to the Saora, and have in recent times become money-lenders who despoil the latter of cash and produce.

There are three main branches of Hill Saora: Jatis, who do not eat beef, and claim that they are pure in blood, custom, and religion; Arsis, from the term for monkey, who wear a long-tailed cloth and eat beef; and Jadus, from a word meaning 'wild', who live on the tops of hills and in the wilder tracts north of Serango. There are also a few occupational groups, whose members live with the other Saora and 'resemble them in every respect except in the special craft they have adopted'. These include basket-makers, potters, brass-workers, and blacksmiths. Different groups are what Elwin describes as 'vaguely endogamous'. A Jati may marry an Arsi or a Jadu without eliciting much comment. The barriers are, however, a little stronger between the cultivating and occupational groups, yet an elopement between a potter and a Jadu cultivator is not taken very seriously and is forgiven after the payment of a small fine. But a Jati hereditary priest or *Buyya* cannot marry an Arsi *Buyya* or Jadu *Buyya*. Members of all these groups look, dress, and behave alike. Even blacksmiths and potters have their fields and cattle. Different groups often live in the same street. A most significant feature of Hill Saora society is the high degree of political autonomy enjoyed by the most important residential unit, the village. It may be said without exaggeration that a sociological analysis of the structural relationships within and between Saora villages would provide an indispensable introduction to Elwin's study of Saora ritual. But his data on village organization and on the demographic aspects of village residence are thin and fragmentary.

Several of the ritual case-histories cited by Elwin refer to quarrels within and between *villages*. Elwin also mentions (p. 57) 'the acrid disputes that occasionally disfigure a Saora *village*'. Before performing a ritual a shaman usually makes an invocation to the unseen beings and powers, which includes the following phrase: 'Let no one in the following *villages*, a, b, c, etc. work evil (i.e. sorcery) against us' (p. 235).

These data suggest that there are stabilized conflicts between villages, perhaps over rights to scarce tracts of fertile land, perhaps as the vestigial traces of feuds forbidden now by the Central Government. We cannot tell from Elwin's account. And it would be important to know the motives for inter-village conflict and the customary mechanisms for restoring order *between* villages from the point of view of our analysis of shamanism – for shamans practise outside as well as inside their own village.

What, then, are we entitled to say about Saora village structure? In the first place we can quote Elwin as saying that Saora villages are, for the most part, 'large', long-established in their present sites, and 'built in the most difficult and inaccessible sites that can be imagined'. But Elwin gives us little indication as to precisely *how* large these villages are. He has made no attempt to discuss in quantitative terms such factors as the magnitude and mobility of villages, and the residential mobility of individuals through villages. We can obtain no information about the *average* magnitude of a Saora village or of the *range* of village size. He does mention tantalizingly that 'shifting cultivation means that some Saora villages are very small, with only three or four houses, high in the hills, lonely and remote, but convenient for the swiddens' – by which term he means ash-gardens. But he has just previously written that 'Saora villages in fact resemble established Gond or Santal settlements rather than the rough and ready camps of Baigas and Konds, for whom shifting cultivation means shifting homes' (p. 39). He does mention that in three of the Ganjam political sub-divisions called *Muttas* there are 104 villages. Now there are, according to Elwin, about 60,000 Hill Saora in Ganjam, living in eight *Muttas*. Putting these figures together, and making the admittedly risky assumption that three-eighths of the Ganjam Hill Saora do in fact live in the *three Muttas* he mentions, we may guess that the average village population in these *Muttas* is about 216. In a later chapter entitled 'The Cost of Religion', Elwin mentions that in one Koraput Hill Saora village there were 80 households, in another 74, and in a third 25. This information is not entirely helpful, since he nowhere discusses the social composition or the average size of a household. But we are able to infer from some of his case histories that certain households – a household may own several houses, for each wife has her own – contain three generations of kin. He also mentions here and there that the Saora practise polygyny and widow-inheritance. 'Polygyny,' says Elwin, 'is fairly common. In Dokripanga I found every married man had at least two wives' (p. 56). Now let us suppose that an average elementary family contains four members. Then let us suppose that various accretions from polygynous marriage, temporary co-residence of adult brothers (Saora are patrilocal), widow-inheritance, etc. account on average for a further four members. The first village would then contain approximately 640 inhabitants, the second 592, and the third 200. The first village he mentions, Boramsingi, he refers to several times as 'large' and divided into 'widely separated hamlets' (p. 51). I think that we would not be too much in error if we assumed that the average size of a Hill Saora village was between 200 and 300 inhabitants, with a range of from about 30 to 800.

I have laid stress on this question of village size since there may well be a functional relationship of some importance between the *size* and the *structure* of an important residential unit in a society like the Saora, which emphasizes kinship as a significant principle of residential organization. Limitations on village magnitude may, for example, impose limits on the number of groups of unilineal kin who can dwell together, and on the size of each group. Such limitations can also control the extent of differentiation of the village into occupational and sub-territorial groups. Village size may significantly influence the relationship between lineal and familial modes of organization. If patrilineal descent is an important principle governing residential affiliation, as it appears to be among the Saora, and if in small villages patrilineages are stunted, it is probable that the social mechanisms for promoting cohesion and reducing conflict in the residential unit will differ from those found in patrilineal societies where a larger village is typical or in social systems, such as the Zulu, where emergent new settlements can move out to found new small villages. Again, the average magnitude of villages may be connected with ecological factors. Above a given population threshold a village may have to split to avoid pressure on resources. And indeed Elwin writes that in the Western Ganjam District 'there is considerable pressure on land' (p. 36). On p. 536, he quotes from the report of a Forestry Officer that already in 1907, in Ganjam, 'denudation of the hills by axe-cultivation had seriously affected the water-supply, and that the pressure of population had already resulted in far too short a rotation in the use of clearings'. In larger-than-average villages one might expect to find tensions between sub-groups and factions. Elwin, indeed, gives cases of quarrels over gardens in such villages. The small villages that he mentions may well result from the fission of villages that have exceeded a certain optimum size. And it is in just such over-large, quarrel-ridden villages that I would have expected to find many performances of curative ritual, a type of ritual that writers on Central African ritual have found to have the latent function often of redressing disturbed social relationships. It may be more than coincidence that many of Elwin's examples of ritual are drawn from villages he describes as 'large' such as Boramsingi, mentioned above.

Since Elwin has emphasized that most Saora villages are long-established and 'have nothing of the nomad about them', and since most are difficult of access, and were formerly 'forts' for defence against the raids of other Saora, we may infer that such villages are social entities with a high measure of cohesion and continuity, towards which their members feel strong sentiments of loyalty. Yet at the same time Elwin shows us that each village is internally divided into a number of local and kinship sub-divisions. In the first place, most Saora villages are divided into a number of groups of houses called *sahis* which Elwin translates as 'quarters' or 'hamlets'. Often these are named after their most important residents. In Saora villages, there are a number of political officials. Each has a quarter named after his office. Thus the *Gamang* or Chief, the *Karji*, and the *Dhol-behera*, other political functionaries, have quarters. So has the village priest or *Buyya*, who has political as well as ritual functions. The nuclear group in each quarter consists of the paternal extended family of the quarter-head. Not infrequently, however, quarters are named by some geographical or occupational term, and not after a political or ritual office.

What is the social composition of a quarter? Here as elsewhere in his introductory section Elwin is extremely vague. He points out that in contrast to all the neighbouring tribes the Hill Saora have no exogamous totemic clans, no phratries, no moieties. 'The one essential unit,' he writes, 'is the extended family descended from a common male ancestor.' This 'extended family', the ***birinda***, is the main exogamous unit of Saora society. It has no name and no totem. It is possible, as I suggested earlier, that the term ***birinda*** refers to two distinct kinds of grouping – a patrilineage and an extended family. If both senses are present in ***birinda***, there may be conflict between the organizing principles of these two kinds of grouping. Members of two or more ***birindas*** may live together in one quarter or hamlet, or members of one ***birinda*** may be divided between two or more quarters. But nearly every ***birinda*** is to be found within a single village. A woman does not change her ***birinda*** membership after marriage, and it appears from several of Elwin's texts that a person's mother's ***birinda*** plays an important part in his or her affairs. There does not appear to be any clear rule of post-marital residence and we hear of married sisters living in the same quarter as their seminal brothers, i.e. brothers by the same father. I suspect that one of the basic conflicts of Saora society is between a woman's husband and father or brother for control over her and over her children's residential allegiance. In other words, the conflict would lie between her husband's ***birinda*** and her own. Furthermore, this indeterminacy with regard to post-marital residence would appear ***prima facie*** to inhibit the development of deep local patrilineages, for a man has the choice of residing with either his father's or his mother's ***birinda***. Residential affiliation would seem in fact to be 'ambilateral', in the sense in which Professor Firth (1957) has defined this term. This view receives support from Elwin's remark that 'if a man migrates to another village and settles there, he can – provided that someone in the relationship of mother's brother, father's sister, or their sons is living there – be admitted to a sort of honorary membership of their family' (p. 361). As Elwin always translates ***birinda*** as 'family', one has now the impression that the local ***birinda*** is a composite group containing a nuclear membership of patrilineal kin of both sexes, with men preponderating, descended from an apical ancestor, perhaps not many generations back from the oldest living members, with a fringe of sisters' children and their children. The fact that cross-cousins are forbidden to marry is also consistent with the view that sisters' children are regarded as 'honorary members' of the *birinda.* One might infer from this feature of residential structure that there is incompatibility between the principles of patrilineal and matrilateral affiliation. Since Elwin points out that there is considerable intermarriage between separate villages, it is possible that this conflict of loyalties underlies the hostility between villages expressed in sorcery accusations. One might also postulate that disappointed claimants for village office and men who have failed to obtain what they considered to be a fair share of their patrimony express their discontent by going to reside with their matrilateral kin in the villages of the latter. They might bring up their children in those villages. Such children might be unable to succeed to office there or inherit *birinda* property – for it would appear that the *birinda* owns the permanent terraced rice-fields supplying the staple crop. If this conception of the structure of the *birinda* is correct, it may help to clarify certain features of the shaman's role. For three shamans, mentioned by Elwin, said that their tutelary wives were brought to them by the tutelaries of their mothers, and one by his mother's brother's tutelary, in other words, from tutelaries associated with their mother's *birindas*. In complementary fashion many shamanins acquire their tutelary husbands from their fathers' sisters' tutelaries, i.e. from members of their fathers' *birinda*. Shamans of one sex stress ritual loyalties to the *birindas* of their parents of the opposite sex. In the case of shamanins, ritual loyalties coincide with secular loyalties and strengthen an attachment which conflicts with that of marriage. Thus many shamanins emphasize the ritual importance of principles other than those which ought to govern their dominant loyalties in secular life; a significant proportion of shamans in Saora society stress matrilateral ties against patriliny and women stress a reinforced patrilaterality against the marriage bond. In this connexion it is interesting to note that funerary shamanins (*Guarkumbois*), who are 'usually trained and initiated by their fathers' sisters, ought not to marry and have children' (p. 146). The patrilateral tie is reinforced in a ritual context at the expense of the secular marriage tie. Such shamanins are 'outsiders' to the customarily expected role of women. Both shamanins and shamans use ritual links with the *birindas* of their parents of opposite sex to place themselves outside their customarily expected group allegiance and emphasize their personal independence from customary claims made upon their loyalties. Freudian analysts might postulate that the shaman's marriage with a matrilateral tutelary spouse represents a barely disguised wish for incest with his mother and that the shamanin's patrilateral spirit-husband is really her father. But this interpretation would have to reckon with the fact that religious beliefs are customs, collective representations, social stereotypes, not private fantasies. It might be argued, however, that the operative residential group among the Saora is not, as it ideally ought to be, strictly patrilineal, but consists of brothers and sisters and their adult children who stand to one another in the relationships of cross-cousin. This bilateral group resists the loss of its women by virilocal marriage. And although in social reality it must recognize the force of exogamy, in the powerful wish-world of ritual, men and women mate in fantasy within the forbidden degrees of kinship, or with surrogate parents, and thus assert the omnipotence of the primary group against the structured, differentiated order, based on exogamy, of adult society. It would seem that some women prefer celibacy as shamanins to relinquishing full participant membership in their father's groups. We can only speculate because Elwin's material is thin on this point, but I suggest that Saora shamanistic beliefs are related to the universal human problem of the basic contradiction in exogamy – the primary kin group wants to *keep* its own members and at the same time to win members from other groups.

Because Elwin was preoccupied with religious custom and belief *sui generis*, he failed to collect the data that would have enabled him to make a prior analysis of the Saora social system, and this has given his book a curiously invertebrate appearance. For the same reason he has been unable to interpret adequately those items of religious custom itself which are directly linked to the social structure. For, as Simmel once wrote (1950, p. 15): 'religious behaviour does not exclusively depend on religious contexts, but it is a generally human form of behaviour which is realized under the stimulus not only of transcendental objects but of other motivations. . . . Even in its autonomy, religious life contains elements that are not specifically religious but social . . . only when (these elements) are isolated by means of the sociological method, will they show what within the whole complex of religious behaviour may legitimately be considered purely religious, that is, independent of anything social.' What kinds of data, then, do we need to collect, in order to understand the Saora rituals in their social context, and even to understand their significance for the individuals concerned with them? What I am about to say may seem elementary, indeed naïve, but the omission of the data I shall list has seriously reduced the value of many otherwise excellent compilations of ritual customs by leading modern anthropologists.

We need census surveys of several complete villages both in Ganjam and Koraput. We need information about the amounts of bridewealth paid or received at every marriage recorded, the amount of compensation paid for adultery or divorce, the number and ages of children of village members, the natal villages and villages of rearing of village members, the quarters of those villages in which they formerly resided, the village, quarter, and *birinda* affiliation of their parents, their own occupation and status, and similar situationally relevant information. We also require full genealogical data from *birinda*-heads and elders, so that we can attempt to link together all members of a *birinda* on a single genealogy. We need records of all the affinal ties interlinking different *birindas* in the same village, and the affinal ties connecting members of census villages with other villages. We should also have hut diagrams of a considerable number of villages, relating the hut-ownership pattern to our village and *birinda* genealogies. From our numerical analysis of census and genealogical data we would then be in a position to infer the effective principles determining village structure. We would then have been able to compare this analysis of 'the situation on the ground' with the ideal pattern as it is stated by Saora informants. Collaterally, we require village histories giving actual cases of succession to various kinds of political and ritual positions. From these we may infer not only the mode of succession but also whether struggles for office follow a definite pattern, so that we may ask, for example, whether the factional groupings that support the main claimants tend mainly to be their patrilineal kin, members of their village quarters, or other categories of persons. We would also like to know the class and occupational attributes of such groupings. It would be reasonable to collect data on the mode of inheritance of movable and immovable property, and on the system of land-tenure. It would be important to have case-histories of disputes over inheritance of property and rights to different categories of land, for quarrels over land are mentioned in Elwin's cases of sorcery-accusation. I consider that information of these sorts, properly analysed and succinctly presented in a couple of introductory chapters, would have enormously enhanced the value of Elwin's *ritual* data. Furthermore, if he had collected systematic information about a series of rituals performed in a single village, or in a neighbourhood cluster of villages over a period of months or even years, he might have greatly illuminated our understanding of the role of ritual in Saora group dynamics. In other words, if he had given us first a general model of Saora social structure, followed by an analysis of actual social processes in significant sectors of Hill Saora society, he would have been able to show us to what extent principles, values, norms, and interests, and the relationships they govern and establish in secular contexts, are represented in ritual, both in its social and in its symbolic aspects. He would then have been in a better position to detach from the whole complex of ritual behaviour and ideas what was 'purely religious', in Simmel's words, and 'independent of anything social'.

Systematic collection of these kinds of data, then, would have given us a firmer foundation for analysing village structure than the morsels of sociological information that Elwin interpolates in his descriptions of religious customs. But let us nevertheless try to construct a model of the Saora village from these scanty bits of information. The village, as we have seen, is divided into quarters or hamlets. The nucleus of each quarter is a *birinda*, which itself has a core of patrilineal kin and a fringe of matrilaterally attached kin, cognates, and affines. Cutting across these groupings is a division between aristocrats and commoners. In most Saora villages, there are titled political functionaries, and in Ganjam there is additionally a village priest or *Buyya*. Each of these functionaries, of whom the most important is the village chief, has his own quarter, named after his title. Elwin does not tell us whether the *birindas* of these functionaries, each member of which may call himself by the title of their head, tend to dominate their quarters or hamlets numerically. The *birindas* of political functionaries and village priests together constitute the aristocracy. It is possible that villages are spatially divided between preponderantly aristocratic and preponderantly commoner sections, each section consisting of several quarters. Each quarter also would appear to have its internal divisions between patrilineal kin and its 'honorary' members. Again, each *birinda* contains separate households, and a household may be divided between the matricentric families of a polygynous household head, or between the families of brothers who live together. Beyond these divisions there is the gradation in descending order of prestige between the three branches of Hill Saora, Jatis, Arsis, and Jadu. Members of all three branches may live in one village. Then there is the distinction in status between cultivators, both aristocratic and commoner, and occupational groups, such as basket-makers and potters. In summary, the Saora village is by no means a homogeneous, undifferentiated unit. It is governed by a number of distinct, and even discrepant principles of organization.

Professor Srinivas, in his book *Religion and Society among the Coorgs of South India*, isolates the various sub-units of Coorg society, village, caste, joint family, domestic family, and lineage, and refers to each of these in different contexts as 'the' basic unit of the Coorg social system. If he had said that each of these sub-units was 'a' basic unit, he would have resolved the discrepancy in his analysis by affirming the existence of discrepancy in social reality. For the structural principles to which he refers in some situations may come into conflict with one another, in others again may operate in isolation from one another. From the point of view of social dynamics a social system is not a harmonious configuration governed by mutually compatible and logically interrelated principles. It is rather a set of loosely integrated processes, with some patterned aspects, some persistencies of form, but controlled by discrepant principles of action expressed in rules of custom that are often situationally incompatible with one another. Similarly in Saora society, we may expect to find conflicts, under varying circumstances, between its different articulating principles: village affiliation, quarter, *birinda*, household, elementary family, social class, and occupation. Within the individual these would take the form of conflicts of loyalty to different social groups.

It is primarily in ritual that discrepancies between structural principles are overlaid or feigned not to exist. One way in which the Saora do this is by ritualizing each crucial principle in isolation from the others. Thus we find periodic rituals each of which celebrates the importance of a different principle of grouping. These rituals are performed at different periods in the annual cycle. Each of them asserts the paramountcy of a particular principle of grouping in connection with a specific set of activities and motivations. The functionaries at the periodic, prescribed rituals that celebrate these structured groupings of Saora society are not, like the shamans, 'outsiders' but 'insiders' to the groups they concern, although shamans also have a role in some of these rituals, as representatives of the most inclusive Saora community.

I have no time to do more than point up the contrast between calendrical rituals of this type, associated with the fixed structure of the Saora system, and curative rituals, associated with the re-establishment of that structure, after breaches have occurred in its critical relationships. Here is an abbreviated list of these regular rituals, the groups they typically involve, and the principal ritual officiants at each.

Most of the Harvest Festivals, which ostensibly celebrate the harvesting of different kinds of crop, involve the whole membership of the village. In that part of Saora country where the institution of village priest exists, this priest or *Buyya* presides over the ritual. His special function is to offer sacrifice for the whole village in the culminating phase of the ritual at one of the public *sadru*-shrines, which are located *outside* the village. These shrines are for the gods; shrines made within the village are for the ancestors of particular households, and for the gods worshipped in private cults.

The *Buyya* priest, who has political and jural, as well as ritual, functions, has the further task of guarding the village lands from the interference of hostile sorcerers, spirits, and gods connected with other localities of Saoraland. He is not usually invited, as the shaman is, to visit other villages to perform ritual. It would seem that his office has to do with maintaining the unity and continuity of the village. A new priest is selected by a shaman in state of trance from among the patrilineal kin of his predecessor. This mode of succession to office conforms to the general Saora pattern, and contrasts with that followed by many shamans. In the Harvest Festivals, presided over by the *Buyya* priests, the principle of the unity of the village is stressed over and above its internal divisions. The emphasis here is on the maintenance of the social order, not, as in curative ritual, on its re-establishment after breaches have occurred. But in the secular interstices of the ritual, as it were, in the intervals between sacred events, and on the margins of sacralized sites, behaviour indicative of conflict in other ranges of behaviour may be observed. To quote Elwin (p. 325): 'A father may choose this moment for the dedication of his daughter as a shamanin; sick people may decide to consult the already excited shamans for diagnosis of their maladies; the ancestors are always breaking in, and their coming affords a convenient opportunity to consult them about domestic and other matters.' Quarrels that have been situationally suppressed by ritual prescription here obtain indirect representation in the idiom of Saora ritual. Both priest and shaman uphold the order of Saora society: the one by positively affirming it, the other by redressing natural misfortune and the consequence of human error or malice. Each has a different social personality and employs different means; but both are devoted to the same ends, social peace and natural prosperity, which Saora, like most pre-industrial societies, regard as interdependent or complementary aspects of a single order. The interdependence of priest and shaman is recognized in the fact that a new priest is selected by a shaman. Again, the priest worships the same gods in their fertility-bestowing aspect that the shaman propitiates or exorcises in their punitive capacity.

Elwin gives little detailed information about ritual associated with the village-quarter, but writes that 'many ceremonies take place within the quarter for its own members who owe a special loyalty to their particular leader'.

The *birinda*, or paternal extended family, has its special ritual autonomy, for it controls certain sacrifices, as well as the ceremonial eating of food in public rituals. The *Doripur* and *Ajorapur* ceremonies, to propitiate respectively the fever-giving god of cattle graziers and the snake god who causes miscarriages, are performed only for and by members of the afflicted person's *birinda*, although I suspect that doctor-shamans initiated into the cults of these gods may also take part regardless of their *birinda* affiliation. Each *birinda* has its own hereditary funerary priests and priestesses, who succeed patrilineally; these cannot function for other *birindas*. At the great funerary rites of the *Guar*, *Karja*, and *Lajap*, at which members of several villages attend, members of the *birinda* of the dead person eat their share of the ritual food in their own homes and obtain more than strangers, who eat out in the fields and obtain less. At the actual cremation of the dead only members of the *birinda* may attend, and each *birinda* has its separate burning-grounds and separate cluster of stone memorials for its dead. But these funerary rituals interlink neighbouring villages, as well as emphasizing the value set on patriliny. For at the *Guar* ritual, which transforms a dangerous wandering shade into a reputable ancestor with a home in the

Under World, certain physical remains of patrilineal *birinda* members who have been residing with matrilateral kin or who have married out in other villages are brought back by their kin. Members of both villages perform roles in the *Guar* ritual cycle. And there is a special class of shamans and shamanins, the *Guarkumbois* (including many celibate women), who officiate at these interconnecting funerary rites.

Some occupational groups are recognized as distinct units in some rituals. For example, at *Karja* ceremonies the Kindal basket-makers ceremonially exchange mats and baskets for a share in the rice and meat of the feast.

The household, in some ritual situations, becomes the effective unit, for the rites of the threshing-floor are performed by each householder separately.

We see how, in these different kinds of rituals, the validity of certain crucial principles of organization is insisted on, outside the specific contexts in which they produce conflicts. These rituals, as it were, feign that the principles are never in conflict, and that there are no antagonisms of interest or purpose between persons and groups organized under each principle. But in social reality, there is much antagonism of principle and purpose. And it is at this point, I think, that we should reconsider the 'outsider' position of the shaman.

For the shaman, as I have said, does not represent a particular group, but, as Elwin says, 'may go wherever he is summoned (p. 131). . . . He is regarded with respect and often with affection, as a man given to the public service, a true friend in time of affliction.' Helped by his tutelary spouse, he has access to the gods, ancestors, and shades who punish the living for sinning, quarrelling, bearing grudges, and failing to remember particular gods and spirits when making invocations during ritual. These mystical agencies afflict with misfortune and illness, and the shaman cures the afflicted. Such afflictions are the common lot of mankind, and ritual directed towards their removal seems to possess in Saora culture a politically integrative function. The widest Saora community is a community of suffering; there is no Saora state with centralized administrative and military institutions. Nor are there great national rituals attended by the whole Saora people. The concept of pan-Saora unity, transcending all the divisions of the secular system, and expressed in beliefs and symbols shared by all Saora, is rather the product of innumerable, fitfully performed occasions of localized ritual, each couched in the idiom of unity through common misfortune. The shamans and shamanins maintain this widest unity, mainly because they are structurally located outside the local and kinship units of their society.

Men and women become diviner-shamans as the result of an experience that Elwin calls 'conversion'. The person who will become a diviner often dreams about a parent's tutelary who comes with a young tutelary, who may or may not be a relative of the latter, to arrange for the intended diviner to marry the spirit. At first he or she refuses and becomes very ill, sometimes to the point of madness. There exists, in fact, the implicit assumption that psychic conflict in the individual prepares him for the later task of divining into the conflicts in society. Such psychic conflict itself may be related, as we have speculated, to the social fact of exogamy. The diviner-elect wanders about the village and out into the woods dancing and singing. This may be said to represent his disaffiliation from the ordered life of village society. Dreams and illnesses of these sorts typically occur during adolescence for diviners-elect of both sexes. When the afflicted person consents to marry his tutelary, he recovers his health and poise and enters on his vocation as a diviner. He then receives additional training from accredited diviners, who are frequently his close paternal or maternal kin.

Through conversion the diviner achieves a socially recognized status as a sacred outsider. But the question remains: was he or she in any sense, social or psycho-biological, an 'outsider' before conversion? Are shamans and shamanins recruited from categories of persons who have either some inherent deficiencies or a low ascribed social status? In the first place, many, but by no means all, diviner-shamans and -shamanins possess some physical or psychical abnormality. For example, Elwin mentions a male eunuch who practised as a shamanin with a male tutelary. This tutelary had formerly been the eunuch's mother's tutelary husband, according to the diviner's account. Another shaman was born 'with a great head that caused his mother much pain'. Another was impotent, 'for all his seed was in his head', as he told Elwin. One shamanin was a leper, another said that 'because she had a child in the other world she did not think she would have one here', and yet another had lived naked from birth, doing a man's work, 'even sowing seed', among the Saora a typically masculine task. But before saying that abnormalities of these kinds mark men and women out to be shamans and shamanins, we should like to know how many abnormal people did not become diviners. For shamanism is a phenomenon of culture and society, not of bodily or psychic abnormality and socio-cultural phenomena are associated with a plurality of motivations and interests. Thus many apparently normal Saora become diviners, and it is possible that many abnormal Saora do not. Again, it looks as though social factors are involved.

Elwin has said that both male and female commoners, as well as aristocrats, can become shamans and shamanins. Village priests, on the other hand, and political functionaries are drawn exclusively from the aristocracy. But he does not tell us what is the ratio of commoner to aristocratic shamans. He writes (p. 449) that 'some shamans come from very poor homes' and mentions 'two Arsi Saora (shamans) in largely Jati villages'. One wonders whether there are significant structural differences between the domestic and *birinda* arrangements of the two social classes and also between the three different branches of the Hill Saora. For Elwin stresses (p. 52) that the aristocrats marry commoners hypergamously. He has also said that polygyny is fairly common, and we have noticed above that he mentions a village where 'every married man had at least two wives' (p. 56). The question arises, where do the Saora obtain the women to enable them to do this? By raiding other tribes? Clearly, no, for tribal warfare is forbidden by the Central Government. Alternatively, there may be a very early marriage-age for girls (and this is indeed the case), and a late marriage-age for men. But Elwin states explicitly (p. 54) that Saora boys commonly marry 'at sixteen or seventeen'. This paradox might be resolved if *male aristocrats* married early, and *male commoners* late. The village with many polygynists might be a village of Jati aristocrats. But this situation would produce numerical imbalance between the married and unmarried of both sexes in the different social classes. For example, under hypergamy, some aristocratic women might not be able to find husbands. Perhaps it is from these women that the celibate funerary shamanins are mainly recruited? It might also mean that there would be a shortage of marriageable commoner women, with corresponding male competition for them. If, in addition, commoner men married fairly late, there might well be sharp tensions between the older and the younger men who might tend to commit adultery with the older men's wives.

We have no information on these important points. Indeed, Elwin regards the 'conversion' of a shaman or shamanin as a general phenomenon of adolescence, instead of considering differences in adolescent reactions between members of different groups and sections of Saora society. It is not a universally human psychological problem but the problem of a specific social system. I have already mentioned earlier that there appears to be a conflict between patrilineal and matrilateral affiliation, and that a certain proportion of patrilineal members of each *birinda* live with their mothers' patrilineal kin. This linking-political role must impose a strain on those who perform it, and so I suggest that a significant proportion of shamans may be recruited from avunculocally resident young men, especially from those who have already a constitutional tendency to psychic abnormality.

All one can safely say is that many shamans may be recruited from groups and categories of persons whose social position debars them from obtaining political or priestly office, substantial wealth, or high secular prestige. Their only path of upward mobility may be through shamanism. As individuals, shamans of this sort may be psychobiologically normal, and may even inherit their shamanistic status patrilineally. On the other hand, some of the shamans who exhibit aberrant psychic or physical characteristics may not be structural outsiders, but may belong to office-holding classes and families. Elwin has introduced a certain amount of confusion by classing under the rubrics of 'shaman' and 'shamanin' the roles of diviner and doctor. Doctors are specialists who do not have tutelaries, and who learn the medicines and practices of particular curative rituals, such as the *Doripur* and *Ajorapur*, from other experts. I would guess, by analogy with African studies, that such doctors were formerly patients themselves in those rituals. Then, when they were successfully treated, they became doctor-adepts in a curative cult to propitiate the god who had afflicted them. Certainly, those who are believed to have been killed by a particular god are thought by Saora to 'become' that god themselves, either by becoming merged in him, or by becoming one of his assistants in afflicting the living. If curative cults do in fact exist, this would mean that cult-ties cut across other forms of affiliation and provide further links between villages and *birindas*.

There remains the problem of how shamanism is made respectable, in view of the fact that many of its exponents withdraw themselves to a considerable extent from the obligations of ordinary group life. In the first place, it is an imperative of Saora culture that the diviner-shaman has to be *coerced* by his tutelary into accepting his vocation. He affects to resist the forces that prevent him from occupying the social position that would have been his in the normal course of social maturation. Everyone believes that the diviner has had little or no choice in the matter, that he is not a diviner by free will but by mystical election. He cannot then be held personally responsible for seeking an exceptional (and indeed often lucrative) status at the expense of many of his normal secular commitments. In the second place, his fantasies of sexual intercourse with his tutelary are legitimized by the belief that he must marry the latter. The value set on marriage in secular society is upheld by the cultural stereotype of spiritual marriage. The tutelary is not an incubus or succubus, a 'demon lover', but a spouse. Yet the illicit nature of a diviner's sexual strivings is sometimes betrayed by his choice of a spirit-mate. For, as we have seen, Elwin mentions several cases of marriage to the child of a parent's tutelary, in other words, to a spiritual half-brother or half-sister. Other Saora shamans married their spiritual cross-cousins, although cross-cousin marriage is prohibited in reality. Diviners' fantasies may thus offer a legitimate outlet for incestuous wishes. They constitute further aspects of the shamanistic syndrome, i.e. compromise-formations between social norms and illicit wishes. A social factor may also be present here: for commoners may have only a few available mates and there may be a high polygyny rate among elders. This situation may encourage sexual relations between forbidden categories of kin in this group.

Several features of the behaviour of a diviner-elect during the period before conversion are consistent with the view that a diviner-shaman is outside and in a sense *opposed to* the structural arrangements of the social order. It is, I think, significant that conversion occurs on the threshold of adult life. I have found no evidence in Elwin's book that the Saora have life-crisis ritual, initiating juniors into adult tribal status. Rather it would seem that most Saora gradually attain social maturity, and that men achieve social and economic independence rather late in life – often after their fathers have died. But for the diviner-shaman there is an abrupt break between his childhood and his adult life as a ritual practitioner. His conversion and spiritual marriage is a life-crisis that sets him outside the normal life-cycle. During the limited period between childhood and divinerhood, he is culturally conditioned to behave as though he were mad. Now, madness in many societies seems to symbolize the negation of all order. In more than one African society, for example, the Nyakyusa, either the simulation of madness as ritual behaviour, or madness as a sanction against breach of ritual taboos, is a feature of several kinds of life-crisis ritual, especially of funerary ritual (Wilson, M., 1957, pp. 46–54). Funerary ritual constitutes a passage from one set of ordered relations to another. During the interim period the old order has not yet been obliterated and the new order has not yet come into being. The effect is analogous to the attempt to photograph two successive family groups on the same negative. Many events of a typical funerary ritual are concerned with the careful disengagement of past from present, and with the systematic reordering of social relations, so that the dead person is converted from a dangerous ghost into a helpful ancestor, while the relationships of the living are reorientated so as to take account of the changes in status and mutual positioning brought about by death. Madness in such a situation may represent the breakdown of a former order or the confusion of two orders. Similarly, the disordered, disorientated behaviour of the shaman-elect is the appropriate accompaniment of his transference from an ascribed position in a local sub-system of social relations to a new position where he will perform a role concerned with the maintenance of Saora tribal values transcending those of household, *birinda*, quarter, and village.

It must, however, be stated that not all diviners completely separate themselves from secular life. Some marry and have children by earthly as well as spiritual spouses. Elwin claims that there is less conflict between a person's role as diviner and as ordinary citizen than might have been expected, yet he gives examples of sharp conflict. One man, whose mother had been a shamanin, treated his shamanin wife with great brutality (pp. 169–170) and felt 'a passionate jealousy and suspicion of his wife whenever she went anywhere to fulfil her duties as a shamanin'. Another (p. 168) 'felt greatly cut off from his wife's inner life. There was always something going on; she had a range of interests into which he could not enter. She had a baby from her tutelary and a lot of her heart was wrapped up in the boy whom she saw only in dreams, but who was as real to her as any human child. Once she wandered out into the jungle and stayed there three days, living entirely on palm wine. She said that she had been with her tutelary and had enjoyed the experience.' 'No wonder,' comments Elwin, 'that some husbands regard their shamanin wives with suspicion.' The earthly wife of a shaman was asked by her husband's tutelary, speaking through his mouth, 'Tell me, will you honour me or no, or are you going to quarrel with me?' (p. 137). These cases indicate, to my mind at any rate, the existence of conflict in the role of a shaman or shamanin who is not a celibate.

To sum up both the section on shamanism and the essay as a whole: Simmel's point that 'even in its autonomy, religious life contains elements that are not specifically religious, but social' would appear to have some justification in the case of Saora shamanism. Conversion and spiritual marriage are better understood not as religious phenomena *sui generis*, but in relation to Saora social structure and to the social maturation of individuals occupying ascribed positions in that structure. It is also possible that investigators trained in psychology and psychoanalysis would have been able to throw further light on those elements of Saora shamanism that appear to be 'independent of anything social'. Only after the sociological and psychological factors influencing religious behaviour have been closely examined, is it justifiable to speak, as Elwin does, following Rudolph Otto, of a 'numinous' element in religion, of 'the recognition of something entirely different from ourselves'. Finally, I would suggest that the notion that the abnormal person and/or the structural outsider is in Saora society allocated the role of representing and maintaining the transcendental, unifying values of the widest social system, might be fruitfully tested out in other ranges of data. It might help to explain, for example, some of the phenomena of mysticism, asceticism, conversion, and holy mendicancy in the higher religions.

A. L. EPSTEIN

The Case Method in the Field of Law

FEW topics in the entire range of anthropological literature can have been so bedevilled by the problems of definition as that of primitive law. Indeed, so much of the discussion in this field has revolved around the terminological wrangles of jurists and anthropologists about the meaning of the term 'law' that it would seem at times as though the critical issues for debate were of a semantic rather than a sociological kind. Where we are dealing with so complex a social institution perhaps some argument about words is unavoidable – after all Western philosophers, theologians, and jurists have been discussing the nature of law for more than two millennia – but in the context of anthropological discourse much barren disputation could surely be avoided if the search for definition were more closely related to purpose and problem. It seems to me that much of the debate about primitive law has been reduced to fruitless verbal exchanges precisely because our concern with the topic has not been made sufficiently explicit. To take but one example: Elias (1956, pp. 31–32) has taken Evans-Pritchard (1940) to task for stating that 'in the strict sense, Nuer have no law', pointing out that they do have obligatory rules of conduct. If the implication of Evans-Pritchard's statement is that the Nuer are a lawless people, then Elias's view must command one's sympathy. Yet it is also clear from the whole of Evans-Pritchard's account that he intended to say no such thing. The argument here between lawyer and anthropologist is essentially sterile because the proponents are at cross-purposes. Each seizes on a different facet as being the distinctive criterion of law so that no common ground of discourse is established, and the road is blocked to further discussion. The dilemma here arises from the way in which the problem is posed. The question whether the Nuer or the Athabascans have law can be answered only in terms of definition, that is to say in terms of the presence or absence of certain formal criteria. If there is no consensus about these criteria the question cannot be satisfactorily answered. Many authorities, for example, have stressed the critical significance of courts in the definition of law. The presence or absence of law is thus readily measured by the presence or absence of forensic institutions. Yet anthropology is essentially a comparative discipline: it is concerned with the principles that underlie the workings of different kinds of society and different social systems. If the institution is to be taken as the point of departure for analysis, then, since not all societies possess courts, comparison is ruled out from the very beginning. If we are to work on a comparative basis and examine the phenomenon of law in the full range of human societies and cultures we have to look for universals: in short, our concern must be with process rather than form. As Elias himself has remarked (p. 31): 'Institutions may differ, processes tend to be everywhere the same.'

With what processes, then, are we concerned in the field of law? For anthropological purposes the more fruitful approach to the problem would appear to begin from the postulate that there is no human society known to us in which men do not quarrel and dispute with their fellows. Disputes are a universal feature of human social life. The central question thus becomes not do the Nuer have law, but, in any given society, in what ranges of social relationships do quarrels arise, what forms do they take, and by what means are they handled? Adopting this standpoint we may then go on to deduce a number of different aspects or facets that we may expect to find in all societies, albeit differing in form and degree, and which together in any one society make up the total complex phenomenon for which I shall henceforth reserve the broad term law (see Gluckman, 1961). This mode of proceeding has the further advantage that, in delineating the aspects of law, we are also able to map out a number of problem areas and suggest topics for further research.

Disputes in any society arise in an endless variety of ways and for a multiplicity of reasons. But underlying every dispute is a sense of grievance that arises out of an assumed or alleged breach of entitlement. This is not to say that a breach of entitlement is always necessary to spark off a quarrel; it is merely to observe that, even where a quarrel has been deliberately courted by some hostile act in the furtherance of self-interest, the tendency is for the aggressor to justify himself by pointing to the other's breach of his entitlement. It is in this sense that one may speak of the logical priority of rules in the dispute process, since every breach implies the prior existence of more-or-less well-recognized norms that set out the expectations we may have of others' behaviour. Where these rules or standards may be enforced through the powers of coercion vested in a legitimate authority, I shall speak of jural rules or rules of law (Epstein, 1966). This body of rules may be regarded as constituting the substantive law of a given community.

Grievances then erupt into quarrels whose source can be attributed by the actors to some breach of a rule or norm of conduct. The first step in redressing the situation must lie in determining whether and what norm has been infringed, and where responsibility lies. This implies in all societies the need for some form of inquisitorial procedure that will be regularly followed in certain given circumstances. In societies that have achieved a degree of centralized political control, the need will most commonly be met through the institution of courts. However, the court represents only one among a number of alternative solutions. In societies lacking forensic institutions, similar basic ends may be achieved by other procedures – divinatory seances, oaths and ordeals, song contests, moots and the like – the distinguishing features of which will be considered later.

The question of inquisitorial procedures is, of course, closely related to that of modes of redress and, indeed, both of these aspects frequently merge, as in our concept of trial. Nevertheless, two processes are involved which should be kept analytically distinct. A diviner's verdict or the findings of a coroner may be very suggestive, but redress and enforcement will have to be sought through other channels. Redress is essentially concerned with the ways in which the situation is readjusted when a breach or norm has been established: this is bound up with the nature and deployment of the system of sanctions within the society. In this context our concern is with law as an instrument of social control and its relation to other agencies working towards similar social ends.

Starting, then, from the idea of disputes, we have isolated three necessary ingredients or universal aspects of law – rules, procedures of inquiry and adjudication, and modes of redress and enforcement. There is, however, another matter that requires mention. Rules of conduct may be regarded as obligatory and binding, but it does not follow that they are invariably obeyed or remain valid for all time. They may be so ignored that they fall into desuetude; they may be amended or discarded and replaced by others. Jural procedures likewise are not automatic in their operation: they have to be initiated by acts of human will, and this may involve winning first the support of others; there is always the possibility, too, that such procedures may be abused and manipulated for personal ends. Hence discussion in this field cannot ignore the element of human aims, purposes, and values. Jurisprudence, it has been said, is a normative science: it is concerned with the realm not of the 'is' but of the 'ought', and what ought to be is determined by a community's scheme of values, including its concepts of equity and justice.

In delimiting these various aspects of law, I have at the same time been indicating a number of problem areas within the field, whose further exploration will be my main concern in the remainder of this essay. But by what methods shall we proceed? It may be expected that the approach of the jurist to the study of primitive law will reflect the biases and emphases of his own legal training, which in turn derive from the character of his national legal institutions. Thus the use of the case method, for example, is likely to be more congenial to the Anglo-American than to the Continental scholar. It is also congenial to the anthropologist. Since I have had some training in both disciplines, it is the one I shall adopt as the chief instrument of attack. In this regard I merely re-echo Hoebel when he remarks (1942, p. 966) that the study of 'primitive law, like common law, must draw its generalizations from particulars which are cases, cases, and more cases'. But what is the case method, and what kind of material does its use involve? Incidents and episodes observed by the anthropologist and recorded in his notebooks are the very stuff from which he builds up his account of the social system; but they may also be used in the ethnographic analysis itself with telling effect to illustrate a general point. One of the best-known instances of this kind in the literature is the expulsion of Namwana Guya'u from the village of his father, the Tabalu of Omarakana, which Malinowski (1926, pp. 102–105) used to illustrate what he called the conflict between mother-right and father-love in the Trobriands. But although the events are set out in some detail, the case serves Malinowski more as a literary device to lend colour to the argument, than as the unit of analysis itself. Where the case method is employed, however, the material is used not so much by way of illustration but as providing the raw data for analysis, the various strands in the skein of facts being teased out and dissected to reveal underlying principles and regularities. The kind and range of data that need to be collected will vary of course with the problem being investigated. In this essay I shall try to show the different uses to which the case method may be put and how, judiciously applied, it may help to illuminate each of the different sets of problems to which I draw attention.

RULES, CONCEPTS, AND CATEGORIES

I have mentioned how Elias, reacting against a view that would deny the existence of law in societies that lack courts, was led to formulate his own definition of law as a body of obligatory rules. Elias, himself a distinguished African lawyer, has here departed to some extent from the views of other legal authorities, yet in another respect he is merely following the biases and concerns of his profession. For the practising lawyer it is the rules of law, and the way in which these may be interpreted or manipulated, which are of primary interest. For many jurists likewise, the central task of jurisprudence appears as the analysis and systematic exposition of legal rules and precepts, and the deduction of the general principles and concepts that underlie them, and the way in which these may be built up into a logical and coherent scheme or system. There seems to be no intrinsic reason why the study of primitive law should not be approached in a similar way. But in fact this aspect of the study has aroused little theoretical enthusiasm among anthropologists, and it is noticeable that studies along these lines have usually been carried out in response to the request of a colonial administration, as in the case of Schapera's classic monograph on Tswana law and custom (1938), or else by administrative officers who had received training in anthropology, of which Howell's *Manual of Nuer Law* provides an instance.

Such studies appear to have arisen out of the felt needs expressed by colonial administrators for the proper recording of customary law. The desirability of carrying out such a task, at least in British territories, was implied to some extent in the policy of Indirect Rule, under which local tribal courts were recognized as an integral part of the territorial legal system, but the problems of applying an unwritten body of rules in rapidly changing circumstances had raised the issue more urgently. As J. P. Moffett, Local Courts Adviser to the Government of Tanganyika, put it in a foreword to Cory's book on Sukuma law and custom (1953, p. ix): '. . . one reason why the recording of customary law is so essential is to enable the courts to refer to a generally approved or an "authorized version" of the law, sanctioned by chiefs and people. Without a written record there can be no certainty in the law, nor is it wise to bring about changes in the law (the necessity of which arises with increasing frequency) without that sure knowledge of it, and of its underlying principles, which only written law can give.'

According to Allott (1953), the eventual aim of this kind of study, best exemplified perhaps in the work of Cory among the Haya (1945) and Sukuma of Tanganyika (1953), must be the production of legal textbooks that can be cited in courts. I do not wish to deny the importance of producing such manuals: at the same time it seems to me that the goal stated is unnecessarily restricted and, in any case, cannot commit the anthropologist. I would argue rather that the recording of customary law is also important as a first step towards the systematic study of tribal systems of law, and so provides the basis for further inquiry into the connexions between legal ideas, concepts, and categories and social structure and culture.

But granted the ends, what of the means? The available accounts are not always very specific on this point, sometimes merely stating that the information was gathered by attending tribal courts and from local informants. However, for his study of the Sukuma, Cory gave a good deal of attention to the question. Cory was faced with the problem of local variation in Sukuma custom, and he was led to work mainly through an assembly of expert and authoritative spokesmen: questions were put to the gathering and the matter was debated and discussed until all agreed on the answer, which was then recorded. Such a method may be valuable for the recording of statements of custom, but I must confess to some doubts as to its adequacy when discussing the finer points of law. In my own fieldwork among the Bemba, and later in the African urban courts of the Copperbelt, I found that court members could expound the points involved in a case they had just been hearing with great command and infinite patience, but they were much less at home in the discussion of hypothetical issues which I would sometimes have to put to them. This was not because they were unintelligent or lacking in legal insight and imagination, but because their mode of legal thinking was particular rather than abstract: the rules of law they expounded were not conceived as logical entities; they were rather embedded in a matrix of social relationships which alone gave them meaning. Since rules and standards have to be applied in an endless variety of circumstances, this suggests that the use of case material for the extracting of rules and principles should take priority over the use of informants. Cory did indeed use such material, but only in a limited way, and mainly as a check on his informants. The result is, I feel, that at times he has fallen into the trap against which there have been ample warnings in the literature. As Julius Lips, for example, rightly cautioned (cited in Hoebel, 1961, p. 428): 'Even a simple description of *facts* pertaining to law in a primitive tribe may, if we use our own legal terminology, cause a distortion of the legal content of primitive institutions.' Thus in his discussion of divorce, Cory sets out at length the various grounds that may be adduced to sustain a suit for divorce in a Sukuma tribal court. He also notes that certain forms of behaviour, such as the cursing of his wife by a husband or vice versa, would not constitute adequate grounds for dissolving a marriage. Such statements, it seems to me, could be quite misleading to someone with a formal legal training, but lacking intimate knowledge of an African tribal court. Thus a magistrate or High Court judge, hearing such a suit on appeal from a local tribal court, and using such a handbook, might be inclined to interpret the statement of the rules in it in terms of his own technical concept of grounds of divorce: this would imply (see Epstein, 1954a) that a marriage could only be dissolved if a proper case was made out, whereas it appears from a case cited by Cory in another context (p. 84) that a Sukuma court may grant a divorce 'without the petitioner giving any grounds for his demand'.

The view that I am putting forward that when working on the descriptive level to formulate the body of rules of law we should proceed mainly through the analysis of cases has also been adopted by Pospisil in his monograph on the law of Kapauku Papuans. The method does have disadvantages. One may have to sit through many long disputes before a case comes up involving some novel or critical point on which one is anxious to have information and, indeed, the whole period of fieldwork may pass without such issues coming up for juridical discussion. In these circumstances, of course, there is no alternative but to make the best possible use of one's informants.

What kind of data then does this use of case material involve? Since Pospisil makes considerable use of cases in his exposition of Kapauku law, it may be helpful to examine his method in some detail. His procedure is to state the rules as these emerged out of discussions with his informants, and then to show how they were applied in particular circumstances. Thus the rules about homicide in Kapauku society follow closely Nadel's concept of the social range of offences, the penalty or mode of redress depending upon the social units involved (1947, p. 501). Hence, for example, killing outside the political unit is not punishable (rule 1*c*), though a war usually results. Case 4 is reported as follows:

Place: Mogu, South Kamu Valley.
Date: June or July, 1954.
Parties:

(*a*) Defendant: Ti Jaj of Mogo
(*b*) Murdered man: Pi Meb of Obaa
(*c*) Authority: Ti Mab of Mogo

Facts: The defendant and Pi Meb had gone into the woods together. In the evening, the defendant returned alone and announced that the other man had fallen from a tree and died. However, he refused to lead the people to the place of the accident. About twenty people combed the forests and finally found the corpse bearing a deep wound in the face, apparently inflicted by a stick. Since the defendant was reluctant to bring the search party to the place, and because the body lay in a very soft terrain full of rotten leaves and moss, which could not account for the deep wound, the defendant was charged with murder.

Outcome: The defendant and the murdered man were from two different political units. To prevent war, the authority ordered blood money to be paid to the Pi people of Obaa. Close relatives of the defendant delivered 180 Km and 240 Tm to the brothers of the victim. The defendant was reprimanded for several days, but he escaped any bodily injury.

This case is used by Pospisil to illustrate one aspect of the principle of liability for homicide among Kapaukans, and it may be seen how case summaries of this kind, particularly when presented in series, may be valuable in working out a tribal *corpus juris*. At the same time, the data presented in the case raise other questions of method. The approach through the cases argues some consistency in the application of the rules from dispute to dispute. Yet even where the rules are capable of fairly precise formulation, it does not follow that the outcome of their application to a given set of circumstances can be predicted with any degree of reliability. Pospisil's cases relate to different communities and to different points of time and his summaries do not indicate the circumstances surrounding a particular dispute. The implication of Case 4, for example, where the defendants were anxious to avoid war, is that either rule 1*c* was not followed to the letter or that it stands in need of further qualification. In point of fact, few disputes centre upon the application of a single unequivocal rule, and the more usual content of a dispute is a dialogue of norm and counter-norm. Thus the process of litigation commonly involves the clarification of issues hitherto obscure, a point made repeatedly by Llewellyn and Hoebel in their now classic study of Cheyenne law, and in particular in their discussion of the Case of Wolf Lies Down (1941, pp. 127–129). If we wish to grasp the *ratio decidendi* of a case, the rule or principle that it exemplifies or embodies, then the summary should also include some reference to the arguments adduced.

The importance of this point emerges even more forcefully when we turn from consideration of the rules themselves to the search for the unifying principles that underlie the rules – the concepts and categories of tribal jurisprudence. In the Anglo-American system of law we are, of course, accustomed to distinguish between civil and criminal law, and within the civil law between tort and contract and other of the law's major branches. Within each of these, further conceptual sub-divisions are recognized. Clearly, it would be absurd to assume *a priori* that these are all universal categories. Beidelman (1961), for example, makes the point that jural classification, like classification of kin, varies with each society and has to be considered on its own terms in each case, and he presents an interesting illustration of a Kaguru local court treating what we would call an unnatural offence with a sheep as an issue of sexual trespass upon another man's property rather than of bestiality *per se*. A similar point lies at the core of Bohannan's (1957) exposition of Tiv jural concepts. Bohannan's view is that, in using the categories of our own legal system to organize the raw social data from other societies, one commits a cardinal ethnographic error. Where the Tiv are concerned the error would be that such an arrangement is not part of their way of looking at things, and hence would be false. Bohannan's general line of approach is best seen in his discussion of debt (*injo*). He points out that the Tiv word *injo* covers a wider range of phenomena and social relations than the English word 'debt' usually does, and it includes matters which to the modern lawyer would fall into the distinct categories of tort and contract.

With Bohannan's insistence on the need to avoid doing violence to indigenous concepts I am fully in sympathy and, at the descriptive level, I applaud his attempts to capture in English the full texture and scope of Tiv legal ideas. My misgivings are that the preoccupation with what is unique in Tiv culture, and the problems of translation that this poses, blind him to problems for comparative analysis. Bohannan appears to feel that he has made his point when he shows that the Tiv idea of *injo* does not fit readily into our own modern categories of tort and contract. To this one can only say that it would be very surprising if it did, for these concepts have been worked out and refined over many centuries of continuous social change and legal growth. On the other hand, if one looks back to earlier phases in the development of the Common Law, it is interesting to discover that no adequate distinction was then drawn between proprietary rights such as an action in debt and remedies for breach of contract, or for wrongs now called torts (Potter, 1943, p. 389). Bohannan himself is thus led into methodological sin because of an over-concern with cultural forms rather than universal processes. Bohannan's technique is to allow the Tiv, so far as possible, to speak for themselves, and their jural concepts are elucidated through the best possible medium – the records of cases heard before Tiv tribunals. But there is another aspect to the use of case material that should not be overlooked. Cases are also concerned with the solution of specific human problems as these arise within a given society – and this is not a static process. Novel circumstances arise which call for new solutions. Hence, as I have suggested earlier, legal ideas have continuously to be clarified and re-defined and new concepts gradually evolved in the process. The process itself is most commonly to be observed in the arguments through which a dispute is conducted. In general, Bohannan pays inadequate attention to this aspect of disputes, and it may be for this reason that when in one case he does discuss the issue explicitly, he provides a shattering instance of what may be termed Tivnocentricity. In this case, the plaintiff, a woman, had been having some trouble driving her goats to market, so she left the nanny in the care of the defendant on the understanding that he would take it to the market-place for her the following day. The woman's complaint was that the man had not done this, and had in fact sold the nanny. She sought compensation for it and for the two kids that it would have borne in the meantime. The defendant, on the other hand, argued that it was really a case of 'releasing livestock', that the nanny had died, and he was not responsible. Bohannan remarks that it would be possible to consider cases that concern 'releasing livestock' as cases of breach of contract, but adds: 'little purpose would be served by so doing, for Tiv do not have a concept "contract".' It may be noted that early English law similarly lacked the concept, and that a bench of early Common Law judges might have handled the case not very differently from the Tiv. Bohannan observes, moreover, how in presenting his case the defendant sought to change the norm involved, so that his action would seem to be in accordance with *some* norm. In this the defendant was, of course, presenting a problem that must be familiar to any bench, and if the argument was in this instance somewhat ingenuous, at least it indicated the path along which the development of legal ideas can take place. In short, what Bohannan has overlooked is that there are certain questions of a legal character that must arise in any human society: What kinds of injury are to be recognized as calling for the right to redress? How is the notion of obligation to be defined: of what kinds are they and to whom are they owed, and in what measure? What is the nature of liability, and how far shall it take account of intention, negligence, or accident? Different societies will offer different solutions to these questions, but at least by posing the problem in these terms we can go on to examine the way in which they are related to other aspects of the social system, and to note the sets of conditions under which refinements of legal doctrine occur and new concepts and categories emerge. In this task the study of cases, in which full attention is paid to the play of argument, is an essential tool. An English legal historian has remarked that in the present state of our knowledge we cannot tell how the forms of action grew up in early English law, and adds that probably we never shall. 'The plea rolls if completely analysed might tell us, but only a record of the discussions in the Inns of Court and of Serjeant's Inn would probably settle the point: such a record almost certainly does not exist' (Potter, p. 267). In the same way, without the adequate recording of tribal case material, we are bound to remain in ignorance of many of the essential features of primitive jurisprudence.

PROCEDURES OF INQUIRY AND ADJUDICATION

I began with the postulate that there is no human group known to us in which men do not have their differences of opinion and quarrels. Friction indeed appears to be an inescapable fact of social life; and not merely because of the individual's concern in promoting his own interests, but also because disputes so frequently have their sources in the arrangements and conflicting norms of society itself (Gluckman, 1955; Turner, 1957). Yet the waging of disputes, if left unchecked, is also apt to be a wasteful and disruptive activity that may obstruct the achievement of other human ends and purposes. The problem, therefore, is not to eliminate dissension and faction but to provide the means through which grievances can be legitimately aired and disputes properly conducted. One of the tasks of the anthropologist is the examination of the various solutions to this problem that have been devised in different societies, and the structural and cultural features with which they are associated.

There are really three aspects to the problem – the inquiry into guilt or responsibility for a particular event; the process of adjudication between conflicting claims; and the modes of redress and enforcement where a breach of entitlement has been established or assumed. These three aspects are closely interrelated: in any given society, therefore, the lines of distinction between them are likely to be blurred and a single procedural arrangement may well cover more than one aspect; alternatively, different procedures may be invoked depending on social context and situation. Thus among ourselves a court of law combines the functions of inquiry and adjudication, and imposes penalties or indicates the mode of redress, and only the actual enforcement is left to other agencies. In tribal communities, on the other hand, where mystical techniques are commonly employed to discover an unknown offender, the merger of functions may in some instances be even more complete. Among the Azande, for example, the *bagbuduma* magic resorted to in cases of homicide where the sorcerer is not known is 'regarded as a judge which seeks out the person who is responsible for the death, and as an executioner which slays him' (Evans-Pritchard, 1937, p. 389). Nevertheless, the importance of the analytical distinctions remains. The Azande, who practise vengeance magic, also recognize divination as a quite distinct procedure, while in English law cases of death in violent or suspicious circumstances are first made the subject of a coroner's inquest. In short, we have to deal with a range of solutions that fall along a continuum, each procedural device having its own distinctive characteristics, but also sharing to some extent the properties of others.

Divination is essentially a mode of inquiry. In some communities it appears to be a purely revelatory process, dependent on the performance of the appropriate techniques, but not otherwise subject to human control. In parts of Melanesia, for example, the procedure is to go to the cemetery after nightfall and there burn a bamboo containing hair cut from the corpse of the murdered man, together with various flowers and leaves. When the last ember is cold the specialist becomes possessed by a spirit which leads him to the house of the sorcerer. Here a tiny light is seen to be shining brightly on the roof, convincing proof that the occupant has had dealings with the spirit world (Hogbin, 1939, p. 89). Elsewhere, however, as Turner

(1961) describes for the Ndembu, the seance includes non-mystical elements, and the interpretation by the diviner of symbolic objects is combined with the interrogation of his clients. Although Turner was unfortunately not able to witness a 'live' consultation, there is a suggestion in his account that the interrogation may approximate to the process of examination in a court of law. On the other hand, divination is largely concerned, in Turner's words, with bringing into the open what is hidden or unknown, in particular with exposing the agents, human or otherwise, of misfortune and death. Divination is thus far from being simply a technical inquiry into the cause of death: a seance is more often a pointer to disturbed social relationships within the community. Indeed, for groups such as the Cewa, the diviner's attribution of misfortune to a witch or sorcerer may be the means by which a defecting group within a village justifies its decision to secede in the face of other social values that stress the importance of village unity and the maintenance of harmonious relations between kinsfolk (Marwick, 1952). The task of the diviner, and hence his technique, is not that of a judge, for he is concerned with events which take place on a mystical plane, and are not amenable to rational scrutiny. For this reason my earlier juxtaposition of the diviner and the coroner may seem at first sight rather odd. Nevertheless, if the differences between them are wide, there are also a number of interesting parallels. Like the diviner, the modern coroner may be called upon in certain circumstances to establish the cause of death. The coroner, moreover, is not necessarily required to have had a legal training, and many in fact are practising doctors: in his court the ordinary rules of evidence are waived, and the proceedings are quite informal. Finally, we may note the liberty which the coroner enjoys, of which many notoriously take advantage, to make pronouncements on the wider issues, frequently moral, raised by the case in ways which would be regarded as quite unfitting in a judge.

But not all grievances relate to what is 'hidden and unknown' and not all disputes have their sources in a crisis of moral choice (Gluckman, 1965). In many instances a man is aggrieved because he feels that he can point to a clear breach of entitlement, and claims to know or can at least guess who the offender is. Here the inquiry takes a different form: it is now more a question of establishing the degree of liability and how it should be apportioned. The appropriate procedure in these circumstances will be some form of hearing, conducted according to well-understood rules, in which the disputants submit their case for arbitrament or adjudication. The essential characteristic of this mode is that it is a contest conducted by way of argument about the norms of entitlement.

The court of law provides the most obvious instance of such a process, but it is also important to remember that adjudication may cover a range of procedures. These vary from society to society, and, even within the same society, the procedure to be adopted depending not only on the nature of the issues in dispute, but on the framework of social relationships within which the dispute arises. For purposes of cross-cultural comparison, clear analytical distinctions are essential. We need to know whether we are observing a judicial process, in which judgment follows the rational assessment of the evidence and the arguments adduced, a tribunal of arbitration, or something else, and this requires that the full conduct of the proceedings. as well as their social context, shall be made absolutely clear. This is a point that Gluckman has repeatedly emphasized, and well illustrated in his discussion of the Eskimo 'song contest' (1961b, p. 6; 1965, pp. 87, 190–191). In his book *The Law of Primitive Man*, Hoebel (1954, pp. 93–99) brings together from the literature a number of accounts of this institution. According to Hoebel, a 'song encounter' occurs when a man who feels aggrieved challenges his opponent to a contest in which they sing an exchange of taunts and gibes which have to be suffered without taking offence. Hoebel speaks of these encounters as 'juridical instruments'. And, indeed, it is apparent from a number of examples that he cites that the contest does involve a dialogue of norms. Unfortunately, the circumstances in which a contest may be held remain a little obscure. However, it cannot be without significance that all the instances he quotes are disputes over deserting wives. In a society that places great stress upon male vigour and initiative, these cases would seem to centre upon the impugning of a man's honour rather than a breach of legal entitlement as such. Again, Hoebel speaks of the contest as producing a 'judgment' in favour of one of the contestants, but there appears to be little information on the way in which points are scored or on the role of the audience in deciding between the disputants: in any case, if the issue raised is one of honour, the kind of arguments led and the ways in which they are assessed will differ from what occurs in a judicial process. Gluckman refers to the Eskimo 'song contest' at one point as a singing-duel, and this term seems more apt, suggesting on the one hand its difference from a 'legal mechanism' and, on the other, its affinities with the kind of institution described by Colson (1953) for the Plateau Tonga, where, for certain kinds of offence involving the moral values and honour of the group, clan joking partners are called in to reprimand the offender by subjecting him to public teasing and ridicule (Gluckman, ibid., pp. 87, 307).

The value of case material in elucidating the distinguishing characteristics of different modes of procedure, and the social contexts in which they are apt to be invoked, is well brought out in a short article by Beattie

(1957) on informal judicial activity in Bunyoro. In Bunyoro, as elsewhere in Africa where centralized political institutions exist, there are more or less institutionalized ways of settling interpersonal disputes below the level of the formal court system. These take the form of 'councils of natives' or 'of neighbours', for whose proceedings the term 'moot' is perhaps appropriate. The body itself consists of a group of neighbours summoned *ad hoc* to adjudicate upon the matter in issue. Membership of the group is not an office: there is no formal appointment to it, nor is it a 'standing committee' with permanent or semi-permanent membership. It only comes into existence when an aggrieved person causes it to be known that he has a dispute. When a dispute arises neighbouring householders are informed, and those who are available and interested will come along.

Beattie describes as a typical sort of case one in which two men quarrelled at a beer party. An older man, Yonasani, who was drunk, insulted a younger man, Tomasi. Tomasi wished to fight with Yonasani, but other people who were present prevented him from doing so. However, he left the party early and waited on the path leading to Yonasani's house, and when Yonasani passed he dealt him a severe blow on the head with a stick and fled, leaving him lying on the ground. The case was brought before the council of neighbours. After a brief discussion it was agreed that Tomasi had struck Yonasani and that he had done wrong to do so, for if he was aggrieved by Yonasani's behaviour he should have brought a case against him, not beaten him. He was accordingly instructed to bring four large jars of banana beer and five shillings' worth of meat to Yonasani's house. The meal was held about a week later, and went off so successfully that soon all were singing and dancing and Tomasi and Yonasani were chatting together in friendly fashion and calling each other by their *mpako* or praise-names.

As in other African kingdoms, the Banyoro also have a system of formal courts of judicature. But the Banyoro would regard it as unneighbourly to take a minor complaint such as the case of Tomasi and Yonasani to the chief's official court. The proper and seemly way of dealing with such disputes is within the neighbourhood itself so that the matter is kept within the community. Even though conventional penalties are imposed, Beattie observes that their effect is to express confidence in the man who has erred and to show that he is still accepted as a member of the local community. On the other hand, the possibility of recourse to the official courts means that these provide a constant background to disputes at the village or neighbourhood level. In the case cited, for example, when Tomasi was first taxed about the assault he denied all knowledge of it, and it was only when Yonasani declared that he intended to take the matter before the chief's court that Tomasi's father said that he and his son were agreeable to a hearing before the council of neighbours (see Hoebel's review, 1961, of Bohannan, 1957).

Beattie's analysis of this and other cases pinpoints some of the differences between the informal moot and the official court. For each operates with different aims, and to this extent their procedures also differ. Like the court, the informal tribunal may impose penalties, and the possibility that these may have a deterrent effect is acknowledged by Banyoro. But this, as Beattie notes, is secondary. The main object, where possible, is to reconcile the parties, remove the bitterness and resentment between them, and thus re-integrate the delinquent into the community. So when an offender is ordered to provide the wherewithal for a feast he himself, as Beattie's informants pointed out, consumes his share and enjoys the feast as much as the others do. By contrast, African tribal courts, though they may similarly aim at the reconciliation of the parties, may wield their power more nakedly, for the judges will be, in a sense, 'strangers' to the disputants. This power of the courts is seen in the belief that they will impose heavier penalties for an offence that would be treated with some leniency by the moot. There is also the further, and basic, difference that whereas submission to the moot is voluntary, the court has the power to compel attendance and to enforce its jurisdiction.

What I am suggesting, then, is that each mode of procedure has to be regarded as possessing its own internal structure in which the physical setting, the personnel involved, the nature of the dispute, and the character of the hearing itself are all interrelated. In terms of fieldwork this means that we must note where the hearing takes place, whether in a court-house or yard or in an open space; what persons are involved and the capacities in which they are present or serve; when and under what circumstances the body is convened; what powers it has and how far these are limited by jurisdiction, by the right of appeal, or otherwise. But the central problem here is the nature of the adjudicatory process itself: the aims which the process is designed to serve, and the means by which they are achieved. Following in the path of Llewellyn and Hoebel, Gluckman (1961b) has done most to illuminate the problem with his exposition of the role of 'the reasonable man' in Barotse jurisprudence. This is not the appropriate place for a detailed discussion of this concept, but a few of the main points relevant to the present analysis may be illustrated by reference to a case I myself recorded in one of the African Urban Courts on the Copperbelt. The case was a suit for divorce filed by the wife. Her story was briefly as follows. One day while she was pounding maize at her mother's house in the compound, her husband arrived and announced that he was on the way to the Beer Hall. He told his wife to meet him there when she had finished her task. On her way to the Beer Hall the wife met a friend who invited her into the house, and asked her to stay a little while she prepared some ground-nuts. When eventually she reached the Beer Hall she missed her husband. When they both finally returned home the husband was very angry and accused his wife of having been with a lover. They quarrelled over the matter for a number of days, and finally the wife decided to seek a divorce at the Urban Court. This statement before the court was substantiated by the husband, but he claimed that the complainant was still his wife.

From these statements made to the court the grounds for divorce would appear rather flimsy. Yet as a matter of fact the court did not concern itself overmuch with this question. Thus it did not even consider whether the husband did beat his wife as she alleged, or whether he had any grounds for believing that she was with a lover. Instead, it concentrated on the 'total' nature of the marital relationship – a relationship that in many African societies involves not only the spouses but also the close kin of the wife. After establishing that the marriage had been properly contracted, the court inquired about previous misunderstandings between the couple. The wife said that there had been trouble in the past, and once before her father had wanted to see the marriage dissolved. She then embarked upon a lengthy account of how her husband had constantly ignored her parents. When her father was ill her husband had not come to offer his sympathy; he did not greet his father-in-law with the customary salutations when the latter returned home from work; on another occasion he had refused to go into the bush to seek medicine for a sick child, and so on. Let us see how the court took up these points.

Court: Is it true that you refused to fetch medicines for a sick child?

Husband: No, I did not refuse to fetch it.

Court: But did you go and get it?

Husband: No.

Court: Do you think the relatives of your wife would have been pleased about that?

Husband: No, they were not very pleased.

Court: Yes, you see. That is where you were very foolish. And don't you know that whenever your father-in-law comes back from work in the evening you should clap before him in accordance with our Bemba custom?

Another member of the court who was of the Kaonde tribe intervened:

Member: According to the customs of the Kaonde, if I were to come to you and seek to marry your daughter, what would you say?

Husband: I would be pleased.

Member: Would you not say this son-in-law of ours will help us in all our difficulties?

Husband: Yes, I would.

Member: Well, that is exactly the point here. You should know that you made a mistake by refusing to go where your father-in-law directed you. Listen now, if your chief came and married my daughter I would be entitled to make him climb trees. [This was a reference to the Bemba custom of performing services for one's in-laws by cutting trees and making gardens for them.] There is a proverb in Bemba that a chief does not marry the daughter of a fellow chief unless he is anxious to cut trees. Now what have you to say about your wife?

The husband still claimed his wife, but she continued to insist on a divorce. As the discussion proceeded it became clear that there was no hope of reconciliation. The husband at length recognized the position, and a certificate of divorce was granted to the woman.

It will be seen here that the points on which the court concentrated had little to do with the statements initially made by the litigants. The court took the view that the complaints made by the wife in her opening remarks were only indices of a deeper rupture in the marriage relationship, and it proceeded to examine the behaviour of the husband within the total context of that relationship. But how is that behaviour to be assessed? The measuring-rod is provided by the notion of the reasonable man. As a member of society each man has a number of roles to fulfil, as husband, father, citizen, and so on. What defines these roles are the expectations we have of how those who occupy them will behave in a given set of circumstances. Thus a husband in many African societies is expected not only to care for his wife and children, but also to show due respect and courtesy to his in-laws and to help them when he can. Since ideas such as 'care' or 'respect' cannot be expressed in absolute terms, the standard set must be one of reasonable expectation, of how a husband might reasonably be expected to behave in a given context. In so far as litigants and judges share the same sets of expectations – and questions and responses make it plain that they frequently do – we can see how this concept of the 'reasonable man' provides a yardstick for measuring behaviour. But that is not all. For when the technique is successfully applied, it does not merely enable the judges to see where the fault lies, it leads the litigant to see for himself the error of his ways. Since so often he stands condemned out of his own mouth, he has little choice but to accept the judgment of the court without harbouring resentment against his opponent in the suit. Thus the way is opened to restoring amity and harmony in social relations.

Detailed analysis of case material can thus throw a great deal of light on the adjudicatory process: the form that juridical reasoning takes in different societies; the assumptions that the judges bring to their task; the way in which decisions are arrived at, and the extent to which they are acceptable to the litigants. But the method may also be used to illuminate a number of other problems, for example, the way in which courts are able to accommodate the law to changing social circumstances (Epstein, 1954b) or such questions as the relationship of law to custom or morality (Gluckman, 1961b). Thus in the case just cited we may see how custom enters into the field of legal action without losing its distinctive identity. In that instance it appears that in Bemba tribal custom the obligations to one's wife's kin are onerous, and not even a chief may always successfully evade them. But such customs are not in themselves legally enforceable. No Bemba, for example, could bring a case against his son-in-law simply because the latter had failed to greet him in the customary fashion. On the other hand, should a more serious dispute arise at a later date, such as a case of divorce, then such incidents might well be recalled and would assume significance as throwing light on the total social relationship in question.

Analyses of these kinds impose special demands on the fieldworker. Involved here are such matters as the way in which the case is presented; the modes of interrogation and examination; the kinds of evidence that may be led and the ways in which it is assessed; the often unspoken assumptions that underlie the judges' approach to their task. All of this requires much more than a summary of the facts and arguments of a case. It demands careful and detailed recording of all that passes at the hearing, including where possible the murmured *obiter dicta* of the judges, as well as the reactions of the audience. This is at the best of times a laborious and time-consuming task, and even where the fieldworker has a fair degree of fluency in the vernacular the use of idiom and metaphor and elliptic references to persons, events, or topography make it all too easy to miss vital points in the cut and thrust of argument. I do not wholly share Bohannan's view (1957, p. vii) that the only sensible gadget for doing anthropological field research is the human understanding and a notebook. Thus my objection to the use of a tape-recorder for recording cases is not so much that it introduces 'gadgetry' into fieldwork, but that under the usual conditions of field research it simply does not work, or raises more problems than it solves. I did not have a machine when I studied urban courts on the Copperbelt, where the circumstances would probably have been quite favourable, but I did experiment with one in the more conventional setting of my fieldwork on the island of Matupit, New Britain. Far from disturbing the flow of action I found on Matupit that as the disputants warmed to their task they forgot all about the presence of the machine, so that in the subsequent attempts at transcription little could be picked out above the din of altercation and mutual abuse. The procedure I have myself adopted has been to train an assistant to record the case in the vernacular as it proceeded or, where this was not possible, to prepare a text on it as soon as possible thereafter. At the same time I myself took notes of the hearing, recording passages or phrases verbatim in the vernacular. The two records were then checked against each other, discussed and clarified, and combined in a final typed record of the case. In this form the record served as a springboard to further inquiry: points that remained obscure or aspects of the case that I wished to pursue further could be taken up with different informants. It scarcely needs adding that this method may also be extremely useful in paving the way for broader ethnographic inquiry. As Oliver (1949) found on Bougainville, material on disputes can be used as a starting-point for gathering information on nearly every other subject.

REDRESS, SANCTIONS, AND SOCIAL CONTROL

In the previous section two aspects of the handling of disputes have been considered: the inquisitorial and the adjudicatory. It remains now to consider a third: the modes of redress by which entitlements are enforced, the validity of norms that have been broken are reaffirmed, and the situation created by breach readjusted. This raises at once a wider range of problems than those considered hitherto. Ideally, perhaps, adjudication and politics represent two distinct fields of action, but probably in no society does the dispute process provide an instance of their complete divorce from one another. Among ourselves, for example, the very decision to go to court may well be prompted by political considerations, and a court trial may on occasion simply provide the legal trappings for what is essentially a political contest (see Barnes, 1961b). Nevertheless, for certain purposes it is legitimate to treat the political factor as marginal: in the analysis of the judicial process, for example, we are concerned with the principles that give structure and coherence to a hearing, not why the case was brought in the first place. But when we treat of law in its aspect of social control we move more directly into the realm of politics itself. In this context our concern with the use of case material also shifts. In the earlier analysis the case was treated, so to speak, as a system in itself from the analysis of which certain regularities of a legal or forensic order could be abstracted. In the present context the case remains the unit of analysis, but in its political aspect as an index of group relationships.

In few societies is there a precise or automatic correspondence between offence and remedy. In primitive societies in particular, as we saw earlier, the reaction to a particular breach of norm is bound up very closely with the nature of the social units involved. Hence, as Gulliver (1963, p. 297) has noted, in societies that lack the organs of centralized government it is the political aspect of the dispute process, rather than the purely forensic, which is the more immediately striking – a point that also emerged very clearly in the course of my own fieldwork on the island of Matupit. There, village meetings were a regular feature of social life, and much of the business of these meetings was taken up with the hearing of cases. I have myself referred elsewhere (1954, p. 2) to the 'necessity of decision' as a primary characteristic of a court of law. The procedure for hearing cases on Matupit had much in common with what I knew of courts in Africa, so I was at first puzzled to find that many of the village meetings at which disputes over land were submitted for public arbitrament had to break up without arriving at any satisfactory resolution of the issues. The fact was that what I was observing was less a judicial hearing than part of an on-going political process. The disputants might point to the wrongs they had been done, and couch their arguments in terms of an appeal to jural norms and precedents, but it was also apparent that they were rival leaders canvassing support and recognition of their authority: such hearings provided a forum for a trial of political strength as between opposed groups and not merely for the adjudication of legal issues and a claim for redress as between individual litigants.

The treatment of disputes within a political frame of reference calls for quite a different kind of case material, and a different mode of analysis. I would argue further that, in the context of discussions of social control, the use of material on disputes that does not take full account of the political aspect is open to serious criticism. In the first place, cases become difficult to follow, often because the reported behaviour of the parties, when not related to an on-going set of relationships, appears as arbitrary and capricious. Secondly, the presence of interesting theoretical problems is obscured. I can best illustrate these points by considering some aspects of a recent study by Berndt (1962) of social control in a New Guinea Highlands society.

Berndt's account provides a superabundance of data on disputes, but he uses it almost entirely for purpose of illustration, and only to a lesser extent as an instrument of analysis. The following is a less dramatic but otherwise fairly typical example of the kind of case material he presents, and the use to which it is put. In a discussion of the 'foci of dissension' Berndt draws attention to the position of co-wives in a polygynous union. As elsewhere, the situation is one that is apt to give rise to dispute. One way in which a wife may seek to express her sense of grievance at her husband's neglect is by leaving him or blatantly engaging in extra-marital liaisons. In taking such action, Berndt points out, the wife may consider herself justified, but the husband does not, and he will proceed against her either by force or through the informal court if this is operative. He then continues (p. 144):

> Another example is the case of Mare^{c}e, originally of Kogu, who was married first to an Asafina man, Agiasa, but was abducted while working in a garden at Goritaopinti (Asafina, near Ora). Two Ora men, Takasu and his age-mate Berebi (both of the *anumpa* clan) saw her. Takasu declared 'I want this woman'. (Takasu called Agiasa *nenafu*, but this did not stop him.) They took hold of her and brought her back to Igivinti in Ora, where Takasu had already had his wife Wabaso (an *anumpa* of Ora). Wabaso resented her coming and fought with her. 'I alone am here. Why do you come to my man?' Takasu tried to make peace between them: 'I can marry her. Why do you two fight?' And Berebi added his opinion (as dominant warrior leader): 'Why do you fight? Takasu wants to marry her, he abducted her for that purpose.' Mare^{c}e pretended to be menstruating and went to the seclusion house. Rain was falling and the villagers remained indoors; Mare^{c}e ran away. Onaba (*anumpa*, who called Berebi and Takasu 'father'), from the men's house at Masagari, saw her running away. He went after her, caught her, and copulated with her. In the meantime the other two men, suspecting that she might go, looked in the seclusion hut and found it empty. They picked up their weapons and went after her. Berebi came first and saw Onaba copulating with her. 'Why do you do that?' he asked. 'She is married to another man.' Onaba replied that he had seen her running away and had consequently caught her. Berebi then improved on the situation and told Onaba to copulate again while he held him at the back. This he did, and Onaba, enjoying it, remarked, 'I am copulating properly now. My penis reaches to her anus . . . I will look after your garden and give you plenty of taro.' Takasu, however, came up and seeing them so engaged was angry. He threw Onaba to the ground and beat him with a stick, asking 'Why do you copulate with her? She is married to me.' But when Onaba managed to explain, Takasu, sorry for what he had done, said, 'She is no wife of mine. I abducted her.' They then each copulated with her. When they had finished, Berebi told her to lie down and taking up his bow shot her in the thigh. By this time others, including Takasu's first wife, had come upon the scene. Wabaso and her husband carried her back to the house, the latter first removing the arrow . . . Some time afterwards Mare^{c}e made the same excuse and went to the seculusion hut; from there she ran away to her first husband, Agiasa. Finding her gone, Takasu and Berebi, fully armed, followed her to Asafina, where they met Agiasa. Agiasa spoke to them: 'You like this woman, and you have copulated with her. She is my woman, and I want her back. I will pay you both.' Berebi and Takasu accepted the offer . . . Agiasa said, as he handed the payment over, 'You two are strong. You take this woman, and now I give you pay. In future you are not to abduct her.'

In a review of *Excess and Restraint*, Paula Brown (1963) expresses the view that some of the cases cited by Berndt may be sheer fantasy, others exaggerated in some respects, still others plain reporting, and she goes on to make the general point that in any discussion of social control it is most important to distinguish hearsay from directly observed events. It is most unlikely that the events recited in the present text could have been directly observed by the anthropologist. On the other hand, if Berndt is quoting the statements of his informants, he gives no indication of the circumstances under which they were recorded, nor does he mention whether his informants were party to the incident and in what ways they were involved, or whether they were themselves mere outside observers. Since Berndt himself does not evaluate his sources, it is difficult to know what meaning is to be given to behaviour which, on the face of it, seems so wilful and capricious. Such points apart, however, the case also reveals a number of other puzzling features. Thus we are told that Takasu called Agiasa, the injured husband, *nenafu*. This is the term for the cross-cousin relationship, and even when the male *nenafu* belong to different villages or districts the relationship is said to typify comradeship and freedom of association. Ideally, where men are concerned, it is a bond founded on mutual trust. But the term is also used in another way. A man has his own close and classificatory female *nenafu*, but there are others whom he calls by the same term by virtue of their marriage to his male *nenafu*. These last he may have sexual access to and later marry. It would seem that the abducted woman Mare^{c}e falls into this category, but Berndt says nothing on this score, nor, indeed, of the prior relations of Takasu and Agiasa.

Another curious aspect of the case is that it is the wronged husband who, visited in his home territory by the abductors of his wife, offers them payment to refrain from repeating the act. There is, of course, no *a priori* reason why such behaviour should not occur in this society: submission to bullying is not unknown elsewhere. Berndt's gloss on the case, however, is that Berebi and Takasu were not in the wrong when they abducted Mare^{c}e. Only force or what is, in effect, bribery could restrain them, and he points out that there is no legal influence to restrain this behaviour, which is simply what is expected between hostile units. But the matter is surely a good deal more complex and subtle than this. As Berndt himself shows in a later context, the seduction of a married woman in another district is likely to lead to violence when both parties have the wholehearted support of their respective units. Agiasa may have been a weak man, anxious only to get his wife back and avoid further trouble, but the question why no further action was taken has also to be considered in the context of the contemporary internal and external relations of the respective groups, including in the present instance Agiasa's affines.

Aggressiveness and male dominance are cardinal values for many of the peoples of the New Guinea Highlands, and one of the basic themes of Berndt's book is the way in which aggression in this society tends towards excess in situations of stress and excitement, and yet at the same time provides a form of social control. This is seen for example in the practice of plural copulation, which may appear simply as an enjoyable act of aggression, but may also display a punitive element. Indeed, where a woman from another district is abducted, as in the case I have quoted, and is then subjected to collective sexual violence when she attempts to run away, Berndt describes the act as a 'legal' procedure from the point of view of those performing it, on much the same basis as inter-district warfare. Yet if the two situations are indeed on the same footing the question that arises is why in the one violence appears to be given free rein, while in the context of warfare, where the tendency towards excess might also be expected, certain controls seem to operate. Warfare between different districts is frequent, but when one group secures an advantage why does it not seek to press it home and exterminate the enemy? Far from this being the case, Berndt points out, the drawing of blood, or the killing of one victim, may be enough to stop the fight. If more than three or four people are killed, there may be an outcry that the enemy 'is shooting us like wild pigs'. 'This is not fighting,' they may say. 'We are men, not pigs or animals!' But if there are such 'rules of the game' through what sanctions are they enforced? There is in the society, Berndt claims, a strongly articulated conception of 'balance' and order, simply framed in terms of reciprocity, or 'backing', and in terms of recurrent sequences. But how this 'balance' is achieved does not emerge very clearly from the evidence of the cases presented. Working among the Plateau Tonga of Zambia, who similarly lacked centralized administrative organs, Colson (1953) was able to elucidate some of the mechanisms of social control underlying the apparent anarchy of indigenous Tongan society by taking a single case of homicide, examining the varying and sometimes conflicting roles of all the relevant parties and groups, and showing how cutting across the lines of cleavage there were also links of co-operation. Berndt, by contrast, uses cases to illustrate particular kinds of violent reaction; he is thus led to ignore the possibility that a case may also represent a process of interaction between groups involved in varying and flexible sets of social relationships.

Berndt's use of the case method in this way has further disadvantages for it obscures the existence of other problems of theoretical interest. Hoebel (1954, p. 15) observes that the entire operating system of sanctioning norms is what constitutes a system of social control. Jural norms and the machinery by which they are enforced constitute an important element in the system, but these still represent only one particular kind of sanction. Here the problem is not merely to distinguish and classify the various types of sanction, but to establish the relationship between them. In what kinds of situation is a particular kind of sanction likely to be invoked and why, indeed, within the one social system are so many different kinds of redressive mechanism necessary? At the end of his book Berndt includes a list of personal names, numbering about a thousand in all, which occur in the cases he cites. But the interesting thing is that in only a handful of instances do the same names recur in different contexts. In short, there is no continuity between the cases, and the disputes are not conceived as arising within some relatively enduring framework of social relationships. This may be contrasted with Turner's concept of the 'social drama', which he developed in his analysis of the social system of the Ndembu (1957, pp. 91–93). Here, each dispute was viewed as one in a series in the context of the competition for power and prestige involving the same persons and groups, but in shifting alignments and circumstances. A large part of Turner's data consists of direct reporting but, like Berndt, he was also compelled at times to rely on the accounts of his informants. For Turner, however, it is the bias of his informants that is of central interest and importance. For the aim of the 'social drama' is not to present a supposedly objective recital of a series of events; it is concerned, rather, with the different interpretations put upon these events, and the way in which these give subtle expression to divergent interests or switches in the balance of power. By examining 'the facts' from different points of view, and discussing them with different informants, the case takes on a multidimensional aspect: the parties themselves are no longer just names, but characters in the round whose motives become intelligible not only in terms of temperament, but also in terms of the multiple roles they occupy simultaneously or at separate times. More than this, Turner's approach to and use of case material brings out how misconceived are those hypotheses of an either/or character as in attempts, for example, to correlate the incidence of sorcery with the presence or absence of 'superordinate justice' (Whiting, 1950; Hogbin, 1958, p. 112). As I have pointed out elsewhere (Epstein, 1966), formulations of this kind pose a false dichotomy. They ignore the fact that sanctions inhere in social relationships, and since, as members of society, we tend to be involved in many different sets of relationships, so we find that in most societies we are confronted with a coincidence of sanctions and modes of redress. Through the systematic and meticulous use of case material, and the careful isolation of issue and context, Turner has been able to suggest for the Ndembu in what circumstances, among a range of alternatives, a particular mode of redress is likely to be invoked. In this way, I believe, he has made an important contribution that opens up the way to furthering our understanding of social control as a dynamic process.

CONCLUSION

In his Presidential Address to the British Association on the theme of African tribal jurisprudence, Gluckman (1961b) has followed Stone and other jurists in recognizing that a term such as 'law' has many referents, and that the search for a single meaning, valid for all purposes, is quite futile. Similarly, in this essay, I have treated law as a complex social phenomenon concerned with a series of problems with which all human groups would appear to be confronted, and for which solutions must be devised. Postulating disputes as a universal feature of social life, I have sought to delimit some of the aspects of law, suggesting how each of them presents a different set of problems for anthropological investigation and research. I then tried to show how the case method, employed both as a field technique and as a tool of analysis, and applied in different ways, may serve to illuminate these problems. The discussion has concentrated on law as a body of rules, as a set of procedures of inquiry and adjudication, and as an instrument of social control. Nor does this, of course, exhaust the topic. Law may also be regarded as embodying a system of values; moreover, as a social institution it is itself subject to evaluation. We are concerned here with the basic assumptions or postulates that underlie the social life of a community, and the ways in which the task and purpose of law may be perceived. These are not easy questions to handle, yet even here the value of taking disputes as a point of departure, and examining them from the different points of view outlined in this essay, should at least be apparent. Thus the very conditions that characterize the hearing of cases contain a statement about the culture of a group that tells us at the same time something of immediate relevance about the place of law within the community. The seeming casualness of the proceedings in some African tribal courts is in marked contrast to the august atmosphere of their English counterparts. But, as Elias has pointed out (1956, p. 30), such informality does not mean that the actual situation is chaotic; rather, it reflects how closely the work of the courts is bound up in the daily lives of the people. I was present on one occasion at the court of the Bemba Paramount Chief when a schoolboy came to complain of being unfairly punished by his teacher. The court members were evidently amused at the lad's precocity, but they maintained a strict judicial gravity, summoned the teacher to appear before them, and dealt with the case in the same way as all the others. The court, in short, is conceived of as a possession of the people, a forum to which all may submit their grievances in the expectation of receiving a full and proper hearing. It is clear, again, that in the hearings themselves the statements of the litigants, the questioning of witnesses, and the deliberations of the judges not only illustrate legal ideas but also provide us with texts that embody many of the basic premises of the group, both implicit and explicit (Gluckman, 1964). But we need not stop at this point. The Bemba have a saying, *mulandu taupwa*, a case never ends. It is not so much that quarrels are never wholly resolved, but rather that cases have their sources in the ceaseless flow of social life and, in turn, contribute to that flow. For certain analytical purposes we carve a sequence of events – which we call a case – out of its matrix and dissect it. But if we are to gain a deeper understanding of the role of law in society, and its relation to justice and other social values, it is not enough to concentrate attention simply on the dispute process. We need to know a great deal more about the impact of judicial decisions, and of the ways they are communicated and received. Perhaps to this end the study of the 'case' needs finally to be reset in the framework of the on-going social process from which it was abstracted.

M. G. MARWICK

The Study of Witchcraft

THE main objective of the modern anthropological fieldworker is to discover principles governing the interaction of the members of the society he is studying. He tries to develop a model of their social behaviour that will economically summarize and account for as many as possible of the instances and episodes that he observes. In this attempt he takes note of any kinds of phenomena likely to illuminate his analysis and perfect his model. Beliefs in witchcraft and sorcery, hitherto sometimes recorded as much for their entertainment value as for their sociological importance, may have this function of contributing to his understanding of total social processes, but only if he records them in such a way that their social relevance can be fully appreciated and their value as indices of social relationships fully exploited.

In seeking material on sorcery and witchcraft that is likely to aid his general sociological analysis, the fieldworker may profitably combine methods traditionally divided between anthropology and sociology. In the early stages, his primary task is to acquire a full qualitative understanding of informants' beliefs and the extent to which these form a consistent system in the sense of being logically interrelated. At this stage he relies heavily on feeling himself as much as he can into his informants' reported experience, and, from this vantage point, on seeing the beliefs in relation to the rest of the social system he is exploring. To the extent that he is able to view them in their full context, he can appreciate the meaning they have to those who hold them and can convey this meaning to his colleagues and other persons outside the culture.

The need for the fieldworker to project himself as fully as possible into his informants' world of belief should not lead to his neglecting an equally important part of his investigations, viz., the collection of specific instances of misfortunes, including those attributed to witchcraft and sorcery. In using these quantifiable data as a check on his qualitative impressions, he is drawn more and more into the traditional realm of sociology with its concern for problems of sampling, the use of rates rather than raw frequencies, and the statistical significance of trends, associations, and differences.

The fieldworker's need to check his qualitative impressions against specific instances of misfortune of all kinds demands an understanding, not only of the realm of witchcraft and sorcery, but also of neighbouring areas of religion, magic, and taboo. This is because the principles employed by the society for explaining misfortunes are likely to have reference both to the machinations of sorcerers and witches and to the actions of ordinary people who break taboos, neglect rituals, become ritually impure or dangerous, offend the spirits of the ancestors, or fall out of harmony with the universe as a result of some public delict such as committing incest or jeopardizing the person of the chief or the fertility of the land by spilling blood. Furthermore, it may be important for the total sociological analysis being made to note which kinds of misfortune are usually attributed to witchcraft and sorcery, and which to other causes. Another reason why the investigator will have to include magic in general in his inquiries and observations is that sorcery (though not witchcraft) is best understood when regarded as a branch of magic, in particular the illegitimate sub-division of the destructive division of magic.

DEFINITIONS

To amplify the last sentence requires a systematic attempt to define terms to be used in this paper, to which I may now turn. Being clear about definitions is important because, in spite of Evans-Pritchard's pioneering work and its influence on anthropologists, there are still some terms, such as 'sorcery', which, when used by Oceanianists, have different meanings from those now widely adopted by Africanists.

In 1931, and more systematically in 1937, Evans-Pritchard, with apparently no necessary intention of standardizing terminology for the whole of Africa or for the whole of the anthropological profession, used terms such as 'witchcraft', 'sorcery', and 'magic' as the English equivalents of concepts that his Zande informants clearly distinguished from one another. Such was the clarity of Zande thought on the logical consequences of their distinctions and such was the mastery of Evans-Pritchard's presentation of the total cosmology of which Zande beliefs form a part, that many anthropologists have tried to cast their field data in what are basically Zande moulds. This has not been as incongruous as it might appear; for, even in those societies such as the Zulu (Krige, E. J., 1936), who conceive of only one kind of mystical evil-doer, or those such as the Ceŵa (Marwick, 1963), who conceive of more than one in certain contexts but lump them together in others, the logical consequences of the distinction may yet be important, and making the distinction may therefore be an aid to analysis.

According to the anthropological tradition started by Evans-Pritchard, magic is a general and morally neutral concept. It consists of (1) the use of substances and objects believed to be imbued with supernatural power, to the accompaniment of (2) verbal addresses (or 'spells' where there is an emphasis on their being word-perfect) by (3) an operator who believes that, provided his procedures have been perfectly performed, the desired result will inevitably follow. The final proviso usually implies that he should be in a state of ritual purity.

The objectives of the magician are varied. He may seek to accelerate a natural process such as the growth of a crop, or to effect a change in someone's status during an initiation ritual, or to ward off evil influences, including the magic of other operators. Firth's classification of magic as productive, protective, or destructive (1956, p. 156) is a convenient one, even if the last two categories may sometimes overlap when, for instance, a man protects his property rights with magic aimed at injuring a thief or guards his marital rights with magic aimed at killing an adulterer.

From the two examples just given it is clear that destructive magic may be applied with social approval. More often, however, destructive magic is conceived as a means by which a person, possibly because there is no way open to him of reconciling a difference, decides to settle a score arising from jealousy or hatred, without the approval of society, by using destructive magic to harm his opponent. Among Africanists, who usually follow Evans-Pritchard's definitions, this illegitimate use of destructive magic is known as 'sorcery'. Among Oceanianists the term 'sorcery' is, following precedents going as far back as Evans-Pritchard's (e.g. Malinowski, 1926, pp. 93–94; Fortune, 1932, pp. 167, 176), still used to refer to the whole realm of destructive magic and not specifically to that part of it deemed illegitimate by the members of the group concerned. However, the need, in analysing Oceanian material, for the distinction long accepted by Africanists is illustrated in the use by recent writers, such as R. M. Berndt (1962) and Meggitt (1962) of the somewhat anomalous expression 'legitimate' or 'retaliatory' sorcery in reference to the division of destructive magic that constitutes, not a public delict, but the socially sanctioned redress of a wrong. This problem of divergent definition in Africa and Oceania is complicated by the fact that, in the latter area, particularly among indigenous Australian and Melanesian peoples, the main context of destructive magic appears to be in inter-societal rather than intra-societal tensions, though I suspect that this emphasis may sometimes have arisen from too great a dependence on informants' statements and too little systematic recording of specific instances of the retrospective explanation of misfortunes (see Marwick, 1964).

The sorcerer (according to the Africanist's usage, which I shall follow in this essay) and the witch are differentiated on the score of personality type, motivation, and method, and classed together on the score of their common social condemnation. This distinction originates in Evans-Pritchard's reporting that, whereas the Azande believe witches to have aberrant personalities permanently addicted to harming others by mystical means, they look upon sorcerers as ordinary folk driven by possibly passing fits of anger or envy and employing destructive magic to attain their antisocial ends; and his summing-up of their social or moral similarity occurs in the statement, 'Both alike are enemies of men', i.e. the believed activities of both are deemed anti-social or illegitimate (Evans-Pritchard, 1937, p. 387).

PRELIMINARY INQUIRIES

As I suggested in the introduction, the methods most appropriate to the earlier phases of the study of witchcraft and sorcery are the traditional ones of social anthropology. The investigator has to establish rapport with his informants, and this he does by 'hanging around' and losing his sharpness of outline by becoming socially invisible through familiarity, as did the postman-murderer in the Chesterton story; by learning the language; by showing in word and deed that, unlike the administrator, missionary, or trader, he has come to learn and not to 'sell' (in the various modern meanings of this word); and by listening sympathetically to what people tell him. This approach, which is necessary for all aspects of his work, will acquaint him with the general nature and the usual contexts of the society's mystical beliefs, including those in witchcraft and sorcery.

The next step probably comes as a natural consequence of his steeping himself in the daily life and reported experience of the people he is studying. This is to lose his own ethnocentric resistance to the premises from which his informants make their deductions.

I had not been long among the Ceŵa before I discovered that virtually every person in the community where I was living believed in *ufiti* (a term which can be translated in Evans-Pritchard's usage as either 'sorcery' or 'witchcraft', depending on context), and that many of my acquaintances, particularly those who were educated or economically advanced, were preoccupied by intense fears of being attacked by sorcerers. When people discovered that I was interested in the practices and characteristics attributed to sorcerers and that I would neither scoff at their beliefs nor try to change them, they spoke freely to me and with a sense of relief at unburdening themselves to a sympathetic listener. It was not difficult for me, therefore, to fall into the Ceŵa habit of asking, when misfortune befell anyone (and the death rate was high), not 'What disease could he have died of?', or 'Could this accident have been avoided?', but rather 'With whom did this unfortunate person quarrel?', 'Who had a grudge against him?' or, in short, 'Who killed him by using sorcery?'

Although I remained fully aware of the unreality of these questions, this habit of asking them helped me to lose the sense of the oddity of the idiom of sorcery and brought home to me how beliefs of this kind must become credible to those who ask such questions as the result, not of scientific curiosity, but of traditional precedent and lifelong habit.

CONFIRMATION OF IMPRESSIONS

In the literature on witchcraft and sorcery there is an abundance of general statements, unsupported even by what Gluckman (1961a) calls 'apt illustrations'. To me this suggests that many fieldworkers go no farther than gaining insight into their informants' beliefs in the manner I have just described. In other words, many anthropologists have in this area of their investigations forgotten the rule that the interrogation of informants must always be supplemented by the observation of events. It is true, of course, that the 'events' informants describe are partly or wholly imaginary depending on whether people ever attempt the actions described, which is possible in a few cases of sorcery but most unlikely in any case of witchcraft.

There are nevertheless episodes involving beliefs in witchcraft and sorcery that are real enough to be observed by the ethnographer. There are, first, the steps people take to protect themselves and the wider community from the believed attacks of sorcerers and witches. These include prophylactic measures, most of them magical, used in hut-building and in bodily protection. Secondly, there are steps taken by individuals such as friends and relatives of the believed victim, or by the leaders of the community, to establish who is to be held responsible for a particular misfortune or a series of misfortunes. These steps may go no farther than gossip, or they may involve the use of oracles and ordeals and the employment of diviners and witchfinders. Thirdly, and most important for sociological analysis, there may be, associated with, or resulting from, these procedures of detection, open accusations of witchcraft or of sorcery.

The sociological importance of the last of these categories of observable events lies in the fact that it provides direct evidence of tense relationships in the society being studied. Accusations of witchcraft and sorcery may be taken as indices of social tension in the relationships in which they occur, i.e. as social strain-gauges.

RELEVANT SOCIOLOGICAL THEORY

In a specific sense, the sociology of witchcraft and sorcery dates from Evans-Pritchard's studies of the Azande. In a more general sense, in that it is an aspect of the sociology of tension and conflict, this subject has earlier origins. Since there is a variety of usage in the works that might be cited, I should make it clear that I shall follow Gluckman's practice (1955a, 1965) of reserving 'conflict' for oppositions of principle and motive that are covert, underlying, and usually inherent in social structure. For their overt manifestations I shall use 'dispute', 'rivalry', 'quarrel', etc.

Evans-Pritchard was the first to appreciate the important point that beliefs in mystical evil-doers explain the course of events by relating the occurrence of misfortune to disturbances in the moral relationships between persons. As I have shown, Evans-Pritchard, while distinguishing between witches and sorcerers on the score of personality type, classed them together on the score of their common social condemnation. His generalizations thus usually apply with equal force to either type. It is true that Middleton and Winter (1963) have attempted to explore the consequences for the sociology of witchcraft and sorcery of Evans-Pritchard's distinction; but to me their attempt is largely an academic logical exercise bearing little relation to field problems in general or even to the ethnography presented in their own book.

The first notable contributor to the sociology of tension and conflict was Simmel (1955) who, unlike the generation of sociologists who followed him, saw conflict, not simply as a pathological phenomenon to be prevented or adjusted, but rather as an essential ingredient in the balance and vitality of group life, a view which has been confirmed by the more recent work of anthropologists such as Gluckman (e.g. 1955a) and Turner (1957) and of sociologists such as Angell (1950), Bernard (1957), and Coser (1956).

An approach somewhat similar to Simmel's and one throwing light on the social processes associated with beliefs in, and accusations of, witchcraft and sorcery, is that of von Wiese (Becker, 1932). This writer specifies the conditions under which competition develops through suspicious opposition ('contravention') to actual violence or the threat of it ('conflict' – in his usage, not Gluckman's which is followed here). To von Wiese, these last two dissociative forms of interaction develop from competition that has got out of hand either because of the strength of motivation towards the scarce power, person, or resource for which the parties compete, or because of the flexibility of the situation in which their competition takes place. Hidden tension or more overt dispute and violence are most likely to develop when motivation is strong and the situation is one in which there is either the possibility of manipulation and jockeying for position or the presence of underlying, built-in conflicts of claims, duties, or loyalties. They are least likely to develop when motivation is weak or when notions of status or social distance or institutionalized avoidance or licensed familiarity prevent, check, or harmlessly discharge any tension that might arise.

The implication of these general principles for the specific instance of witchcraft and sorcery is that accusations and believed instances will tend to occur when competition for highly desired goals, such as political office, sexual favours, or property, is not kept in check by social distance, nor harmlessly played out by joking relationships, nor resolved by judicial arbitration. Sometimes conflicts (in Gluckman's sense) cannot be resolved because they are deep-lying contradictions inherent in the social structure. The position of the daughter-in-law among the Zulu is a good example (Gluckman, 1955a, pp. 98–99). Through her fecundity the lineage gathers strength; yet she is, by this very attribute, providing the means by which her husband's independent interests are extended and by which his lineage's differentiation may be hastened. Conflicts of this kind tend, according to Gluckman and Turner, to be expressed in mystical beliefs, including those in witchcraft and sorcery, which ascribe the surface disturbances associated with these deeper conflicts to the wickedness of individuals. The inherent disharmonies in the social system are thus cloaked under an insistence that there is harmony in the values of a society. Similarly, Nadel (1952) has asserted that witch beliefs enable a society to continue functioning though it is fraught with conflicts and contradictions that it is helpless to resolve.

ASSUMED HYPOTHESES IN THE LITERATURE

The sociological approach I have been detecting and developing in the last section is one of the many approaches made to the analysis of beliefs in witchcraft and sorcery; and before I deal with some of its implications for the fieldworker, I shall try to place it with other hypotheses that have been assumed by some of the anthropologists, historians, and psychologists who have written on witchcraft and sorcery.

If one examines the literature on sorcery and witchcraft, both in the history of Western society and among contemporary non-literate societies, one finds that writers appear to make, explicitly or implicitly, several types of assumption, and that they may subscribe to them singly or in combination. Such assumptions include the following:

(a) *Beliefs in witchcraft and sorcery provide outlets for repressed hostility, frustration, and anxiety:*

This assumption is a derivative of Freud's theory of the displacement of affect and is a specific variant of the general theory of magic advanced by Malinowski, who illustrated his theory by reference to 'witchcraft' performed by a 'sorcerer' (1948, p. 52). This proposition need not detain us. First, since it is concerned with the dynamics of individual behaviour, i.e. with the manner in which a human personality generates, converts, and disposes of aggression, it is a psychological theory largely irrelevant to the problems of sociological analysis. Secondly, even if it were relevant, it is not, as a scientific hypothesis should be, testable. As yet we have no satisfactory measures of frustration, of aggression, or of anxiety that could be used for establishing a relationship between these largely subjective conditions and their release or alleviation in the standardized delusions of a system of sorcery or witchcraft. In spite of this fact it has been, in whole or in part, the theoretical foundation of a number of analyses – perforce somewhat speculative – of the functions of witchcraft and sorcery, of which Kluckhohn's study of Navaho witchcraft (1944) perhaps provides the most notable example.

(b) *Beliefs in witchcraft and sorcery serve as media through which real or imagined episodes dramatize and reinforce social norms, in that antisocial or socially inadequate conduct is attributed, sometimes retrospectively, either to the accused witch or sorcerer or to his believed victim:*

This is the assumption that is best illustrated in the literature, not only on the witchcraft of simpler societies, but also on that of Europe; and it is exemplified by modern forms of witch-hunting such as McCarthy-ism. It may spring, in part at least, from people's desires to be blameless for their own misfortunes. In retrospectively explaining misfortunes, people often imply that the witches and sorcerers who are to blame are so much 'the enemies of men', or the personification of evil, that they may be detected by their having previously shown minor aberrations such as short-temperedness, meanness, or an array of delinquencies whose definition is specific to the society concerned; this leads to a trial by reputation. Or informants may imply that the victim of a believed attack was himself to blame either through having committed some act of foolishness, social inadequacy, or moral torpidity, or through having been responsible for some major delict such as adultery, in which case the revenge of the sorcerer, while still not socially sanctioned, is at least better understood as the human reaction of someone who would find formal redress of his wrong too mild a means of satisfaction. This hypothesis has some relevance to changing social situations. Those persons who may have been exposed to the values of an alien society may develop acute fears of attack by witches or sorcerers in their own society as a result of their new attitudes. For instance, there may be a conflict between their newly acquired proprietary attitude towards the fruits of paid employment and older traditional values, such as the notion of corporate ownership by a kinship group. In the same sort of situation the person who deviates, either from the traditional system of values, or from an introduced but dominant one, may be regarded not as the victim but as the perpetrator of the misfortune. For instance, in the history of English witchcraft, heretics have been identified with witches, and Christian leaders have thus been able to gain the support of a pre-Christian moral indignation against the religiously unorthodox (Hole, 1945).

(c) *Accounts that informants give of attacks by witches or sorcerers reflect their estimates of, and insight into, the incidence of social tension in their society:* This assumption seems to be implicitly made by two categories of anthropologists. First, there are those who, without indicating whether they depend on informants' statements or on recorded instances, report a general tendency for believed attacks to be between persons in particular social relationships such as between co-wives or between paternal half-brothers (father's sons) (e.g. Ashton, 1952, p. 81; Kuper, 1947, p. 175). Secondly, there are those who present tables of 'cases of witchcraft' in which the alleged evildoer, his believed victim, the relationship between them, and the nature of their quarrel may be shown (e.g. Krige, E. J. and J. D., 1953, pp. 264–267). The main implication of this assumption seems to be that informants are aware of the social tensions prevailing in their society, and are influenced by their insights when, in reference to particular misfortunes, they identify witches and sorcerers, on the one hand, and victims, on the other, by considering the quarrels that may have occurred between them or that, given their relationship, could have occurred between them. The merit of this assumption where it leads to the compilation of tables of 'cases' of witchcraft and/or sorcery is that it goes beyond a reliance on informants' general statements alone and requires a summary of – if not actual, then at least specific – instances. My experience shows that the two views may give very different results. For instance, although Ceŵa informants, in making general statements, asserted that most sorcerers were women, they gave me a series of believed instances in which the majority of the sorcerers identified were men. The disadvantage of considering relationships between the victim and his alleged attacker is that it deals with what are, by and large, imaginary events, i.e. attacks by witches and sorcerers, and thus relationships involving at least one imaginary participant. It therefore illustrates the people's own assessments of the tensions prevailing in their social structure rather than the external observer's assessments of them.

(d) *Accusations of witchcraft and sorcery are indices of tense relationships between the accuser, on the one hand, and the sorcerer or witch, on the other:*

The method called for by this assumption has the advantage of providing a direct index of tense relationships rather than an indirect one through informants' own estimates of who might have attacked the victim. Accusations are not matters of informants' beliefs but of the investigator's direct observation. Even if the ethnographer does not observe the accusation himself, he is often able to determine who made it. In either event, he then has an index of the hostility existing in a particular relationship. If he records a number of accusations, their distribution in categories of relationship gives him a picture of the incidence of tension in the society concerned. And he can go further than merely constructing a static model of the behaviour he has observed and had described to him. If he follows the extended-case-study method exemplified and recommended by Turner (1957; 1964), he can set his model in motion to represent 'the vicissitudes of given social systems over time'; and, in these, accusations will reveal, 'not only the structure of the group and sub-groups to which the accuser and accused belong, but also their extant division into transient alliances and factions on the basis of immediate interests, ambitions, moral aspirations, etc.' (1964, p. 316).

These complex developments that are punctuated by accusations may, in less sensitive hands than Turner's, prove to be beyond the grasp of the social scientist who, rather than become an historian, still looks for recurrent relationships that can be brought within the compass of a scientific theory; but the possibility of their being used in the way Turner suggests should alert the fieldworker to the great variety of situations and social contexts in which they occur.

RECORDING CASES OF MISFORTUNE

What are the practical steps an ethnographer needs to take if he is to collect data that will have a bearing on the assumptions that have been listed?

Assuming that he has gained, by the traditional method of empathic exploration, a reasonably full knowledge of the idiom of belief, of the actions witches and sorcerers are said to carry out, of the methods they are believed to use, of the ways in which they are said to acquire their craft or the material substances they are believed to use in practising it, what is his next step?

If any of the assumptions set out in the previous section are to be tested, it will be necessary for the ethnographer to use a schedule, not for collecting his case material, but for checking its completeness to ensure that from it he may abstract a standard set of variables and then compare, tabulate, and analyse these. My practice was, whenever a misfortune such as a death occurred, to ask an informant with first-hand knowledge of the person concerned to tell me about it. I recorded what he said in Ceŵa, almost verbatim, though I found I could write down his statement faster if I used a mixture of English and Ceŵa. I then went through the account he had given me and tabulated it in the columns of a specially prepared notebook, keeping one part of it for misfortunes attributed to sorcery and another part for those attributed to such categories as natural causes ('deaths of God', as the Ceŵa sometimes called them), the consequences of breaking taboos, and the actions of matrilineage spirits.

In the section of the notebook devoted to misfortunes attributed to sorcery, I cut a strip from the side of each alternate sheet and recorded the name, age, and sex of the believed victim in the first column from the left of the first page of the set of four pages so formed, in such a way that details of his case could be entered in columns extending over all four pages opposite his name. The headings of these columns included such entries as: the identification and personal details of the alleged sorcerer and his relationship to the believed victim; the name and personal details of the accuser and his relationship, not only to the victim whose cause he had espoused, but, most important, to the alleged sorcerer; the method the sorcerer was believed to have used in harming the victim; a genealogy summarizing kinship (if any) between the three main characters in the drama; the nature of the quarrel, if any, that had preceded the believed attack and/or accusation, including the object of the competition between the contestants; the grounds for suspicion of the accused; and the steps taken to identify him or in some other way to avenge the victim's misfortune. A point I omitted to record systematically, this leading to some difficulty afterwards, was the informant's opinion whether the accused person was a 'killer-for-malice' (***mphelanjilu***, 'sorcerer', in Evans-Pritchard's terminology) or a witch (***nfiti yeni-yeni***).

ANALYSIS OF DATA

After I had left the field, I transferred the information from the columns of the notebook to specially prepared cards which could be sorted quickly (by hand) according to any of the attributes or variables that have been mentioned, including a classification of social relationships into such categories as 'unrelated', 'belonging to the same matrilineage segment', 'belonging to different matrilineage segments', and so on. This permitted cross-tabulations of a large number of attributes and variables likely to be of relevance to various hypotheses that could be examined, for instance: relative age of sorcerer and victim or of accuser and sorcerer; whether sorcerer and victim, or accuser and sorcerer, or accuser and victim, belonged to the sam matrilineage segment or to different segments, or whether they were related but not matrilineally, or whether they were unrelated; the sex of the sorcerer was tabulated against the method he or she used, and this threw some light on the proposition that witches, indicated by the use of largely mystical, supernatural means, were more often women; and sorcerers, indicated by the use of more clearly magical, or even physical, means, were more often men.

The cross-tabulations made and the correlations emerging from a study of this kind made it possible to test a variety of propositions such as whether there is a tendency for accusers to be younger than those whom they accuse and for alleged sorcerers to be older than their believed victims. Objects of competition can be classified with a view to estimating the extent to which modern influences are expressed in the quarrels preceding the believed attack or the accusation. If the cases are arranged chronologically, methods of divination may show historical changes. For instance, in Central Africa, the banning of the poison ordeal seems to have resulted in a greater reliance, where sorcery is suspected, on diviners who formerly seem to have confined their activities to determining which of the lineage spirits was demanding a libation.

The chi-square test can be applied to most of these tables to ascertain the statistical significance of the associations and trends that they reveal. In a few instances, those involving continuous variation, e.g. estimated age, rather than the mere enumeration of attributes, a test for the significance of the difference between two means is more appropriate.

RATES *v.* RAW FREQUENCIES

Some of the results from an investigation of this kind have to be interpreted with caution. Let us suppose we are testing an hypothesis to the effect that, owing to the structure of the matrilineage, in particular owing to the conflict that occurs between the recognized succession rule and the claims of personal qualification for leadership, accusations of sorcery are more common between members of different segments than they are between members of the same segment.

At first sight the raw data required to test this hypothesis will be a table showing the distribution of accuser-sorcerer coincidences in various categories of relationship, summarized in such a way as to make possible a comparison of frequencies for (*a*) accusers and sorcerers belonging to the same segment and (*b*) accusers and sorcerers belonging to different segments. If (*a*) is considerably greater than (*b*) the hypothesis appears to be sustained. But such a conclusion may be the result of a premature interpretation of statistics. It is conceivable that the difference between the frequencies for the two relationship categories could be attributed, not necessarily to an inherent difference in the tension-generating potentialities of the two types of relationship, but merely to the fact that Ego has many more relatives such as matrilateral parallel cousins than he has relatives such as siblings.

Clearly, comparisons must be made between rates of occurrence rather than raw frequencies of incidence. Accusations of sorcery in each relationship category must somehow be expressed as proportions of the total amount of interaction characteristic of that category before comparisons can safely be made. The number of persons to whom Ego bears a particular relationship is but one of the bases for estimating the universe of social interaction characteristic of the relationship category concerned. Another might be the amount of time he spends with persons of that relationship; and another, the extent to which his interaction with them, as against, say, with his own siblings, is circumscribed by notions of etiquette, avoidance, or familiarity. One point seems clear: the fieldworker in a society that is kin-based should have full genealogical and demographic data about persons involved in believed instances of witchcraft and/or sorcery; for it is from these data that paradigms for estimating universes of interaction will have to be built.

SUMMARY

The main points to be remembered in assembling data for a sociology of witchcraft and sorcery are: that the investigator should become familiar with the idiom of the beliefs of the people he is studying and also with the assumptions implied or expressed by those who have made similar studies of other societies or of other periods; that he should devise some method such as the use of schedules or of a ruled notebook, for ensuring that verbatim accounts he is given of specific instances of misfortune contain uniform and therefore comparable attributes and variables; that he should not confine his attention to witchcraft and sorcery but should explore other modes of explaining misfortunes, too; and that he should collect adequate demographic and genealogical data for meeting some of the problems involved in the statistical analysis of his results.

PART THREE

APPENDIX

THE RHODES–LIVINGSTONE INSTITUTE CENSUS CARD

A(rea)………… V(illage)………… H………… Ref. N……… N…………………

Name …………………, …………………, …………………, ……………………

Inherited Name………………… Date……………… Relationship………………

Sex………… R.H.H.………E(thnic) G(roup)……… Clan………………………

F. (P., G.)…………………………E.G……………… Clan………………………

M. (M., P.)…………………………E.G……………… Clan………………………

Born, Date………… Place……………Rearing…………… Died, Date………

Spouse Name	*Rel.*	*Mar.*	*Div.*	*Death*	*Origin*
……					
……					
……					

Child Name	*Sex*	*Born*	*Died*	*Child Name*	*Sex*	*Born*	*Died*
……							
……							
……							
……							

Rank………Religion………Ex-religion………Education……… Occupation………

Rel. Vill. Headman………………… Reason Residence …………………………

Phy. Character……………………… Residence (if temp. away)……………………

Household ………………………………………………………………………………

Comments ………………………………………………………………………………

Inf…………… Obs…………… Rel…………… Date……………

REFERENCES OF WORKS CITED

ABERLE, D. F. 1951. *The Psychosocial Analysis of a Hopi Life-history.* Comparative Psychology Monographs **21** (1).

ACKERMAN, C. 1964. Structure and Statistics: The Purum Case. *American Anthropologist* **66** : 53–65.

ALLAN, W., *et al.* 1948. *Land Holding and Land Usage among the Plateau Tonga of the Mazabuka District.* Rhodes–Livingstone Paper no. 14.

ALLOTT, A. N. 1953. Methods of Legal Research into Customary Law. *Journal of African Administration* **5** : 172–177.

AMERICAN ANTHROPOLOGICAL ASSOCIATION, PUBLICATIONS POLICY COMMITTEE. 1964. *Some Foundations for Publication Policy.* Washington: American Anthropological Association.

ANGELL, R. C. 1950. *Unesco and Social Science Research.* Paris: Unesco (roneo).

ARDENER, E. 1962. *Divorce and Fertility: An African Study.* Nigerian Social and Economic Studies no. 3. London: O.U.P. for Nigerian Institute of Social and Economic Research.

ASHTON, H. 1952. *The Basuto.* London: O.U.P. for International African Institute.

BAILEY, F. G. 1957. *Caste and the Economic Frontier.* Manchester: Manchester University Press.

BANTON, M. 1956. A Technique for Tabulating the Kinship Structure of Households. *Man* : 60–62.

BARNES, J. A. 1947. The Collection of Genealogies. *Rhodes–Livingstone Journal* **5** : 48–55.

—— 1949. Measures of Divorce Frequency in Simple Societies. *Journal of the Royal Anthropological Institute* **79** : 37–62.

—— 1951. *Marriage in a Changing Society.* Rhodes–Livingstone Paper no. 20.

—— 1954. *Politics in a Changing Society.* Cape Town: O.U.P. for Rhodes–Livingstone Institute.

—— 1958. Social Anthropology in Theory and Practice: Inaugural Lecture at Sydney University. *Arts, the Proceedings of the Sydney University Arts Association,* **1** : 47–67.

—— 1960. Marriage and Residential Continuity. *American Anthropologist* **62** : 850–866.

—— 1961a. Physical and Social Kinship. *Philosophy of Science* **28** : 296–299.

—— 1961b. Law as Politically Active: an Anthropological View. In Sawer, G. (ed.), *Studies in the Sociology of Law.* Canberra: Australian National University Press.

—— 1962 African Models in the New Guinea Highlands. *Man* **62**: 5–9

—— 1963. Some Ethical Problems in Modern Fieldwork. *British Journal of Sociology* **14** : 118–134.

BARRON, O. 1961. Genealogy. In *Encyclopaedia Britannica.*

BARTON, R. F. 1949. *The Kalingas.* Chicago: University of Chicago Press.

BEATTIE, J. 1957. Informal Judicial Activity in Bunyoro. *Journal of African Administration* **9** : 188–196.

References of Works Cited

BECKER, H. 1932. *Systematic Sociology on the Basis of the Beziehungslehre* and *Gebildelehre of Leopold von Wiese*. New York: John Wiley.

BEIDELMAN, T. O. 1961. Kaguru Justice and the Concept of Legal Fictions. *Journal of African Law* **5**: 5–20.

BENHAM, F. 1948. *Economics*. 4th edn. London: Pitman.

BERNARD, J. 1957. The Sociological Study of Conflict. In International Sociological Association, *The Nature of Conflict*. Paris: Unesco, pp. 33–117.

BERNDT, R. M. 1962. *Excess and Restraint*. Chicago: Chicago University Press.

BETTISON, D. G. 1959. *Numerical Data on African Dwellers in Lusaka, Northern Rhodesia*. Rhodes–Livingstone Communication 16.

BLACKSTONE, W. 1800. *Commentaries on the Laws of England*. Book the second. 13th edn. with notes and additions by E. Christian. London: Cadell and Davies.

BOHANNAN, L. 1952. A Genealogical Charter. *Africa* **22**: 301–315.

BOHANNAN, P. J. 1954. The Migration and Expansion of the Tiv. *Africa* **24**: 2–16.

—— 1957. *Judgment and Justice among the Tiv*. London: O.U.P. for International African Institute.

BROWN, PAULA. 1963. Review of Berndt, R. M., *Excess and Restraint*. *British Journal of Sociology* **14**: 292–293.

BURKE, B. 1864. *Royal Descents and Pedigrees of Founders' Kin*. London: Harrison.

BURLING, R. 1962. Maximization Theories and the Study of Economic Anthropology. *American Anthropologist* **64**: 802–821.

—— 1964. Cognition and Componential Analysis: God's Truth or Hocus-pocus? *American Anthropologist* **66**: 20–28, 120–122.

CAHEN, A. 1932. *A Statistical Analysis of American Divorce*. New York: Columbia University Press.

CALVIN, J. 1951. *Commentary on the Book of the Prophet Isaiah*. Vol. 2. Edinburgh: Calvin Translation Society.

CANNELL, C. F. 1953. The Collection of Data by Interviewing. In Festinger, L. and Katz, P. (eds.), *Research Methods in the Behavioral Sciences*. New York: Dryden Press, pp. 327–380.

CHARLES, E. and FORDE, D. 1938. Notes on Some Population Data from a Southern Nigerian Village. *Sociological Review* **30**: 145–160.

COHEN, R. 1961. Marriage Instability among the Kanuri of Northern Nigeria. *American Anthropologist* **63**: 1231–1249.

COLSON, E. 1951. Residence and Village Stability among the Plateau Tonga. *Rhodes–Livingstone Journal* **12**: 41–67. Reprinted in Colson, E., 1962. *The Plateau Tonga of Northern Rhodesia*. Manchester: Manchester University Press.

—— 1953. Vengeance and Social Control in Plateau Tonga Society. *Africa* **22**: 199–212. Reprinted in Colson, E., 1962, *The Plateau Tonga of Northern Rhodesia*. Manchester: Manchester University Press.

—— 1958. *Marriage and the Family among the Plateau Tonga of Northern Rhodesia*. Manchester: Manchester University Press for the Rhodes–Livingstone Institute.

COLSON, E. and GLUCKMAN, M. (eds.) 1951. *Seven Tribes of British Central Africa*. London: O.U.P. for the Rhodes–Livingstone Institute.

CONKLIN, H. C. 1964. Ethnogenealogical Method. In Goodenough, W. H. (ed.), *Explorations in Cultural Anthropology*. New York: McGraw-Hill, pp. 25–55.

CORY, HANS. 1953. *Sukuma Law and Custom*. London: O.U.P. for the International African Institute.

CORY, H. and HARTNOLL, M. M. 1945. *Customary Law of the Haya Tribe*. London: Lund Humphreys for the International African Institute.

References of Works Cited

COSER, L. A. 1956. *The Functions of Social Conflict*. London: Routledge and Kegan Paul.

CULWICK, A. T. 1932. Standardization of Pedigree Charts. *Man* **32**: 272.

CULWICK, A. T. and CULWICK, G. M. 1938–1939. A Study of Population in Ulanga, Tanganyika Territory. *Sociological Review* **30**: 365–379; **31**: 25–43.

CUNNISON, I. G. 1950. *Kinship and Local Organization on the Luapula*. Rhodes–Livingstone Communication no. 5.

—— 1957. History and Genealogies in a Conquest State. *American Anthropologist* **59**: 20–31.

—— 1959. *The Luapula Peoples of Northern Rhodesia: Custom and History in Tribal Politics*. Manchester: Manchester University Press for the Rhodes–Livingstone Institute.

DALTON, G. 1961. Economic Theory and Primitive Society. *American Anthropologist* **63**: 1–23.

DAY, L. H. 1963a. Divorce in Australia. *Australian Quarterly* **35** (2): 57–66.

—— 1963b. A Note on the Measurement of Divorce with Special Reference to Australian Data. *Australian Journal of Statistics* **5**: 133–142.

DEACON, A. B. 1927. The Regulation of Marriage in Ambrym. *Journal of the Royal Anthropological Institute* **57**: 325–342.

DEAN, J. P. 1954. Participant Observation and Interviewing. In Doby, J. T., *et al.* (eds.), *An Introduction to Social Research*. Harrisburg, Pa.: Stackpole.

DEANE, P. 1949. Problems of Surveying Village Economics. *Rhodes–Livingstone Journal* **8**: 42–49.

DEVONS, E. 1956. The Role of the Myth in Politics. *The Listener*, **55**: 843–844.

DOMAT, J. 1777. *Les loix civiles dans leur ordre naturel; le droit public, et legum delectus*. Nouvelle édition. Paris: Knapen. 2 vols.

DORJAHN, V. R. 1958. Fertility, Polygyny and their Interrelations in Temne Society. *American Anthropologist* **60**: 838–860.

DRIVER, H. E. 1953. Statistics in Anthropology. *American Anthropologist* **55**: 42–59.

EGGAN, F. 1960. Lewis H. Morgan in Kinship Perspective. In Dole, G. E. and Carneiro, R. L. (eds.), *Essays in the Science of Culture in Honor of Leslie A. White*. New York: Crowell, pp. 179–201.

ELIAS, T. O. 1956. *The Nature of African Customary Law*. Manchester: Manchester University Press.

ELKIN, A. P. 1933. Totemism in North-west Australia (the Kimberley Division). *Oceania* **3**: 257–296.

—— 1953. Murngin Kinship Re-examined, and some Remarks on some Generalizations. *American Anthropologist* **55**: 412–419.

ELWIN, VERRIER. 1955. *The Religion of an Indian Tribe*. London: Cumberlege.

EPSTEIN, A. L. 1954a. Divorce Law and the Stability of Marriage among the Lunda of Kazembe. *Rhodes–Livingstone Journal* **14**: 1–19.

—— 1954b. *Juridical Techniques and the Judicial Process*. Rhodes–Livingstone Paper no. 23.

—— 1963. The Economy of Modern Matupit: Continuity and Change on the Gazelle Peninsula, New Britain. *Oceania* **33**: 182–215.

—— 1966. Sanctions. In *Encyclopaedia of the Social Sciences*. New York: Crowell–Collier.

EPSTEIN, T. S. 1962. *Economic Development and Social Change in South India*. Manchester: Manchester University Press.

—— 1965. Economic Change and Differentiation among the Tolai of New Britain. *Economic Record* **41**: 173–192.

EVANS-PRITCHARD, E. E. 1931. Sorcery and Native Opinion. *Africa* **4**: 22–55.
—— 1937. *Witchcraft, Oracles and Magic among the Azande*. Oxford: Clarendon Press.
—— 1940. *The Nuer*. Oxford: Clarendon Press.
FALLERS, L. 1957. Some Determinants of Marriage Stability in Busoga: A Reformulation of Gluckman's Hypothesis. *Africa* **27**: 106–123.
FINER, S. E. 1956. In Defence of Pressure Groups. *The Listener*, **55**: 751–752.
FIRTH, R. 1936. *We, the Tikopia*. London: Allen and Unwin.
—— 1946. *Malay Fishermen*. London: Kegan Paul.
—— 1954. Social Organization and Social Change. *Journal of the Royal Anthropological Institute* **84**: 1–20. Reprinted in Firth, 1964, *Essays on Social Organization and Values*. London: Athlone Press.
—— 1955. Some Principles of Social Organization. *Journal of the Royal Anthropological Institute* **85**: 1–18. Reprinted in Firth, 1964, *Essays on Social Organization and Values*. London: Athlone Press.
—— 1956. *Human Types*. Revised edn. London: Nelson.
—— 1957. A Note on Descent Groups in Polynesia. *Man* **57**: 4–8.
—— 1959. *Social Change in Tikopia*. London: Allen and Unwin.
FORTES, M. 1936. Ritual Festivals and Social Cohesion in the Hinterland of the Gold Coast. *American Anthropologist* **38**: 590–604.
—— 1937. Communal Fishing and Fishing Magic in the Northern Territories of the Gold Coast. *Journal of the Royal Anthropological Institute* **67**: 131–142.
—— 1943. A Note on Fertility among the Tallensi of the Gold Coast. *Sociological Review* **25**: 99-113.
—— 1945. *The Dynamics of Clanship among the Tallensi*. London: O.U.P. for the International African Institute.
—— 1949a. Time and Social Structure: An Ashanti Case Study. In Fortes, M. (ed.), *Social Structure: Studies Presented to A. R. Radcliffe-Brown*. Oxford: Clarendon Press, pp. 54–84.
—— 1949b. *The Web of Kinship among the Tallensi*. London: O.U.P. for the International African Institute.
—— 1953. The Structure of Unilineal Descent Groups. *American Anthropologist* **58**: 17–51.
——1958. Introduction. In Goody, J. (ed.), The Development Cycle in Domestic Groups. *Cambridge Papers in Social Anthropology* **1**: 1–14. London: Cambridge University Press.
—— 1959. Unpublished paper presented at seminar on non-unilinear kinship systems, 27 February, Palo Alto. Cited by kind permission.
FORTUNE, R. F. 1932. *Sorcerers of Dobu*. London: Routledge.
FREEDMAN, M. 1958. *Lineage Organization in Southeastern China*. London: Athlone Press. L.S.E. Monographs on Social Anthropology 18.
FREEMAN, J. D. 1961. On the Concept of the Kindred. *Journal of the Royal Anthropological Institute* **91**: 192–220.
—— 1964. Some Observations on Kinship and Political Authority in Samoa. *American Anthropologist* **66**: 553–563.
GARBETT, G. K. 1960. *Growth and Change in a Shona Ward*. Occasional Paper No. 1. Dept. of African Studies, Salisbury. University College of Rhodesia and Nyasaland.
—— 1965. A Note on a Recently Introduced Card System for Processing Numerical Data. *Man* **65**: 120–121.
GATES, R. R. 1946. *Human Genetics*. Vol. 1. New York: Macmillan.

References of Works Cited

GEERTZ, H. and GEERTZ, C. J. 1964. Teknonymy in Bali: Parenthood, Age-grading and Genealogical Amnesia. *Journal of the Royal Anthropological Institute* **94**: 94–108.

GIBSON, G. D. 1959. Herero Marriage. *Rhodes–Livingstone Journal* **24**: 1–37.

GIFFORD, E. W. 1926. *Clear Lake Pomo Society*. University of California Publications in American Archaeology and Ethnology **18**: 287–390.

GLUCKMAN, M. 1950. Kinship and Marriage among the Lozi of Northern Rhodesia and the Zulu of Natal. In Radcliffe-Brown, A. R. and Forde, C. D. (eds.), *African Systems of Kinship and Marriage*. London: O.U.P. for the International African Institute, pp. 166–206.

—— 1955a. *Custom and Conflict in Africa*. Oxford: Blackwell.

—— 1955b. *The Judicial Process among the Barotse of Northern Rhodesia*. Manchester: Manchester University Press for the Rhodes–Livingstone Institute.

—— 1958. *Analysis of a Social Situation in Modern Zululand*. Rhodes–Livingstone Paper no. 28. Reprinted from *Bantu Studies* (1940) and *African Studies* (1942).

—— 1961a. Ethnographic Data in British Social Anthropology. *Sociological Review* **9**: 5–17.

—— 1961b. African Jurisprudence. *Advancement of Science* **74**: 1–16.

—— 1964. Natural Justice in Africa. *Natural Law Forum* **9**: 25–44.

—— 1965. *Politics, Law and Ritual in Tribal Society*. Oxford: Blackwell.

GLUCKMAN, M. (ed.) 1964. *Closed Systems and Open Minds*. Edinburgh: Oliver and Boyd.

GOLDENWEISER, A. A. 1937. *Anthropology: An Introduction to Primitive Culture*. New York: Crofts.

GOLDMAN, I. 1937. The Kwakiutl of Vancouver Island. In Mead, M. (ed.), *Co-operation and Competition among Primitive Peoples*. New York: McGraw-Hill, pp. 180–209.

GOODE, W. J. 1962. Marital Satisfaction and Instability: a Cross-cultural Class Analysis of Divorce Rates. *International Social Science Journal* **14**: 507–526.

GOODE, W. J. and HATT, P. 1952. *Methods in Social Research*. New York: McGraw-Hill.

GOODENOUGH, W. H. 1951. *Property, Kin and Community on Truk*. New Haven: Yale University Press. Yale University Publications in Anthropology 46.

GOODFELLOW, D. M. 1939. *Principles of Economic Sociology*. London: Routledge.

GRANQVIST, H. N. 1931, 1935. Marriage Conditions in a Palestine Village. *Societas Scientiarum Fennica, Commentationes Humanarum Litterarum* **3** (8) and **6** (8).

GREY, SIR G. 1841. *Journals of Two Expeditions in North-west and Western Australia during the Years 1837, 38 and 39*. London: T. & W. Boone. 2 vols.

GULLIVER, P. H. 1955. *The Family Herds: A Study of Two Pastoral Tribes in East Africa, the Jie and Turkana*. London: Routledge and Kegan Paul.

—— 1963. *Social Control in an African Society*. London: Routledge and Kegan Paul.

HAGOOD, M. J. and PRICE, D. O. 1952. *Statistics for Sociologists*. New York: Holt, Rinehart and Winston.

HAJNAL, J. 1950a. Rates of Dissolution of Marriage in England and Wales, 1938–39. In Royal Commission on Population. Reports and selected papers of the Statistics Committee. *Papers* **2**: 178–187. London: H.M.S.O.

—— 1950b. Births, Marriages and Reproductivity, England and Wales, 1938–1941. Ibid.: 303–422.

HALE, SIR M. 1820. *The History of the Common Law of England and An Analysis of the Civil Part of the Law*. 6th edn. London: Butterworth.

HAMMOND-TOOKE, W. D. 1962. *Bhaca Society*. Cape Town: Oxford University Press.

HENRY, L. 1952. Mesure de la fréquence des divorces. *Population* **7** : 267–282.

HERSKOVITS, M. J. 1952. *Economic Anthropology*. New York: Knopf.

HOEBEL, E. A. 1942. Fundamental Legal Conceptions in Primitive Law. *Yale Law Journal* **51** : 951–966.

—— 1954. *The Law of Primitive Man*. Cambridge: Harvard University Press.

—— 1961. Three Studies in African Law. *Stanford Law Review* **13** : 418–442.

HOEBEL, E. A. and LLEWELLYN, K. 1941. *The Cheyenne Way*. Norman: University of Oklahoma Press.

HOGBIN, H. I. 1939. *Experiments in Civilization*. London: Routledge.

HOLE, CHRISTINA. 1945. *Witchcraft in England*. London: Batsford.

HOLLEMAN, J. F. 1949. *The Pattern of Hera Kinship*. Rhodes–Livingstone Pape no. 17.

HOLMBERG, A. R. 1950. *Nomads of the Long Bow: The Siriono of Eastern Bolivia* Washington, D.C. Smithsonian Institute. Publications of the Institute of Socia Anthropology 10.

HOWELL, P. P. 1954. *A Manual of Nuer Law*. London: O.U.P. for the International African Institute.

HSU, F. L. K. 1949. *Under the Ancestor's Shadow*. London: Routledge and Kegan Paul.

JACOBSON, P. H. 1949. Total Marital Dissolutions in the United States: Relative Importance of Mortality and Divorce. In Mair, G. F. (ed.), *Studies in Population* Princeton: Princeton University Press, pp. 3–16.

—— 1950. Differentials in Divorce by Duration of Marriage and Size of Family *American Sociological Review* **15** : 235–244.

—— 1959. *American Marriage and Divorce*. New York: Rinehart.

JASPAN, M. A. 1964. *From Patriliny to Matriliny: Structural Change among the Redjang of South-west Sumatra*. Ph.D. thesis, Australian National University Canberra.

KABERRY, P. 1957. Malinowski's Contribution to Fieldwork Methods and the Writing of Ethnography. In Firth, R. (ed.), *Man and Culture*. London: Routledge and Kegan Paul, pp. 71–92.

KATZ, D. 1953. Field Studies. In Festinger, L. and Katz, D. (eds.), *Research Methods in the Behavioral Sciences*. New York: Dryden Press, pp. 56–97.

KISH, L. 1953. Selection of the Sample. In Festinger, L. and Katz, D. (eds. *Research Methods in the Behavioral Sciences*. New York: Dryden Press, pp 175–239.

KLUCKHOHN, C. 1939. Theoretical Basis for an Empirical Method of Studying the Acquisition of Culture by Individuals. *Man* **89** : 1–6.

—— 1944. *Navaho Witchcraft*. Cambridge, Mass.: Papers of the Peabody Museum of American Archaeology and Ethnology 22.

KÖBBEN, A. J. 1952. New Ways of Presenting an Old Idea: The Statistical Method in Social Anthropology. *Journal of the Royal Anthropological Institute* **82** : 129–146.

KRÄMER, A. 1902. *Die Samoa-Inseln*. Erster Band: *Verfassung, Stammbaüme und Überlieferungen*. Stuttgart: Schweizerbartsche Verlagsbuchhandlung.

KRIGE, E. J. 1936. *The Social System of the Zulus*. London: Longmans Green.

KRIGE, J. D. 1947. The Social Functions of Witchcraft. *Theoria* **1** : 8–21.

References of Works Cited

KRIGE, E. J. and KRIGE, J. D. 1953. *The Realm of a Rain Queen*. London: O.U.P. for the International African Institute.

KROEBER, A. 1954. Critical Summary and Commentary. In Spencer, R. F. (ed.), *Method and Perspective in Anthropology*. Minneapolis: University of Minnesota Press, pp. 273–299.

KUCZYNSKI, R. R. 1944. Population Movements: the Contribution of Demography to Social Problems. *Rhodes–Livingstone Journal* 2: 16–34.

KUPER, HILDA. 1947. *An African Aristocracy*. London: O.U.P. for the International African Institute.

LANE, B. S. 1960. Varieties of Cross-cousin Marriage and Incest Taboos: Structure and Causality. In Dole, G. E. and Carneiro, K. L. (eds.), *Essays in the Science of Culture in Honor of Leslie A. White*. New York: Crowell, pp. 288–300.

—— 1962. Jural Authority and Affinal Exchange. *Southwestern Journal of Anthropology* **18**: 184–197.

LEACH, E. R. 1963. Comment on McEwen, Forms and Problems of Validation in Social Anthropology. *Current Anthropology* **4**: 174.

LÉVI-STRAUSS, C. 1962. *La Pensée sauvage*. Paris: Plon.

MACCOBY, E. and MACCOBY, N. 1954. The Interview: a Tool of Social Science. in Lindzey, Gardner (ed.), *Handbook of Social Psychology*. Cambridge: Addison-Wesley, pp. 449–487.

MCCULLOCH, M. 1956. *A Social Survey of the African Population of Livingstone*. Rhodes–Livingstone Paper no. 26.

MCEWEN, W. J. 1963. Forms and Problems of Validation in Social Anthropology. *Current Anthropology* **4**: 155–183.

MCLENNAN, J. F. 1896. *Studies in Ancient History*. 2nd series. London: Macmillan.

MALINOWSKI, B. 1922. *Argonauts of the Western Pacific*. London: Routledge and Kegan Paul.

—— 1926. *Crime and Custom in Savage Society*. London: Kegan Paul.

—— 1927. *Sex and Repression in Savage Society*. London: Routledge; New York: Harcourt Brace.

—— 1929. *The Sexual Life of Savages*. London: Routledge.

—— 1948. *Magic, Science and Religion and Other Essays*, ed. by Robert Redfield. Glencoe: Free Press.

MARWICK, M. G. 1948. African Witchcraft and Anxiety Load. *Theoria* **2**: 115–129.

—— 1952. The Social Context of Ceŵa Witch Beliefs. *Africa* **22**: 120–134, 215–233.

—— 1956. An Experiment in Public-opinion Polling among Preliterate People. *Africa* **26**: 149–159.

—— 1963. The Sociology of Sorcery in a Central African Tribe. *African Studies* **22**: 1–21.

—— 1964. Witchcraft as a Social Strain-Gauge. *The Australian Journal of Science* **9**: 263–268.

MEAD, M. 1937. The Arapesh of New Guinea. In Mead, M. (ed.), *Co-operation and Competition among Primitive Peoples*. New York: McGraw-Hill, pp. 20–50.

MEGGITT, M. J. 1962. *Desert People*. Sydney: Angus and Robertson.

MIDDLETON, J. 1960. *Lugbara Religion*. London: O.U.P. for the International African Institute.

MIDDLETON, J. and WINTER, E. H. (eds.). 1963. Introduction to *Witchcraft and Sorcery in East Africa*. London: Routledge and Kegan Paul, pp. 1–26.

MITCHELL, J. C. 1949a. An Estimate of Fertility in some Yao Hamlets in Liwonde District of Southern Nyasaland. *Africa* **19**: 293–308.

MITCHELL, J. C. 1949b. The Collection and Treatment of Family Budgets in Primitive Communities as a Field Problem. *Rhodes–Livingstone Journal* **8**: 50–56.

—— 1954. *African Urbanization in Ndola and Luanshya*. Rhodes-Livingstone Communication no. 6.

—— 1956. *The Yao Village*. Manchester: Manchester University Press for Rhodes–Livingstone Institute.

—— 1957. Aspects of African Marriage on the Copperbelt of Northern Rhodesia. *Rhodes–Livingstone Journal* **22**: 1–30.

—— 1960. *Tribalism and the Plural Society*. Inaugural Lecture, University College of Rhodesia and Nyasaland. London: Oxford University Press.

—— 1961. Measures of Marriage Stability. In Northern Rhodesia Council of Social Service. Marriage and the Family: Report of the Annual Conference. Lusaka: Government Printer, pp. 16–20.

—— 1963a. Marriage Stability and Social Structure in Bantu Africa. *Proceedings of the International Union for the Study of Population*. Vol. 2: 255–263.

—— 1963b. Quantitative Methods and Statistical Reasoning in Social Anthropology. *Sudan Society* **2**: 1–23.

MITCHELL, J. C. and BARNES, J. A. 1950. *The Lamba Village: A Report on a Social Survey*. Communication no. 24. School of African Studies, University of Cape Town.

MONAHAN, T. P. 1940. The Changing Probability of Divorce. *American Sociological Review* **5**: 536–545.

—— 1962. When Married Couples Part. *American Sociological Review* **27**: 625–633.

MORGAN, L. H. 1870. *Systems of Consanguinity and Affinity of the Human Family*. Washington, D.C.: Smithsonian Institute. Smithsonian Contributions to Knowledge 17 (2).

MOSER, C. A. 1958. *Survey Methods in Social Investigation*. London: Heinemann.

MULVANEY, D. J. 1955. The Australian Aborigines 1606–1929: Opinion and Fieldwork. *Historical Studies Australia and New Zealand* **8**: 131–151, 297–314.

MURDOCK, G. P. 1947. Bifurcate merging: a Test of Five Theories. *American Anthropologist* **49**: 56–68.

—— 1949. *Social Structure*. New York: Macmillan.

—— 1950. Family Stability in non-European Cultures. *Annals of the American Academy of Political and Social Science* **272**: 195–201.

—— 1951. Foreword. In Goodenough, W. H. *Property, Kin and Community on Truk* (q.v.), pp. 5–8.

MYBURGH, C. A. L. 1956. Estimating the Fertility and Mortality of African Populations from the Total Number of Children ever Born and the Number of these still Living. *Population Studies* **10**: 193–206.

NADEL, S. F. 1947. *The Nuba*. London: Oxford University Press.

—— 1951. *The Foundations of Social Anthropology*. London: Cohen and West.

—— 1952. Witchcraft in Four African Societies. *American Anthropologist* **54**: 18–29.

OLIVER, D. 1949. *Studies in the Anthropology of Bougainville, Solomon Islands*. Cambridge: Peabody Museum Papers Vol. 29.

OSGOOD, C. 1955. Ethnographical Field Techniques. In Hoebel, E. A. *et al.* (eds.), *Readings in Anthropology*. New York: McGraw-Hill, pp. 13–17.

PEI TE HURINUI. 1958. Maori Genealogies. *Journal of the Polynesian Society* **67**: 162–165.

PETERS, E. L. 1960. The Proliferation of Lineage Segments among the Bedouin of Cyrenaica. *Journal of the Royal Anthropological Institute* **90**: 29–53.

PETERS, E. L. 1963. Aspects of Rank and Status among Muslims in a Lebanese Village. In Pitt-Rivers, J. A. (ed.), *Mediterranean Countrymen*. The Hague: Mouton, pp. 159–200.

PIDDINGTON, R. O. 1956. A Note on the Validity and Significance of Polynesian Traditions. *Journal of the Polynesian Society* **65**: 200–203.

PLATT, B. S. 1962. *Tables of Representative Values of Foods Commonly used in Tropical Countries*. London: H.M.S.O.

POLLOCK, SIR F. and MAITLAND, F. W. 1898. *The History of English Law Before the Time of Edward I*. 2nd edn. Cambridge: Cambridge University Press. 2 Vols.

PONS, V. 1956. The Growth of Stanleyville and the Composition of its African Population. In Forde, D. (ed.), *Social Implications of Industrialization and Urbanization in Africa South of the Sahara*. Paris: UNESCO. pp. 229–275.

POSPISIL, L. 1958. *Kapauku Papuans and their Law*. New Haven: Yale University Publications in Anthropology 14.

POTTER, H. 1943. *Historical Introduction to English Law*. 2nd edn. London: Sweet and Maxwell.

POWELL, H. A. 1960. Competitive Leadership in Trobriand Political Organization. *Journal of the Royal Anthropological Institute* **90**: 118–145.

QUAIN, B. 1948. *Fijian Village*. Chicago: Chicago University Press.

RADCLIFFE-BROWN, A. R. 1910. Marriage and Descent in North Australia. *Man* **10**: 55–59.

—— 1930. A System of Notation for Relationships. *Man* **30**: 121–122.

—— 1930–1931. The Social Organization of Australian Tribes. *Oceania* **1**: 34–63, 206–246, 322–341, 426–456.

—— 1952. *Structure and Function in Primitive Society*. London: Cohen and West.

READ, M. 1942. Migrant Labour in Africa and its Effect on Tribal Life. *International Labour Review* **14**: 605–631.

READER, D. 1961. *The Black Man's Portion*. Cape Town: Oxford University Press.

RICHARDS, A. I. 1935. The Village Census in the Study of Culture Contact. *Africa* **8**: 20–33.

—— 1939. *Land, Labour and Diet in Northern Rhodesia*. London: O.U.P. for the International African Institute.

—— 1940. *Bemba Marriage and Present Economic Conditions*. Rhodes–Livingstone Paper no. 4.

—— 1950. Some Types of Family Structure amongst the Central Bantu. In Radcliffe-Brown, A. R. and Forde, C. D. (eds.), *African Systems of Kinship and Marriage*. London: O.U.P. for the International African Institute, pp. 207–251.

RICHARDS, A. I. and REINING, P. 1954. Report on Fertility Surveys in Buganda and Buhaya: 1952. In Lorimer, F. (ed.), *Culture and Human Fertility*. Paris: UNESCO, pp. 351–403.

RIVERS, W. H. R. 1900. A Genealogical Method of Collecting Social and Vital Statistics. *Journal of the Royal Anthropological Institute* **30**: 74–82.

—— 1904. Genealogical Tables *and* Genealogies. In Cambridge Anthropological Expedition to Torres Straits. *Reports*. Cambridge: Cambridge University Press. Vol. 5, pp. 122–128.

—— 1906. *The Todas*. London: Macmillan.

—— 1908. Genealogies. In Cambridge Anthropological Expedition to Torres Straits. *Reports*. Cambridge: Cambridge University Press. Vol. 6, pp. 64–91.

—— 1910. The Genealogical Method of Anthropological Inquiry. *Sociological Review* **3**: 1–12.

RIVERS, W. H. R. 1914. *The History of Melanesian Society*. Cambridge: Cambridge University Press. 2 vols.

ROBBINS, L. 1935. *An Essay on the Nature and Significance of Economic Science*. 2nd edn. London: Macmillan.

ROSE, F. G. 1960. *Classification of Kin, Age Structure, and Marriage: a Study in Method and a Theory of Australian Kinship*. Berlin: Akademic Verlag. Deutsche Akademie der Wissenschaften zu Berlin, Völkerkundliche Forschungen 3.

ROUND, J. H. 1895. The Etymology of 'Pedigree'. *Athenaeum* 3514 (March 2) 283–284.

—— 1930. *Family Origins and Other Studies*. London: Constable.

ROYAL ANTHROPOLOGICAL INSTITUTE. 1951. *Notes and Queries on Anthropology*. 6th edn. London: Routledge and Kegan Paul.

—— Sociological Research Committee. 1932. The Standardization of Pedigree Charts. *Man* **32**: 120–121.

SAHLINS, M. D. 1960. Political Power and the Economy in Primitive Society. In Dole, G. E. and Carneiro, R. L. (eds.), *Essays in the Science of Culture in Honor of Leslie A. White*. New York: Crowell, pp. 390–415.

SALISBURY, R. F. 1956. Unilineal Descent Groups in the New Guinea Highlands. *Man* **55**: 2–7.

—— 1962. *From Stone to Steel*. Melbourne: Melbourne University Press for the Australian National University.

SCHAPERA, I. 1938. Contact between European and Native in South Africa. In *Methods of Study of Culture Contact*. International African Institute Memorandum 15, pp. 25–37.

—— 1940. *Married Life in an African Tribe*. London: Faber.

—— 1943. *Native Land Tenure in the Bechuanaland Protectorate*. Lovedale: Lovedale Press.

—— 1947. *Migrant Labour and Tribal Life*. London: Oxford University Press.

—— 1950. Kinship and Marriage among the Tswana. In Radcliffe-Brown, A. R. and Forde, C. D. (eds.), *African Systems of Kinship and Marriage*. London: O.U.P. for the International African Institute, pp. 140–165.

—— 1955. *A Handbook of Tswana Law*. 2nd edn. London: O.U.P. for the International African Institute.

SCHNEIDER, D. M. and ROBERTS, J. M. 1957. Zuñi Kin Terms. Lincoln: University of Nebraska. *Laboratory of Anthropology. Notebook No.* 3, *Monograph* 1.

SCHWAB, W. B. 1954. An Experiment in Methodology in a West African Community. *Human Organization* **13**: 13–19.

—— 1961. Social Stratification in Gwelo. In Southall, A. (ed.), *Social Change in Modern Africa*. London: O.U.P. for the International African Institute, pp. 126–144.

SERVICE, E. R. 1960. Kinship Terminology and Evolution. *American Anthropologist* **62**: 747–763.

SHAH, A. H. and SHROPP, R. G. 1958. The Vahīvancā Bārots of Gujerat: a Caste of Genealogists and Mythographers. *Journal of American Folklore* **71**: 246–276.

SIMMEL, G. 1950. *The Sociology of Georg Simmel*. Translated and ed. by Kurt H. Wolff. Glencoe: Free Press.

—— 1955. *Conflict*, trans. by Kurt H. Wolff. Glencoe: The Free Press.

SMITH, M. G. 1956. On Segmentary Lineage Systems. *Journal of the Royal Anthropological Institute* **86**: 39–80.

SMITH, W. ROBERTSON. 1903. *Kinship and Marriage in Early Arabia*. New edn. London: Black.

SMITHSONIAN INSTITUTE. 1862. Circular in reference to the degrees of relationship among different nations. Washington, D.C.: Smithsonian Institute. *Smithsonian Miscellaneous Collections* **2** (10).

SOMMERFELT, A. 1958. *Politisk kohesjon i et statløst samfunn: Tallensienne i nordterritoriet av Gullkysten* (*Ghana*). Oslo: Brøggers. Studies honouring the centennial of universitetets etnografiske museum 1857–1957, vol. IV.) (Pp. 170–215, English summary.)

SOUTHALL, A. W. and GUTKIND, P. C. W. 1956. *Townsmen in the Making: Kampala and its Suburbs.* E. African Studies No. 9. Kampala: E. A. Institute of Social Research.

SPINDLER, G. and GOLDSCHMIDT, W. 1952. Experiment and Design in the Study of Culture Change. *Southwestern Journal of Anthropology* **8**: 68–83.

SRINIVAS, M. N. 1952. *Religion and Society among the Coorgs of South India.* Oxford: Clarendon Press.

STANNER, W. E. H. 1936. Murinbata Kinship and Totemism. *Oceania* **7**: 186–216.

—— 1960. On Aboriginal Religion. II. Sacramentalism, Rite and Myth. *Oceania* **30**: 245–278.

STEED, GITEL. 1955. Personality Formation in a Hindu Village in Gujerat. In Marriot, M. (ed.), *Village India.* Chicago: University of Chicago Press, pp. 102–144

STREIB, G. F. 1952. The Use of Survey Methods among the Navaho. *American Anthropologist* **54**: 30–40.

SWEET, C. 1895. 'Pedigree'. *Athenaeum* 3518 (March 30): 409.

TURNER, E. L. B. and TURNER, V. W. 1955. Money Economy among the Mwinilunga Ndembu: a Study of some Individual Case Budgets. *Rhodes–Livingstone Journal* **18**: 19–37.

TURNER, V. W. 1957. *Schism and Continuity in an African Society.* Manchester: Manchester University Press for the Rhodes–Livingstone Institute.

—— 1961. *Ndembu Divination: its Symbolism and Techniques.* Rhodes-Livingstone Paper no. 31.

—— 1964. Witchcraft and Sorcery: Taxonomy versus Dynamics. *Africa* **34**: 314–325.

TYLOR, E. B. 1889. On a Method of Investigating the Development of Institutions. *Journal of the Royal Anthropological Institute* **18**: 245–269.

UBEROI, J. SINGH. 1962. *The Politics of the Kula Ring.* Manchester: Manchester University Press.

UNITED NATIONS. 1959. *Handbook on Data Processing Methods.* Part 1. New York: Statistical Office of U.N., and Rome: Food and Agriculture Organization.

UNITED NATIONS. 1962. *Handbook on Data Processing Methods.* Part 2. New York: Statistical Office of U.N., and Rome: Food and Agriculture Organization.

VAN VELSEN, J. 1964. *The Politics of Kinship.* Manchester: Manchester University Press for the Rhodes–Livingstone Institute.

—— 1965. History or Nostalgia? *African Studies* **24**: 63–66.

WAGNER, A. R. 1960. *English Genealogy.* Oxford: Clarendon Press.

WALLAGE, A. F. C. and ATKINS, J. 1960. The Meaning of Kinship Terms. *American Anthropologist* **62**: 58–80.

WARNER, W. LLOYD. 1958. *A Black Civilization: a Social Study of an Australian Tribe.* Rev. edn. New York: Harper.

WATSON, W. 1958. *Tribal Cohesion in a Money Economy.* Manchester: Manchester University Press for the Rhodes–Livingstone Institute.

WHITE, C. M. N. 1959. *A Preliminary Survey of Luvale Rural Economy.* Rhodes–Livingstone Paper no. 29.

—— 1960. *An Outline of the Luvale Social and Political Organization.* Rhodes–Livingstone Paper no. 30.

WHITE FATHERS. 1954. *Bemba–English Dictionary.* Rev. edn. London: Longmans Green.

WHITING, B. 1950. *Paiute Sorcery.* New York: Viking Fund Publications in Anthropology no. 15.

WILSON, G. 1941–1942. *An Essay on the Economics of Detribalization in Northern Rhodesia.* Rhodes–Livingstone Papers 5 and 6.

WILSON, MONICA. 1951. *Good Company.* London: Oxford University Press for the International African Institute.

—— 1957. *Rituals of Kinship among the Nyakyusa.* London: O.U.P. for the International African Institute.

YALMAN, N. 1963. On the Purity of Women in the Castes of Ceylon and Malabar. *Journal of the Royal Anthropological Institute* **93**: 25–58.

YATES, F. 1960. *Sampling Methods for Censuses and Surveys.* 3rd edn. London: Charles Griffin.

YULE, G. U. and KENDALL, M. G. 1958. *An Introduction to the Theory of Statistics.* 14th edn. London: Griffin.

FURTHER SELECT FIELDWORK BIBLIOGRAPHY

1. GENERAL WORKS

BARTLETT, P. C. *et al.* (eds.) 1939. *The Study of Society: Methods and Problems.* London: Kegan Paul.

BENNETT, J. W. 1948. The Study of Cultures: a Survey of Technique and Methodology in Field Work. *American Sociological Review* **13**: 672–689.

JAHODA, MARIE *et al.* (eds.) 1951. *Research Methods in Social Relations.* New York: Dryden Press. 2 vols.

KLUCKHOHN, FLORENCE. 1940. The Participant-observer Technique in Small Communities. *American Journal of Sociology* **46**: 331–343.

LEWIS, OSCAR. 1953. Controls and Experiment in Field Work. In Kroeber, A. L. (ed.), *Anthropology Today.* Chicago: University of Chicago Press, pp. 452–475.

MADGE, J. H. 1953. *The Tools of Social Science.* London: Longmans.

MEAD, MARGARET. 1933. More Comprehensive Field Methods. *American Anthropologist* **35**: 1–15.

NADEL, S. F. 1951. Observation and Description. *The Foundations of Social Anthropology.* London: Cohen and West, pp. 35–55.

ROWE, J. H. 1953. Technical Aids in Anthropology: a Historical Study. In Kroeber, A. L. (ed.), *Anthropology Today.* Chicago: University of Chicago Press, pp. 895–940.

WILSON, G. B. and HUNTER, M. 1939. *The Study of African Society.* Rhodes-Livingstone Paper no. 2.

2. POPULAR ACCOUNTS OF LIFE IN THE FIELD

BOWEN, ELENORE S. 1954. *Return to Laughter.* London: Gollancz.

OAKES, MAUD. 1951. *Beyond the Windy Place: Life in the Guatemalan Highlands.* London: Gollancz.

3. MONOGRAPHS CONTAINING ACCOUNTS OF FIELDWORK METHODS

BERNDT, R. M. and BERNDT, C. H. 1942. A Preliminary Report of Field Work in the Ooldea Region, Western South Australia. *Oceania* **12**: 305–315.

EVANS-PRITCHARD, E. E. 1932–1933. The Zande Corporation of Witchdoctors. *Journal of the Royal Anthropological Institute* **62**: 291–336 and **63**: 63–100.

MALINOWSKI, B. 1922. *Argonauts of the Western Pacific.* London: Routledge and Kegan Paul, pp. 1–26.

—— 1935. *Coral Gardens and their Magic.* Vol. I. London: Allen and Unwin, pp. 317–340, Chap. XI. The method of fieldwork and the invisible facts of native law and economics.

MEAD, MARGARET. 1956. *New Lives for Old: Cultural Transformation – Manus, 1928–1953.* London: Gollancz, pp. 481–501, Appendix I: Methods used in this study.

QUAIN, B. 1948. *Fijian Village.* Chicago: University of Chicago Press, pp. 1–11.

4. INTERVIEWING AND THE USE OF INFORMANTS

BECKER, H. S. 1954. A Note on Interviewing Tactics. *Human Organization* **12**: 31–32.

CAMPBELL, D. 1955. The Informant in Quantitative Research. *American Journal of Sociology* **60**: 339–342.

PAUL, B. D. 1953. Interview Techniques and Field Relationships. In Kroeber, A. L. (ed.), *Anthropology Today*. Chicago: University of Chicago Press, pp. 430–451 (Bibliography).

5. LANGUAGE

BLOOMFIELD, L. 1942. *Outline Guide for the Practical Study of Foreign Languages.* Baltimore, Md.; Linguistic Society of America.

CAPELL, A. 1940. Language Study for New Guinea Students. *Oceania* **11**: 40–74. as *Oceania monograph* 5.

—— 1945. Methods and Materials for Recording Australian Languages. *Oceania* **16**: 144–176.

—— 1952. Methods and Materials for Recording Papuan and New Guinea Languages. Port Moresby; Territory of Papua and New Guinea, Department of Education, viii, 67 pp. *Official Research Publication* no. 2.

ELKIN, A. P. 1941. Native Languages and the Fieldworker in Australia. *American Anthropologist* **43**: 89–94.

HENRY, J. 1940. A Method for Learning to Talk Primitive Languages. *American Anthropologist* **47**: 635–641.

LOWIE, R. H. 1940. Native Languages as Ethnographic Tools. *American Anthropologist* **42**: 81–89.

MEAD, MARGARET. 1939. Native Languages as Fieldwork Tools. *American Anthropologist* **41**: 189–206.

NIDA, E. A. 1947. Field Techniques in Descriptive Linguistics. *Int. J. Amer. Linguistics* **13**: 138–146.

—— 1949. *Morphology*. 2nd edn. Ann Arbor; University of Michigan Press. Chap. 7: Field procedures, pp. 175–190.

—— 1950. *Learning a Foreign Language*. New York: Committee on Missionary Personnel of the Foreign Missions Conference of North America.

PIKE, K. L. 1947. *Phonemics: a Technique for Reducing Languages to Writing*. Ann Arbor: University of Michigan Press. Part I: Analysis and production of phonetic units, pp. 3–56.

VOEGELIN, C. F. and VOEGELIN, F. M. 1959. Guide for Transcribing Unwritten Languages in the Field. *Anthropological Linguistics* **1** (6): 1–28.

WARD, IDA CAROLINE. 1937. Practical Suggestions for the Learning of an African Language in the Field. London: Oxford University Press. *Memor. Int. Inst. Afr. Lang.* **14**.

WESTERMANN, D. and WARD, I. C. 1933. *Practical Phonetics for Students of African Languages*. 2nd edn., 1949. London: Oxford University Press.

WURM, S. A. (forthcoming). *How to Record New Guinea Languages: a Manual.* Canberra: Australian National University.

Further Select Fieldwork Bibliography

6. LIFE HISTORIES

DOLLARD, JOHN. 1935. *Criteria for the Life History*. New Haven: Yale University Press.

DU BOIS, C. A. 1944. *The People of Alor*. Minneapolis, Minn.: University of Minnesota Press, pp. 191–551. Part 3, Autobiographies.

GOTTSCHALK, L. R. *et al.* 1945. The Use of Personal Documents in History, Anthropology and Sociology. *Social Science Research Council Bulletin* no. 53.

PERHAM, M. F. (ed.) 1936. *Ten Africans*. London: Faber and Faber.

SMITH, M. F. 1954. *Baba of Karo: a Woman of the Muslim Hausa*. London: Faber and Faber.

TALAYESVA, D. C. 1942. *Sun Chief: the Autobiography of a Hopi Indian*. Simmons, L. W. (ed.).

7. ECONOMICS

ALLAN, W. 1949. *Studies in African Land Usage*. Rhodes–Livingstone Paper no. 15.

8. PSYCHOLOGICAL INQUIRIES

HENRY, J. and SPIRO, M. 1953. Psychological Techniques: Projective Tests in Fieldwork. In Kroeber, A. L. (ed.), *Anthropology Today*. Chicago: University of Chicago Press, pp. 417–429 (bibliography).

NADEL, S. F. 1939. The Application of Intelligence Tests in the Anthropological Field. In Bartlett, F. C. *et al.* (eds.), *The Study of Society*. London: Kegan Paul, Trench, Trubner, pp. 184–198.

4. LIFE HISTORIES

DOLLARD, JOHN. 1935. Criteria for the Life History. New Haven: Yale University Press.

DU BOIS, C. 1944. The People of Alor. Minneapolis: University of Minnesota Press, pp. 191–548 Part 3 'Autobiographies'.

GOTTSCHALK, L. et al. 1945. The Use of Personal Documents in History, Anthropology and Sociology. Social Science Research Council, Bulletin no. 53.

PERHAM, M. F. (ed.) 1936. Ten Africans. London: Faber and Faber.

SMITH, M. F. 1954. Baba of Karo, a Woman of the Muslim Hausa. London: Faber and Faber.

TALAYESVA, DON C. 1942. Sun Chief, the Autobiography of a Hopi Indian. SIMMONS, L. W. (ed.).

7. ECONOMICS

ALLAN, W. 1949. Studies in African Land Usage. Rhodes-Livingstone Paper no. 15.

8. PSYCHOLOGICAL ENQUIRIES

HENRY, J. and SPIRO, M. 1953. Psychological Techniques: Projective Tests in Field Work. In Kroeber, A. L. (ed.), Anthropology Today. Chicago: University of Chicago Press, pp. 417–429 (Bibliography).

NADEL, S. F. 1939. The Application of Intelligence Tests in the Anthropological Field. In Bartlett, F. C. et al (eds.), The Study of Society. London: Kegan Paul, Trench, Trubner, pp. 184–198.

NOTES ON CONTRIBUTORS

A. L. EPSTEIN

Professor of Social Anthropology at the University of Sussex. Formerly Professor and Head of Department of Anthropology at the Australian National University Canberra, he has done fieldwork in New Guinea and Central Africa. Author of *Matupit : Land, Politics and Change among the Tolai of New Britain* (1969). Editor, *Contention and Dispute : Aspects of Law and Social Control in Melanesia* (1975).

ELIZABETH COLSON

Professor of Social Anthropology at the University of California, Berkeley. She has devoted many years to research among the Tonga of Mazabuka and of the Gwembe Valley on both of which groups she has written extensively.

J. CLYDE MITCHELL

Formerly Director of the Rhodes-Livingstone Institute and then Professor of Urban Sociology at the University of Manchester. Currently, he is a Research Fellow of Nuffield College, Oxford.

JOHN BARNES

Formerly Chairman of the Department of Anthropology and Sociology, Australian National University, Canberra, Barnes is currently Professor of Sociology at Cambridge University.

J. VAN VELSEN

Formerly Director of the Institute of African Studies at the University of Zambia, van Velsen is now Professor of Anthropology at the University of Wales at Aberystwyth.

T. SCARLETT EPSTEIN

Presently Professorial Fellow in the School of African and Asian Studies, University of Sussex. She has carried out field research in South India and New Guinea.

V. W. TURNER

Formerly Professor of Anthropology, Cornell University, Turner is now Chairman of the Committee on Social Thought, University of Chicago.

M. G. MARWICK

Formerly Professor of Anthropology and Sociology at Monash University, Melbourne. He currently holds a similar Chair at the University of Stirling, Scotland.

MAX GLUCKMAN

He was, until his recent death, Professor of Social Anthropology at the University of Manchester.

Index

Index

Index

Index

Index